Camino
Catalan
The Tranquil Route towards Santiago de Compostela

Walking routes from Catalonia to La Rioja and Navarre

Barcelona • Montserrat • Girona • Lleida • Huesca • Puente la Reina • Tortosa • Zaragoza • Logroño

Callum J. Christie

Acknowledgements

This guide's completion would not have been possible without the financial support of the Catalan Tourism Board and the provincial Tourist Boards of Catalunya. Their generosity and patience has been outstanding. Thanks also to Huesca Provincial Delegation and the Government of Navarra Tourist Board, as well as to Foment Torisme Val d'Aran and Barcelona Turisme. There are many folk who have shared their knowledge and expertise, both during the years of ground work, as well as during the process of pulling the book together. Their kindness, patience and professionalism are evident within these two covers.

Special thanks

Juan Carlos Borrego Pérez has been an untiring and great travelling companion from start to finish, sharing his insights into the local customs and history of the landscapes we have travelled together; not to mention the travails of F.C. Barcelona! To Gemma Liesa Ezquerra for her eagle eyed mapping skills and to Rosa Adroer Martori and Carola Ribas Fernàndez for their care and attention to the detail of the book design. To Joan Rossinyol Miralles of Editorial Piolet for introducing me to all of the team already mentioned. Hélène Gaujac and Júlia Romeo Liesa deserve mention for their outstanding translation skills and Mike Digby for his 20:20 eyesight, good taste, and selfless friendship! To Clare, for her love and support.

The hand drawn illustrations within this guide are all originals by my good friend, the polymath Robert Louth. The illustrations in the Val d'Aran section are by Rafa Piñeiro Romero, "un colega" from El Burgo.

Of the many folk I met along the Way, I should like to mention these few who shared their companionship as well as their love and enthusiasm for the Camino and their local surrounds; to Jaime of the Amics de Girona, Bautista Antorán Zabay, Daniel Vallés Turmo and Marcel Iglesias Cuartero.

A note from the author regarding place names in this guide:

In many cases the Camino passes through places that possess more than one official or unofficial name. Often official toponyms have a different version in other languages (aragonese/aranese/castillian/catalan/basque). This is not surprising as the pilgrim passes through a variety of linguistically enriched landscapes. I have always chosen the place name used by the Town Hall of each village or city. In some cases where there are two official place names that differ greatly I have included both. I do hope not to have offended the sensibility of any reader.

First edition: March 2021

© Text and maps: Callum J. Christie

© of this edition: Editorial PIOLET SL

© Photography: all images have been used with the permission of the original author or the tourist organisation, including the Catalan Tourist Board (ACT) and la Comarca Hoya de Huesca (afCHH).

© Art illustrations:
Robert Louth and Rafael Piñero Romero

Design and layout:
Estudi Claris. www.estudiclaris.com

Fieldwork & Research:
Juan Carlos Borrego Pérez and Callum Christie

Mapwork:
Gemma Liesa Ezquerra

Cover photo:
"Montserrat" ©ACT.Sergi Boixader

Print:
Impremta Pagès

ISBN: 978-84-121880-5-9
Legal Deposit: B 6467-2021

This publication is protected by law. The reproduction of any or all of the contents either in print, or by photographical or digital means, is forbidden without the express permission of Editorial PIOLET©. www.editorialpiolet.com

There are no foreign lands. It is the traveller only who is foreign.
R.L. STEVENSON

¡Salud, dinero y amor!
JUANA DE SAN MARTÍN DEL TESORILLO

Bring me my scallop shell of quiet.
SIR WALTER RALEIGH

This book is dedicated to my parents who instilled in me their love of the big outdoors, and to my children Sandy and Lucia who can already name more birds and plants than I ever could when I was their age.

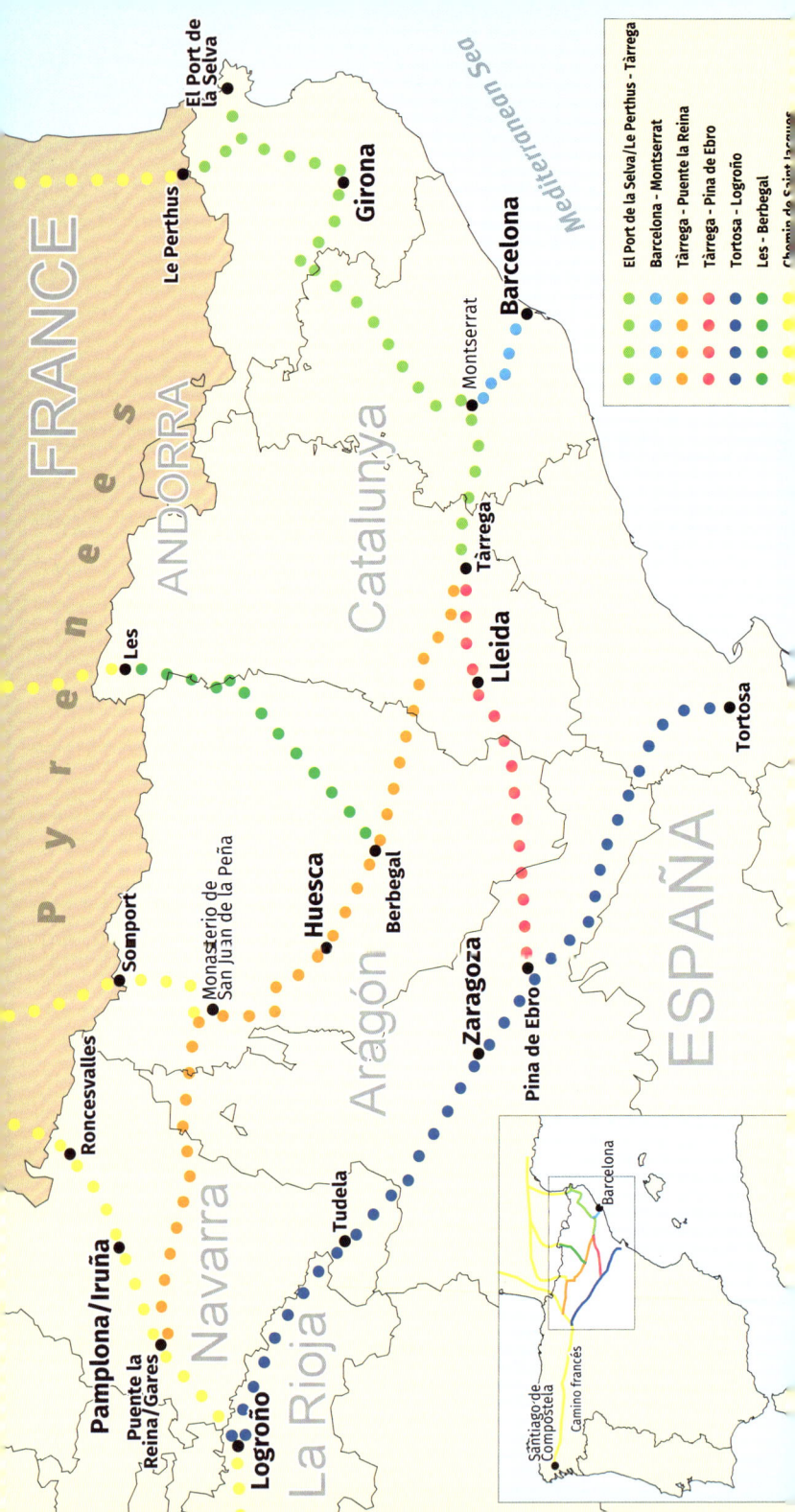

INDEX

Notes from the Author 6
Introduction 8

1. EL PORT DE LA SELVA/LE PERTHUS - TÀRREGA

- **1A** 28.3km El Port de la Selva - Vilabertran 13
- **1B** 33.6km Le Perthus - Vilabertran 16
- **2** 19.3km Vilabertran - Bàscara 21
- **3A 3B 3C** 30.8/27.6km Bàscara - Girona (via Orriols/Vilademuls) 24
- **4** 26.6km Girona - Amer 30
- **5** 23.1km (+9.2km). Amer - Sant Esteve d'en Bas (+Olot) 33
- **6** 21.4km Sant Esteve d'en Bas - L'Esquirol 36
- **7** 18.7km L'Esquirol - Vic 39
- **8** 20.1km Vic - L'Estany 42
- **9** 23.5km L'Estany - Artés 45
- **10** 21.7km Artés - Manresa 48
- **11** 25.5km Manresa - Montserrat 52
- **12** 26.4km Montserrat - Igualada 55
- **13** 22.5km Igualada - La Panadella 58
- **14** 27.7km La Panadella - Tàrrega 61

2. BARCELONA - MONTSERRAT

- **1A** 17.2km Barcelona - Sant Cugat del Vallès 67
- **1B** 30.9km Sant Cugat del Vallès - Esparreguera 71
- **2A** 21.0km Barcelona - Molins de Rei 75
- **2B** 24.8km Molins de Rei - Esparreguera 78
- **3** 12.1km Esparreguera - Montserrat 81

3. TÀRREGA - PUENTE LA REINA

- **1** 23.9km Tàrrega - Linyola 85
- **2** 30.2km Linyola - Algerri 88
- **3** 21.5km Algerri - Tamarite de Litera 91
- **4** 21.0km Tamarite de Litera - Monzón 94
- **5** 20.1km Monzón - Berbegal 97
- **6** 28.7km Berbegal - Pueyo de Fañanás 100
- **7** 18.0km Pueyo de Fañanás - Huesca 103
- **8** 21.6km Huesca - Bolea 107
- **9** 29.1km Bolea - La Peña Estación 110
- **10** 31.9km La Peña Estación - Santa Cilia 114
- **11** 27.2km Santa Cilia - Artieda 117
- **12** 32.1km Artieda - Sangüesa 120
- **13** 26.9km Sangüesa - Monreal 123
- **14** 31.4km Monreal - Puente la Reina 126

4. TÀRREGA - PINA DE EBRO

- **1** 23.2km Tàrrega - El Palau d'Anglesola 131
- **2** 24.6km El Palau d'Anglesola - Lleida 134
- **3** 34.7km Lleida - Fraga 138
- **4** 26.5km Fraga - Candasnos 142
- **5** 20.0km Candasnos - Bujaraloz 145
- **6** 38.2km Bujaraloz - Pina de Ebro 148

5. TORTOSA - LOGROÑO

- **1** 22.7km Tortosa - Estació de Benifallet 154
- **2** 31.0km Estació de Benifallet - Batea 158
- **3** 17.7km Batea - Fabara 161
- **4** 21.6km Fabara - Caspe 164
- **5** 30.5km Caspe - Escatrón 167
- **6** 35.0km Escatrón - Quinto 170
- **7** 16.6km Quinto - Fuentes de Ebro ... 174
- **8** 30.8km Fuentes de Ebro - Zaragoza 177
- **9** 29.0km Zaragoza - Alagón 181
- **10** 30.9km Alagón - Mallén 184
- **11** 29.9km Mallén - Tudela 187
- **12** 24.3km Tudela - Alfaro 190
- **13** 24.7km Alfaro - Calahorra 193
- **14** 19.9km Calahorra - Alcanadre 196
- **15** 34.7km Alcanadre - Logroño 198

6. LES - BERBEGAL

- **1** 20.0km Les - Vielha 204
- **2** 15.5km Vielha - Conangles 208
- **3** 31.9km Conangles - Bonansa (+Vall de Boí) 211
- **4** 35.1km Bonansa - La Puebla de Roda 215
- **5** 33.1km La Puebla de Roda - Graus 219
- **6** 38.1km Graus - Barbastro 223
- **7** 19.9km Barbastro - Berbegal 227

NOTES FROM THE AUTHOR

Callum has spent most of his adult life in Spain and his great fascination with this land and its spirited people continues to this day. This curiosity along with a love for the outdoors led him to spend the last 20 years working mainly as a walking guide all around this diverse country, discovering its magnificent landscapes, colourful local traditions, warm hospitality and delicious culinary offerings. During his years in Spain he has also grown commercial horticultural specimens in green houses, and called 'Action'! on a film set of 'Don Quijote'.

WRITING A BOOK

November 2020

A year ago to the day on a clear Pyrenean morning in the Val d'Aran, I set out on the very last stage of researching this guide book. However, I certainly didn't anticipate how this last dramatic chapter would unfold.

Almost a decade ago, while climbing a steep winding path through vineyards to the remote monastery of St Pere de Rodes in the Cap de Creus nature park, I came across a waist high wooden marker pole with a round blue waymark and a yellow scallop in its midst. Later on, I was scrambling around the rocky slopes overlooking the sparkling Mediterranean far below. Whilst delving into the undergrowth to look for lost dolmens, I came across a boulder of granite, which was scored with a mass of simply gouged out cross shapes.

These half hidden clues that sprang out whilst exploring provided the creative spark that led me to trace the 'Cami de San Jaume', the Catalonian section of the Camino de Santiago pilgrimage route. I was lucky enough that others shared my enthusiasm for, and vision of, creating a guidebook to help fellow walkers find their way from the Catalonian shores toward the far flung rugged Atlantic corner of Galicia.

That November morning a year ago, setting out from Vielha with my walking buddy Juan Carlos, we stopped to talk with two local farmers and promised to look out for their missing cow. They were concerned by the recent weather forecast. We climbed up through forests of firs as vultures circled overhead. It was a bright sunny day as we approached the higher ridges topped with a dusting of snow. After a hasty lunch whilst briefly admiring the views of the Val d'Aran towards the French border, we headed up to the Port de Vielha pass. On turning a corner, the wind and rain hit us quite suddenly but we decided to push on. The path disappeared as a mist descended and we could only see a few yards ahead. The rain turned to snow and we struggled up the rocky slopes, often having to guess at where the zig zag path was trying to lead us. The painted waymarkings of the GR long distance route were hidden from view under a blanket of snow. Eventually we succeeded in finding the pass itself and managed to descend this most treacherous of sections on its icy path. Many hours later, soaked to the skin and in the last light of the day, we entered the warm and comforting confines of the Conangles mountain refuge in the company of Asier, its friendly guardian. It was a rewarding end to an arduous day and much appreciated after the humbling trek across the wild majestic heights, though we never did find the missing cow!

The long journey taken to create this book has led to the discovery of new landscapes. It has forged many new friendships and renewed some old ones. From lush mountain pastures to the shadeless steppes and fertile river floodplains, the trails I found were as varied as the countryside they traversed. Due to the largely unfrequented nature of many of these trails the way-marking in many areas is nowhere near as clear as on the Camino Francés, hence the need for a guidebook with detailed directions. An important element in the process of creating this book came from the pride and passion that local folk hold for their history and surroundings.

The Catalans love their land and their rich cultural heritage. They are fiercely proud of their language and identity, but the walker should also realise that this is a region that knows how to warmly welcome the curious traveller. The guide book of course ventures out of Catalonia, and I can personally vouch for the kind heartedness and the generosity of the villagers and townsfolk all along the Way. If you ask for help you will receive it!

NOTES FOR THE TRAVELLER

Try to remember to obtain your 'Credencial' before setting out. It is a type of pilgrim passport that you can get stamped every day at churches, town halls or accommodation you stay in. It also serves as a timely reminder after your journey, of all the places you have visited on your Camino.

A sun hat, a large water container, a basic first aid kit including blister plasters, and a head torch are a good idea. Aim to carry a backpack that weighs no more than 10 kilos. If you can, plan to wash your clothes as you go. **Definitely do not set off without having broken in your footwear!**

This is not meant to be a flippant opener. When planning to undertake a journey along an unknown route there are some helpful key factors to consider.

> **Preparation** - It is all-important and shouldn't in any way diminish the anticipation and enjoyment of the adventure. Some sort of gradual prior training is essential. Taking ever longer walks to build up your levels of stamina really helps and also breaks in your footwear. Carefully choose what type works best for you.
> P.S. your feet will really appreciate a pair of comfy sandals to wear at the end of each day's hike.
>
> **'Less is more'**- It's an ago old adage for the long distance walker and probably the hardest to adhere to. If you plan to carry everything you need, remember that not only will your back feel the strain, but ultimately the soles of your feet will take the impact of the combined load.
>
> **Hydrate** - Each walking stage in the book gives some guidance to the type of terrain, the amount of shade and whether drinking water is available en route. Bear in mind that it is generally only safe to drink from water fountains in towns and villages. The distances between these can sometimes be pronounced, so carrying enough liquid refreshment should be part of your daily planning.
>
> **Supplies** - When stocking up on provisions be aware that shops tend to shut for a long lunchtime between the hours of 2-5pm as well as all day on a Sunday. Some eateries will not serve a proper sit down meal until 2pm at lunchtime or 8.30 pm in the evening. However, snacks (*tapas*), and sandwiches (*bocadillos*) are generally available at any time throughout the day.

Is there a secret to avoiding self inflicted pain on a long distance walk?
You bet there is! Listen to your body. Take a day off from walking when you feel the pressure building. Take some time to relax and get to know the local folk and your surroundings; these are the moments that will remain with you long after your final destination has been reached. Remember there is no right or wrong way to undertake a pilgrimage, there is only your way. It matters not a jot whether you carry all your own belongings, or whether you overnight under the stars or in a hotel. You are following in the footsteps of kings and paupers. The very act of leaving your home, for whatever the reason, to travel along an unknown Camino makes you an intrepid pilgrim!

INTRODUCTION

Pilgrimage has always been a part of human history. To visit a site that was considered sacred often involved a journey of discovery. These travels would take the pilgrim, either alone or in a group, through remote unknown landscapes, dependent on the hospitality of the local inhabitants. When great distances were involved, a pilgrimage meant a dramatic break, a slowing down from the routine of daily life, and lengthy exposure to nature and its challenges. If they survived and managed the return journey home, this once in a lifetime experience provided the travellers with stories that could be passed on for generations.

In Europe, during the Middle Ages, the cult of St. James the apostle grew to such an extent that Santiago de Compostela became the third most important Christian pilgrimage destination, after Jerusalem and Rome. It brought people from all over Europe, along a myriad of routes, to travel along what we now call the Camino de Santiago. This 'Way of St James', or Cami de Sant Jaume in Catalan, led to Galicia in far northwestern Spain.

Saint James, the Apostle

Prior to his martyrdom in Jerusalem in 44CE, tradition has the apostle James 'the Greater' sent to preach across the Iberian peninsula. His legend includes the miraculous journey of his body to Galicia in a stone boat and his subsequent burial by local Christians on a hill. Around the year 813 the next mention of his remains materialises with the Christian hermit Pelayo, drawn by music and shining lights to discover the saint's tomb. Authenticated by the local bishop and later the Pope, the discovery led to the building of a church and shrine, in turn giving rise to the city of 'Santiago de Compostela', meaning St James of the starry field (*Campus stellae*).

This site of veneration attracted pilgrims from far and wide. Belief in the power of saintly relics was prolific in medieval times. During the time of the crusades, the 'appearance' of St James on a white steed leading the Christian forces into battle against the Moors led to the saint being portrayed as both a pilgrim and a Moor-slayer, ('Santiago Matamoros'). The military Order of St. James was formed for the protection of pilgrims and assisted in the expansion of Christian territories southwards. St James eventually became the patron saint of Spain, and is celebrated annually on the 25th of July.

From the beginning of the C9th, this influx of pilgrims and settlers into northern Spain slowly led to an increase in infrastructure aimed at meeting their needs. Pilgrim hostels, hospices and churches sprang up along The Camino. It also led to an increased Christian presence in this region at a time when most of the Iberian peninsula was dominated by the Moors.

The routes included in this guide all start in modern-day Catalonia and cross the less well trodden lands of northeastern Spain. In medieval times this region was a constantly moving frontier territory between the emerging Christian kingdoms of the north and the gradually receding territory of Al Andalus.

The Moors

The C7th western expansion of Islam converted the peoples of north Africa and propelled some of them to cross the straights of Gibraltar in 711. Arriving from the old Roman province of Mauritania, this collection of peoples became known as Moors. Overrunning the Christian Visigothic rule that had been in place since the late C5th, these great warriors dominated the majority of the Iberian peninsula in just seven years, save for some small mountainous enclaves in the northwest. The Moors went on to cross the formidable physical barrier of the Pyrenees, threatening the Christian kingdoms of France and reaching the city of Poitiers only to be driven back over the mountains by the forces of Charles Martell.

The Moors ruled their territory, 'Al Andalus' for nearly 800 years. This civilisation developed a rich culture with advances in art, science, technology and learning. With advanced use of hydraulics they irrigated alluvial plains and terraces, producing an astonishing variety of fruit and vegetables. Their school of philosophy brought ancient Greek works into Europe thus ensuring their preservation. However, the Christian enclaves in the north grew more powerful. These kingdoms steadily pushed the frontier further south until, with the fall of Granada in 1492, the long rule of the Moors came to an end.

The trails described in detail in this guide, all lead eventually to the busier, well established pilgrim route known as the Camino Francés. It enters Spain via the western reaches of the Pyrenees. Today, the lands encountered within this book are predominantly rural and agricultural, with varied and dramatic terrains and equally diverse climates. They reach from the impressive peaks of the Pyrenean mountain chain to the vast flat expanses of the Ebro valley. As one travels across this remote inland region, the traces of its long history can still be discovered; from Iberian tribal settlements, Roman roads and bridges and feudal castles to today's peaceful rural villages, historical towns and high speed trains.

Camino Francés

Subsequent to the creation of the shrine of St James the safest possible route for pilgrims was across the very north of Spain. The danger faced at times of war with the Moors led to the development of one principal route that was more easily defended. This route became known as the Camino Francés, leading pilgrims directly from the French border at Roncesvalles to Santiago de Compostela.

The Codex Calixtinus (written c.1140 by Aymeric Picaud, a French monk and scholar) is often considered today as one of the very first European guide books ever written. It included information about monuments, shrines, terrain and suggestions for the pilgrim. This book, along with the steadily improving safety of the area, led to a phenomenal increase in the number of pilgrims and the subsequent growth of the local economy and political standing of its towns during medieval times.

After a long demise, The Camino Francés now enjoys a new and invigorated popularity. Its plethora of surviving medieval monuments and Romanesque churches, along with its abundance of eateries and hostelries, attracts visitors and pilgrims in their thousands, almost all year round. Nowadays, in the peak summer months, the official pilgrim hostels find themselves full by midday and it is not uncommon to see pilgrims racing ahead to gain a bed!

Tracing these almost forgotten pilgrimage routes, you may well experience some of the same feelings as those ancient travellers. Following in their footsteps you'll discover these enriching and peaceful trails for yourself. Leaving their daily lives behind them, pilgrims embarked upon this venture for many reasons. To fulfil a vow or to honour the last will and testament of a loved one, to be healed, to attain the plenary indulgence offered by the Pope or give thanks to the Apostle on behalf of their parish. Pilgrims were even paid by others to participate on their behalf. Vagabonds and runaways donned a robe and scallop in order to gain free food and accommodation. Some were serving sanctions for committing serious crimes and others were even spies from enemy kingdoms.

Medieval Catalonia

Charlemagne wrested Barcelona from the Moors in 801 making it the bastion of his southern territories, creating a military buffer zone, the 'Marca Hispanica', against the Moorish incursions into Frankish lands. Loyal local counts were eventually left to control these counties, charged with defending the frontier. These 'condados' were united by Wilfred (c840-98), founding the dynasty of the 'Casal de Barcelona'. Under attack from the Moors in 985, the requested aid from the ruling Frankish king was not forthcoming, independence was declared and the Counts were free to forge their own destiny.

A flowering culture of enterprise and learning spread southwards via conquests over the Moors and north of the Pyrenees through marriage. Catalonia's language is Catalan, which developed from popular latin during these years. Important seminal works such as 'Tirant lo Blanc' from this time mark the beginning of a long and rich literary history.

With the marriage of Count Ramon Berenguer IV to the heiress of the throne of Aragón in 1137 the new kingdom expanded eastwards becoming known as the 'Crown of Aragón'. The incorporation of Corsica, Sardinia, Naples and Sicily spread Catalonia's influence across the Mediterranean. This, along with its trading ports brought riches back to the fast developing cities of Barcelona and Valencia. Through the marriage in 1469 of Ferdinand of Aragón to Isabel of Castille, Catalonia became entwined with the future of Spain.

Of course today your journey is a far safer one. The dangers of medieval times were many; illness, bandits, precarious shelter and lack of food to name but a few. The pilgrims faced not only the hitherto unknown physical challenge of a tough journey on foot but also being far away from home and everything they knew. One cannot help but think that they would have gradually felt part of something greater than their own lives as they met fellow pilgrims, shared stories, heard of far off lands and received hospitality from the towns and villages along the route. The obligation to provide food and board to pilgrims must also have given local people along the Way a similar sense of connection to this historic journey and the wider world; the same sense of connection that folk living along the many routes of the Camino share today. Whatever your intentions, whether they be spiritual or simply the opportunity to challenge yourself by exploring these 'Tranquil Routes' you are sure to enjoy its people and places.
Bon Camí !

El Port de la Selva / Le Perthus - Tàrrega

The dramatic setting of the Sant Pere monastery and the strategic border pass at Col de Panissars both make for impressive starting points. From the monastery, perched high above the glittering waters of the Mediterranean or from the Roman border post ruins overlooking the great cork oak forests, this section of the Way of St. James follows ancient trails through the green heart of northern Catalonia. The nearby remains of the Greek colony of Empuries attests to the importance of ancient Mediterranean trade routes to this area. Here the Romans first landed on the Iberian peninsula in 218 BCE.

In medieval times pilgrims making their way to Rome, Jerusalem and Santiago de Compostela all crossed paths at Vilabertran, making the town and its nearby monastery an important gathering place. The route features many peaceful moments, including the remote pastoral uplands of the Collsacabra with their timeless charm and inspiring views of the Pyrenean mountains.

Girona - Built at the confluence of four rivers, this Iberian settlement became the citadel of *Gerunda* in Roman times. A site of strategic importance, the city was fiercely fought over by both Moors and Christians, repeatedly changing hands. In later centuries it was besieged several times by the French. The impressive eastern fortifications can still be admired today.

The Hebrew community flourished in the C12th. Girona became the seat of the Great Rabbi of Catalonia. Its Jewish Quarter is extremely well preserved and the old town is full of beautiful cobbled streets, some of which still bear the names of the trades that existed in this important merchant city. The Cathedral is approached by a steep Baroque stairway and its treasury holds the Romanesque Tapestry of Creation. Colourful painted houses line the banks of the river Onyar which is crossed by several picturesque bridges including one designed by Gustave Eiffel.

El Port de la Selva (©ACT. Georama)

1A. El Port de la Selva - Vilabertran: 28.3km

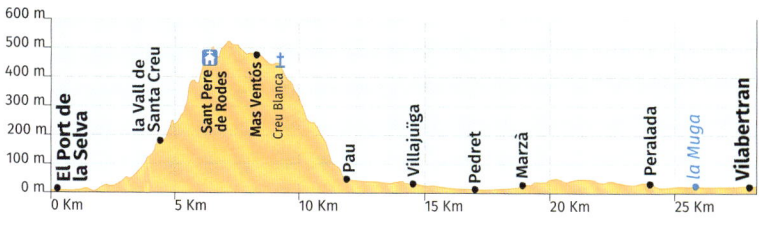

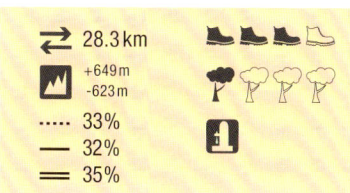

- 28.3 km
- +649m / -623m
- ····· 33%
- — 32%
- = 35%

Presents impressive views over the Cap de Creus Nature Park. The Way includes various cobbled pathways that journey through hamlets, passing vineyards, cork oaks, abandoned terracing and occasional olive groves. The Romanesque monastery of Sant Pere de Rodes is well worth a visit.

Observations: Some steep paths on the ascent to the monastery as well as during the descent to Pau.

El Port de la Selva - pop. 980. Alt Empordà. Situated in a scallop shell shaped bay on the Cap de Creus coast, historical records of 974 refer to it as the port of the Rodes Monastery. Not until the beginning of the C18th do records show a stable thriving fishing town. During the mid C19th the town enjoyed a flourishing trade in olive oil and wine, which by the end of the same century was severely diminished due to the phylloxera disease killing off most of the vines. Today, Port de la Selva remains as a charming fishing village that thrives mainly from tourism.

0km Seafront El Port de la Selva. From the tourist information office leave the town following the attractive seafront walkway. Just after passing the entrance to a campsite, turn left onto a path.

2.3km/2.3km GI-612 Road. Turn left to cross a road bridge and immediately look for a track to follow on the opposite side of the road. The way soon narrows to a path with cobbled stretches.

2km/4.3km La Vall de Santa Creu. Climb through the streets of this pretty hamlet.

2.1km/6.4km Sant Pere de Rodes. After climbing a steep narrow winding section surrounded by old terracing, the path levels out at the magnificent monastery. Follow the road away from the monastery past the former medieval pilgrim's hospice to a car park. Climb steps to the Santa Helena church and the ruins of the village of Santa Creu de Rodes. Turn right, following a path through pines down to Mas Ventós and its picnic area. With the Mas to your left pick up a path that descends and passes the large white cross of Creu Blanca.

5.2km/11.6km Pau. Descend through this small village to enter a flatter area of vineyards and olive groves.

2.6km/14.2km Vilajuïga. Continue through the village to take the road to Marzà. After 200m take a track on the left towards Pedret.

4.6km/18.8km Marzà. After Pedret the camino enters the village of Marzà.

4.7km/23.5km Peralada. Village with an impressive castle. From the roundabout at the entrance follow the outer wall of the castle precinct. Reach a roundabout on the far side of the village on the road to Vilabertran. Exit the village by this road and cross the river Llobregat.

2.6km/26.1km Río Muga. Cross the road bridge and take the second track on the left.

2.2km/28.3km Vilabertran. The Way passes through the heart of this village to arrive at the Monastery of Santa Maria.

Vilabertran - pop. 900. Village of the Alt Emporda region. Once an important gathering place for pilgrims making their way to the Holy Lands. The monastery had its own hospital to provide shelter and medical help for pilgrims.

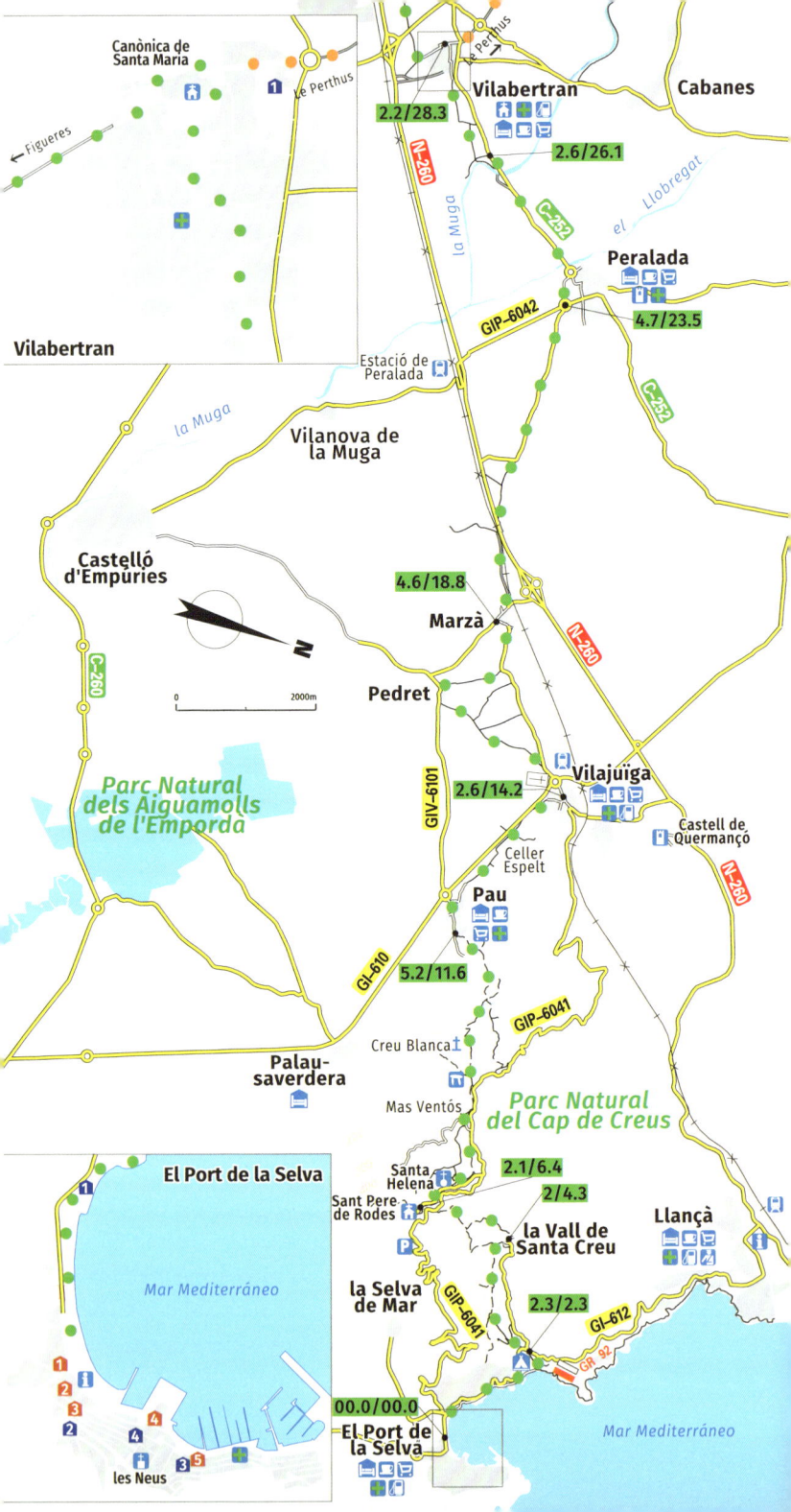

Monestir de Sant Pere de Rodes (©ACT. M.A.S.)

El Port de la Selva
1 Pensió Arola
Tel. 972 387 005
2 Pensió German
Tel. 972 388 005
3 Pensió Sol i Sombra
Tel. 972 387 060
4 Hostal la Tina
Tel. 972 387 149
1 Hotel Mariner
Tel. 972 388 005
2 Hotel Agora
Tel. 972 387 062
3 Hotel Porto Cristo
Tel. 972 387 062
4 Hotel Spa Cap de Creus
Tel. 972 388 107
5 Hotel Boutique Mar d'Amunt
Tel. 972 387 062

Palau-Saverdera
Hotel Niu de Sol
Tel. 671 600 303

Pau
Ca la Sònia
Tel. 615 814 385
Pensió Paó Blau
Tel. 972 190 970 - 652 242 608
Hotel Mas Lazuli
Tel. 872 222 220

Vilajuïga
Mas Gelamà
Tel. 972 531 926
Casa Armengol
Tel. 972 498 030
Celler l'Espelt
Tel. 972 531 727

Peralada
Hostal Cal Palol
Tel. 972 538 074
Hotel de la Font
Tel. 972 538 507
Hotel Peralada Wine Spa Golf
Tel. 972 538 830
Can Genís
Tel. 625 017 420
Casa Convent
Tel. 972 670 920

Vilabertran
1 Ca la Glòria
Tel. 659 447 020

Church of Santa Maria de les Neus, El Port de la Selva. Houses a C15th statue of Saint Peter that was saved from the sacking of the Monastery of St. Pere de Rodes.

Sant Pere de Rodes. Originally a Benedictine monastery built in the Romanesque style on the Verdera mountain, today watched over by the ruins of a castle. The monastery's medieval splendour was gradually eroded by deadly plagues, plundering corsairs, banditry, wars with France, and a state promoted dissolution, resulting in complete abandonment in the C18th.

Santa Helena de Rodes. A C9th parroquial church for the very small village of Sant Creu de Rodes, that grew and diminished along with the fortunes of the nearby monastery.

La Creu Blanca. An ancient cross and sole surviving boundary marker of the monastery's former lands.

Peralada Castle. Originally a C9th fortification and seat of the Counts of Peralada.

Monastery de Santa Maria de Vilabertran. Romanesque Augustine monastery dating from the C10th.

1B. LE PERTHUS - VILABERTRAN: 33.6KM

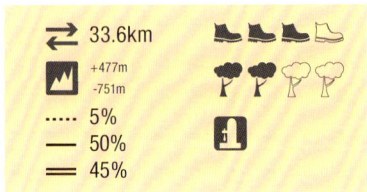

- 33.6km
- +477m / -751m
- 5%
- 50%
- 45%

Le Perthus, situated in a key pass of the eastern Pyrenees, has welcomed pilgrims for centuries. It was the meeting point of the ancient Roman roads, the Via Domitia and the Via Augustina, linking southern Gaul to Hispania. From these slopes, cloaked in cork oaks, the Way crosses a plateau of heathland and abandoned terraces, before descending to the alluvial plain of the river Muga.

Observations: - Option A: Extreme caution should be taken when crossing the N-II before La Jonquera.
- Option B: The Llobregat d'Empordà river at the entrance to La Jonquera avoids the N-II but carries the risk of seasonal flooding.
- Exiting Pont de Molins; crossing the N-II requires great caution.

0km Le Perthus. Starting at the highest point of the main street follow a sign indicating Fort de Bellegarde. Exit the town uphill.
1.1km/1.1km Fork. Follow the asphalted track on the right towards the military cemetery.
0.8km/1.9km Military Cemetery. Leave the asphalt track (it is worth following this track for about 300m to the Roman site marking the beginning of the Via Augusta) to go around the cemetery wall then take the dirt track that crosses a cattle grid and descends through cork oak woodland. Turn left after 300m, heading downhill and after 700m at a fork, take the right hand earthen track.
2.1km/4km AVE Rail Tunnel. Reach a fenced off railway area and continue downhill where an asphalted track passes through a tunnel under the railway. Continue across a bridge over the Llobregat river (*here it is advisable to take note of whether this river carries water or not*).
0.2km/4.2km Track after Bridge. A few metres along, turn right onto a track that runs parallel to the river. After 400m it joins a wider well maintained track where you turn right. After 100m the track forks.
0.7km/4.9km Fork. Here you can choose between two alternatives to get to La Jonquera. Both have their drawbacks;
OPTION A. Take the track on the left to approach the N-II where it runs below the AP-7. ATTENTION ! Cross the N-II (very carefully) under both lanes of the motorway and join a local road that leaves the N-II. As soon as you step onto this road, leave it by turning right, to walk between the guardrail of the N-II and the woods. Here you find the beginning of a path which takes you along parallel to the N-II. This then widens to form a narrow earthen track running between cork oaks. On the outskirts of La Jonquera it links into a wider track. Turn left to go around a truck parking area, after which you reach C. Nord. This street ends at Av. Pau Casals where you turn left and continue.
OPTION B. At the fork, go straight on (right) along the path marked as 'Bike Route 8' until you cross under the AVE train track. After 900m this track narrows, becoming a path and again crosses under the train tracks. In a few metres it approaches the Llobregat d'Empordà river just below the AP-7 overpass. ATTENTION! This is a seasonal flood risk area. There is a concrete ford over the Llobregat river. If it is covered with water it is advisable to go back and take Option A. After crossing the river it joins a well defined track that continues between the overhead rail tracks and the AP-7. After about 150m

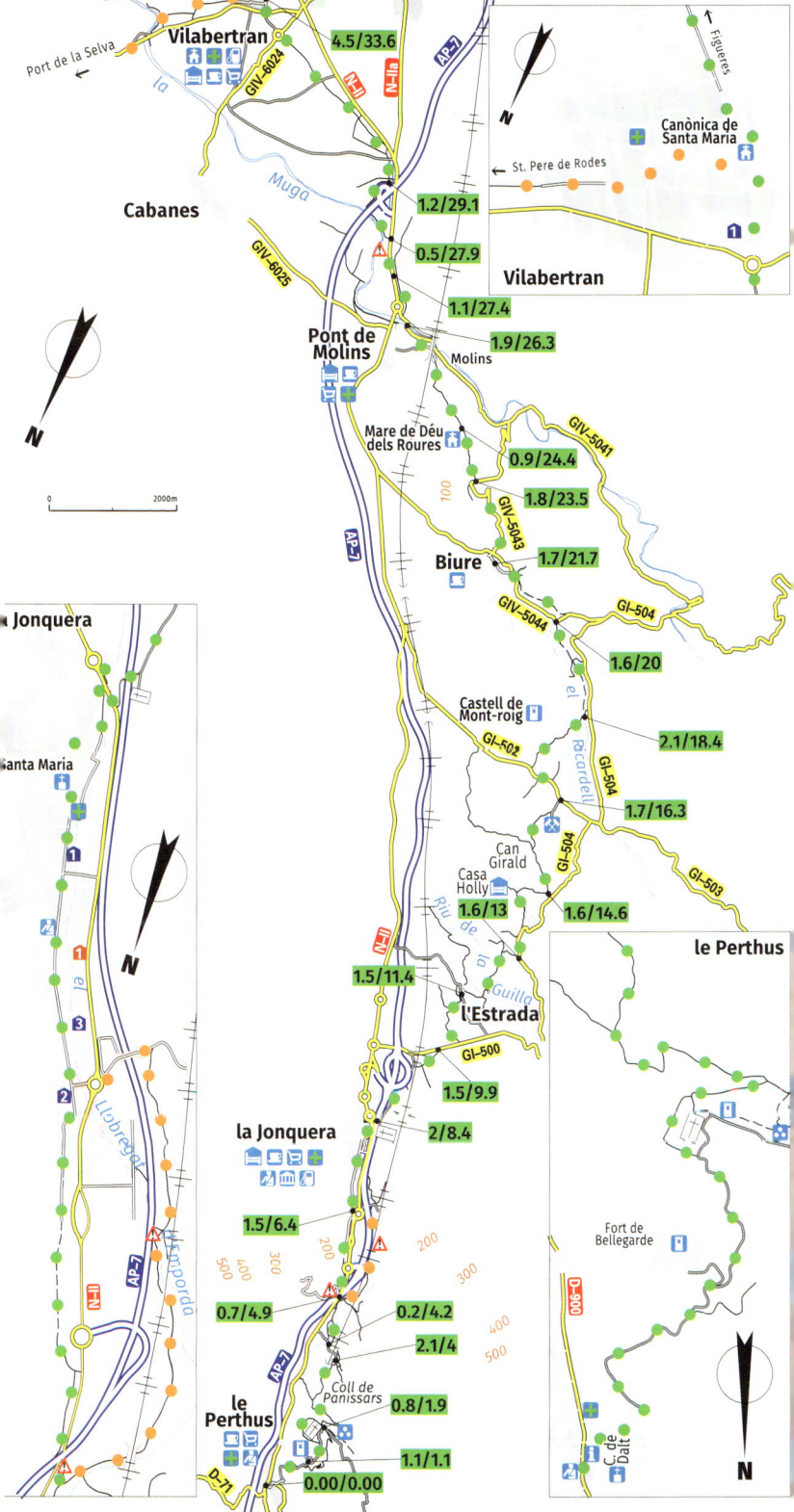

you continue straight on (left) along a rutted path (still between the two main roadways). In 500m you join a wider track. Turn left to cross the AP-7 over a bridge, taking you to a large roundabout on the N-II. Use the zebra crossings and take the second exit, then cross a bridge over the Llobregat river and reach Av. Pau Casals. Turn right.

1.5km/6.4km Av. Pau Casals. Continue straight ahead, now along C. Major, passing the church of Santa Maria de la Jonquera. A little further on, take an alley to the right that leads to C.del Pont. Turn left, continue and cross under the N-II. Emerge at a parking lot next to a roundabout. Turn sharp left onto the walkway of the N-II to cross the Llobregat river. Take the first road on the left which goes up towards a bridge that crosses the AP-7.

2km/8.4km Bridge over the AP-7. On the other side of the bridge, turn left and continue on the asphalt, parallel to the highway. Follow this local road finding a narrow foot tunnel on the right that passes under the AVE train tracks. At the exit of the tunnel, turn left and then immediately right onto a defined track. 400m further on, join the GI-500 road.

1.5km/9.9km GI-500. Turn right. At 300m exit the road to take a narrow track to the left. After 700m continue to the right to reach a local road and the first houses of l'Estrada. Turn left to enter the town.

1.5km/11.4km L'Estrada. Pass by the church of Sta. Maria and turn right to leave the village gently downhill on a track to reach a house. Leave the track and take a path to the left, descending to cross the Guilla stream by a stone walkway. The path climbs through a dense and shady woodland of oaks. After 400m you reach an asphalted track, where you turn right, continuing uphill until you reach a large road.

1.6km/13km GI-504. Turn left proceeding about 200m. Take a well defined track to the left that runs through mixed woodland. All tracks to the left are ignored.

1.6km/14.6km Junction. Leaving the woodland, turn left uphill between agricultural fields and trees. You pass Can Girald and after 300m take the earthen track on the right. Continue along this well defined way and after another 400m descend to join a wide asphalted track that gives access to a quarry. Turn left to descend to the GI-502.

1.7km/16.3km Junction GI-502. Follow the road left for 700m to take a track on the right towards Castell de Mont-roig. Turn right after 300m onto a wider and more defined track. This descends through woods surrounding a couple of agricultural fields and crosses the river Ricardell. The track levels out and continues around a field. At a bend (50m before meeting a road), keep straight on along a path next to the river Ricardell.

2.1km/18.4km El Ricardell. Follow the stream, crossing the water various times until the path leaves the stream climbing up to a gap between low hills. Descending, take the rutted way through a farm field until you exit at the GIV-5044.

1.6km/20km GIV-5044. Turn right to cross a nearby road bridge over the Ricardell and after 25m take a narrow track on the left. About 50m on, look for a narrow path to the left through the trees that follows the Ricardell downstream. The river is crossed by a wooden bridge and the path ends at the road, on the outskirts of Biure.

1.7km/21.7km Church of Biure. Continue up to the town on the street opposite. After passing in front of the church, turn right, downhill on C. Mare de Deu and upon reaching the road again, turn left. After about 100m turn right on the GIV-5043 towards Pont de Molins. Climb steeply, passing through rugged terrain with abandoned terraces devoid of trees and crops. Just after a curve, the road reaches a plateau and about 50m further on take a dirt track to the left.

1.8km/23.5km Dirt Track. Follow this track across a heathland area of abandoned agriculture, which presents good views of the Emporda plain and the Pyrenees.

0.9km/24.4km Mare de Déu del Roure. Passing a few metres from this hermitage (to your left), start a long descent on this track which eventually becomes paved. The Way meets an asphalt lane and turns left. After 300m it passes under the AVE viaduct and descends to a crossroads. Continue to the right to enter Pont de Molins.

Quercus suber

1.9km/26.3km Pont de Molins. Upon reaching the town, turn left towards a bridge over the river Muga. Cross the bridge and turn left. Leave the town and take a narrow track to the right, just after the last house (about 100m before a roundabout). 700m on, leave this track and turn left onto a less defined track that ends in a few metres on the N-II road. Here you have to be very careful due to the high volume of traffic.
1.1km/27.4km N-II. ATTENTION. Turn right and follow the hard shoulder for 500m.
0.5km/27.9km Track to Vilabertran. Look for the first track starting on the opposite side of the N-II road. ATTENTION. You have to cross the asphalt main road, which must be done with great care due to the occasional high volume of traffic. In a few metres the track veers right, closely following the river Muga. After 600m pass under the A-7, then turn to the right, leaving the river behind. Continue on to a crossroads where there is an irrigation canal opposite.
1.2km/29.1km Canal. Turn left, walking parallel to the irrigation canal. Continuing straight on at the next intersection, the track now runs parallel to the N-II. A few metres along, ignore a track on the left, then immediately veer left, taking a dilapidated asphalt track. Stay on this track ignoring all options (either to the right or to the left). After crossing a minor road (with a warehouse on the left), continue straight on. Arriving at a large roundabout, go straight over to enter Vilabertran. At a small roundabout, you continue straight on.
4.5km/33.6km Vilabertran Monastery.
Vilabertran pop. 900. Alt Empordà.
From the 10th century onwards an important nucleus for pilgrims travelling to Rome. The monastery had its own hospital to provide shelter and medical help for pilgrims.

Col de Panissars (©Callum Christie)

La Jonquera
- **Pensió Marfil**
  Tel. 972 554 378
- **Hostal Europa**
  Tel. 972 555 534
- **Hostal Frontera**
  Tel. 972 671 898
- **Hotel Nacional**
  Tel. 972 554 100

Agullana
- **El Suro**
  Tel. 972 535 178

Capmany
- **Casa Holly**
  Tel. 972 535 164

El Pont de Molins
- **Hotel la Masia**
  Tel. 972 529 063

Vilabertran
- **Ca la Glòria**
  Tel. 659 447 020

Fort de Bellegarde. C16th fortification built to safeguard Vallespir and France from possible attacks from the south. It features many bastions, a large moat and drawbridge.

Military Cemetary. Built in the C18th, it contains the burial site of 40 French soldiers.

Torre dels Burots. Fortified tower from the C16th-C17th which functioned as housing for the officials in charge of collecting border taxes.

Roman Ruins, Via Augusta. Archaeological remains where the Via Domitia and the Via Augusta met. This pass has been of strategic importance for more than two thousand years.

Church of Santa Maria de La Jonquera. A single nave C15th Gothic temple

Canónica of the Mare de Déu del Roure. A medieval monastery from the end of the C11th which was abandoned in the late 1700s.

Pont Vell de Molins. C18th bridge.

Canónica of Santa Maria de Vilabertran. Romanesque Augustinian monastery dating from the C10th.

2. VILABERTRAN - BÀSCARA: 19.3KM

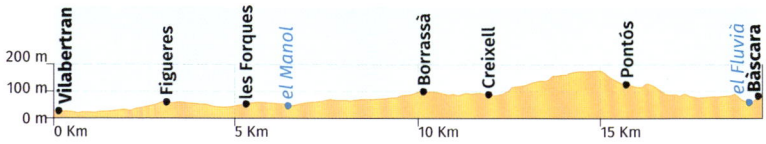

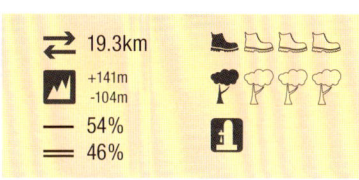

- 19.3km
- +141m / -104m
- 54%
- 46%

The Camino passes through Figueres, a highly visited town given its link with the painter Salvador Dalí. Figueres lies on a plain featuring many small ridges; crowned with occasional pine or holm oak woods and farm fields.

Observations: Precaution needed on the short approach to Bàscara when walking along the N-II.

0km Vilabertran. Leaving the Collegiate Church of Santa María behind you, continue to the left along C. de l'Abat Hortolà.

0.5km/0.5km Dirt Track. At the end of the tree lined promenade turn right onto a dirt track.

1.3km/1.8km Figueres. You enter Figueres passing by the Salvador Dalí school, turning right and then left into C. Compositor Coll. Arriving at the urban section of the C-252, turn left to take C. Tapís. Cross the road and follow C. Peralada to the Pl. Ajuntament.

1.2km/3km Plaça Ajuntament. Turn left at the Town Hall then cross the tree lined Rambla to go straight along C. Sant Pau. Once at the N-IIa roundabout turn left and at the next roundabout turn right to leave Figueres along the Camí de les Forques.

3.7km/6.7km Roundabout Sta. Llogaia. After Les Forques, you cross the river El Manol and at the first roundabout turn right to take an asphalt track. It passes under the AVE train tracks. Later you pass under the AP-7.

3.3km/10km Borrassà. From the Pl. Major you follow the C. de la Plaça. Turn right to take C. de Baix for a few metres, then turn left onto C. Dalmau de Creixell towards Creixell. At the C. del Migdia turn left and at the end of this street turn right onto Camí dels Pujols and exit the town on a dirt track passing under the C-26 to reach the village of Creixell. Turn left towards the bridge of the Riera d'Àlguema.

2.2km/12.2km Crossroads. Turn right onto a dirt track, uphill.

2.1km/14.3km Junction. Turn right onto a road for 200m and then leave it, taking a dirt track on the left.

1.3km/15.6km Pontós. At the far end of the village, turn right by a cross.

2.9km/18.5km N-II. After passing the AVE train line again, turn right to gradually approach the N-II, a busy road.

ATTENTION. The next section requires caution, since you have to walk on the roadside edge.

0.8km/19.3km Bàscara. After crossing the river Fluvià you enter this walled town.

Figueres - pop. 46.000. Capital of Alt Empordà region. Economic centre of the region, it enjoys a privileged location between Barcelona and Rosselló and also between the coast and the Pre-Pyrenees.

Bàscara - pop. 900. Municipality in the Alt Empordà region. Some sections of the former defensive walls remain intact.

©Callum Christie

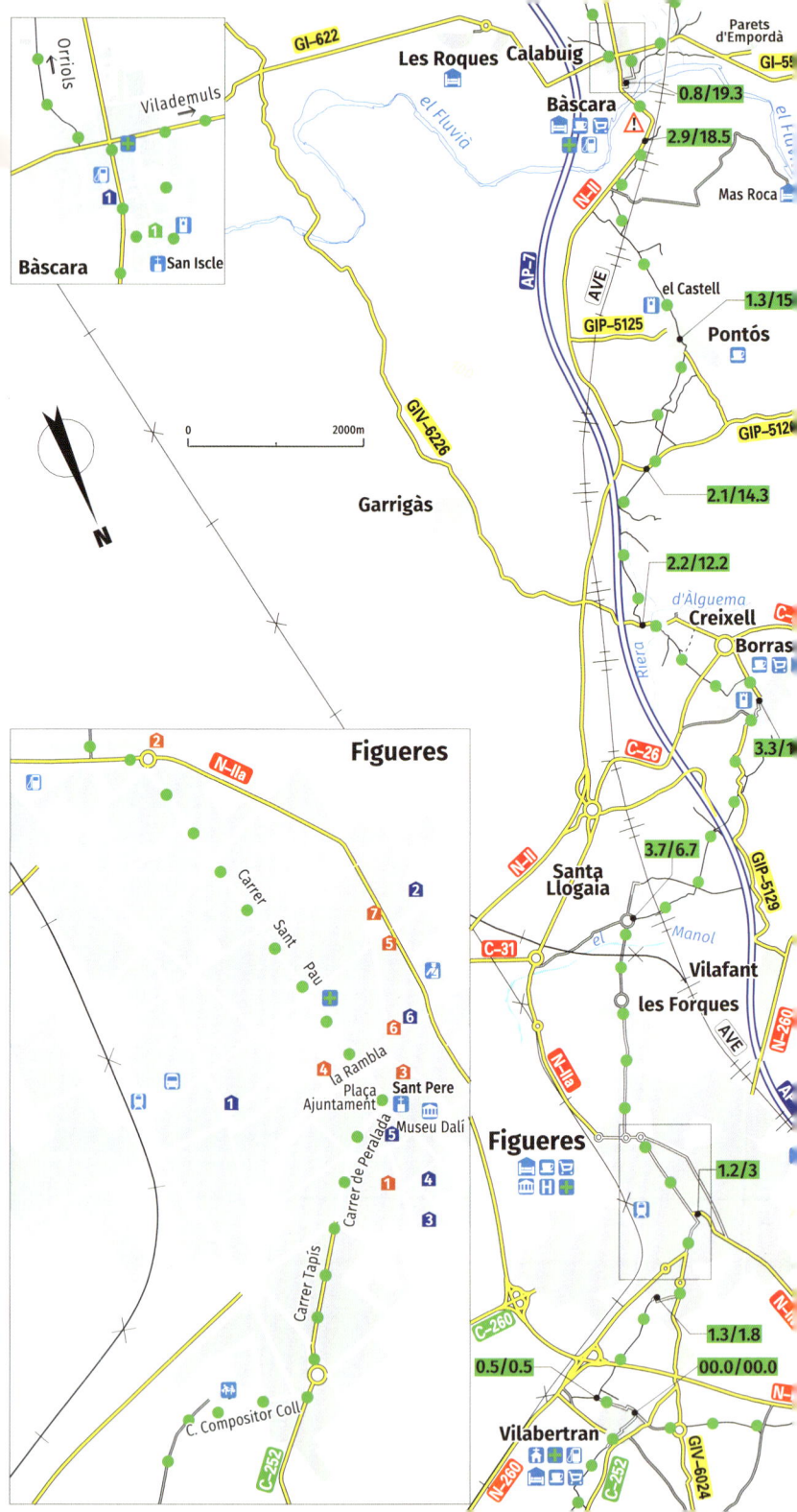

Teatre-museu Dalí. Figueres (©ACT. Nano Cañas)

Figueres
- **Pensió Bartis**
  Tel. 972 501 473
- **Pensió Amiel**
  Tel. 972 504 968
- **Hostal Sanmar**
  Tel. 972 509 813
- **Hostal Isabel II**
  Tel. 619 076 093
- **Hostal Figueres**
  Tel. 630 680 575
- **Hostal la Barretina**
  Tel. 972 676 412
- **Hotel Los Ángeles**
  Tel. 972 510 661
- **Hotel Ronda**
  Tel. 972 676 020
- **Hotel Plaza INN**
  Tel. 972 514 540
- **Hotel Rambla**
  Tel. 972 676 020
- **Hotel President**
  Tel. 972 989 671
- **Hotel Duran**
  Tel. 972 501 250
- **Hotel Pirineos**
  Tel. 972 500 312

Bàscara
- **Hotel Mas Roca**
  Tel. 610 463 055
- **Pensió Fluvià**
  Tel. 972 560 014
- **Ca la Maria**
  Tel. 652 415 797

Calabuig
- **Hotel Les Roques**
  Tel. 972 560 251

Teatre-Museu Dalí. A mid-C19th building that had functioned as a theatre, suffering a fire that completely destroyed it in 1939. In 1974 it was remodelled as a museum to house the legacy of the painter Salvador Dalí.

Sant Pere de Figueres. A C14th Gothic church probably built on top of an early Christian one that was replaced by a Romanesque church of which some walls remain.

Church of Sant Iscle de Bàscara. A late Romanesque and Gothic style church with a single nave.

Bàscara Castle. A square shaped fortification that protected both the town's populace as well as the Camino de Santiago.

3. BÀSCARA - GIRONA: 30.8KM/27.6KM

In Bàscara the Camino divides before meeting up again at Medinyà. Both of the mapped options are specified below.

3A. BÀSCARA - MEDINYÀ via ORRIOLS: 19.8km

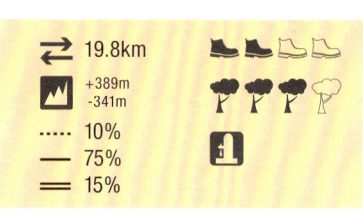

The Camino via Orriols features small villages surrounded by cultivated fields, native woodland and extensive poplar groves along the Ter river. The Monastery of Santa Maria in Cervià de Ter was an important ecclesiastical centre and retains a charming simplicity.

0km Bàscara. Proceed along the main street (the N-II) to a crossroads. Turn left towards Sant Mori and after 100m turn right. Now on a narrow dirt track, arrive at the extensive farmhouse of Mas d'Espollà and continue to the left. Coming to some woodland, take the rough track to the right that ends at a crossroads, where you turn left.

4.4km/4.4km Orriols. From the church, continue on, leaving the village by taking a farm track between fields. You eventually pass under the AP-7.

1.9km/6.3km Road GIV-6234. 400m after the AP-7 turn right onto the GIV-6234. After 1km take the first asphalted lane on the left. After 250m there is a bend where you take a dirt road straight on. After 350m turn right to reach a group of houses and the chapel of Sant Martí de la Móra. Continue to the right, along the asphalt track.

3.2km/9.5km Viladasens. Reaching this village, go around the back of the church. In the C. de la Font turn left and continue, passing the Cemetery.

1.5km/11km GIV-6234. When you reach this road, take a dirt track that begins in front of you (left). Proceed through fields to return to GIV-6234 and cross it, continuing on a rough track that passes by a farm.

2.2km/13.2km Raset. Entering through the Veïnat de Dalt neighborhood you turn left to go down to the Veïnat de Baix. As soon as you meet a small square, take the narrow street to the right going uphill. This changes into a rough track through sheltered woodland and then becomes a path. Entering Cervià de Ter turn right towards the walls of the Monastery of Santa María.

1.4km/14.6km Santa Maria Monastery. Continue ahead on C. Priorat to Pl. de l'Església and then reach the Pl. Generalitat with its striking Torre de les Hores. Turn right taking C. Girona to the outskirts of town and a crossroads. It forks left, just before a stone cross to reach the road GI-633 where you turn right.

1km/15.6km Bridge. In a few metres, just before a bridge over the l'Arner stream, turn left onto a dirt lane. After 200m it forks to the left entering a poplar plantation; a stretch with little signage for the Camino. After 500m it forks to the right to continue between the poplars

1.7km/17.3km Chain. You come to a chain across the path. Continue about 50m and take an earthen track to the left between more rows of poplars. After 200m turn right, crossing a stream, then continue between the trees for about 350m until you come to the banks of the river Ter.

0.6km/17.9km River Ter. Turn right, following the river.

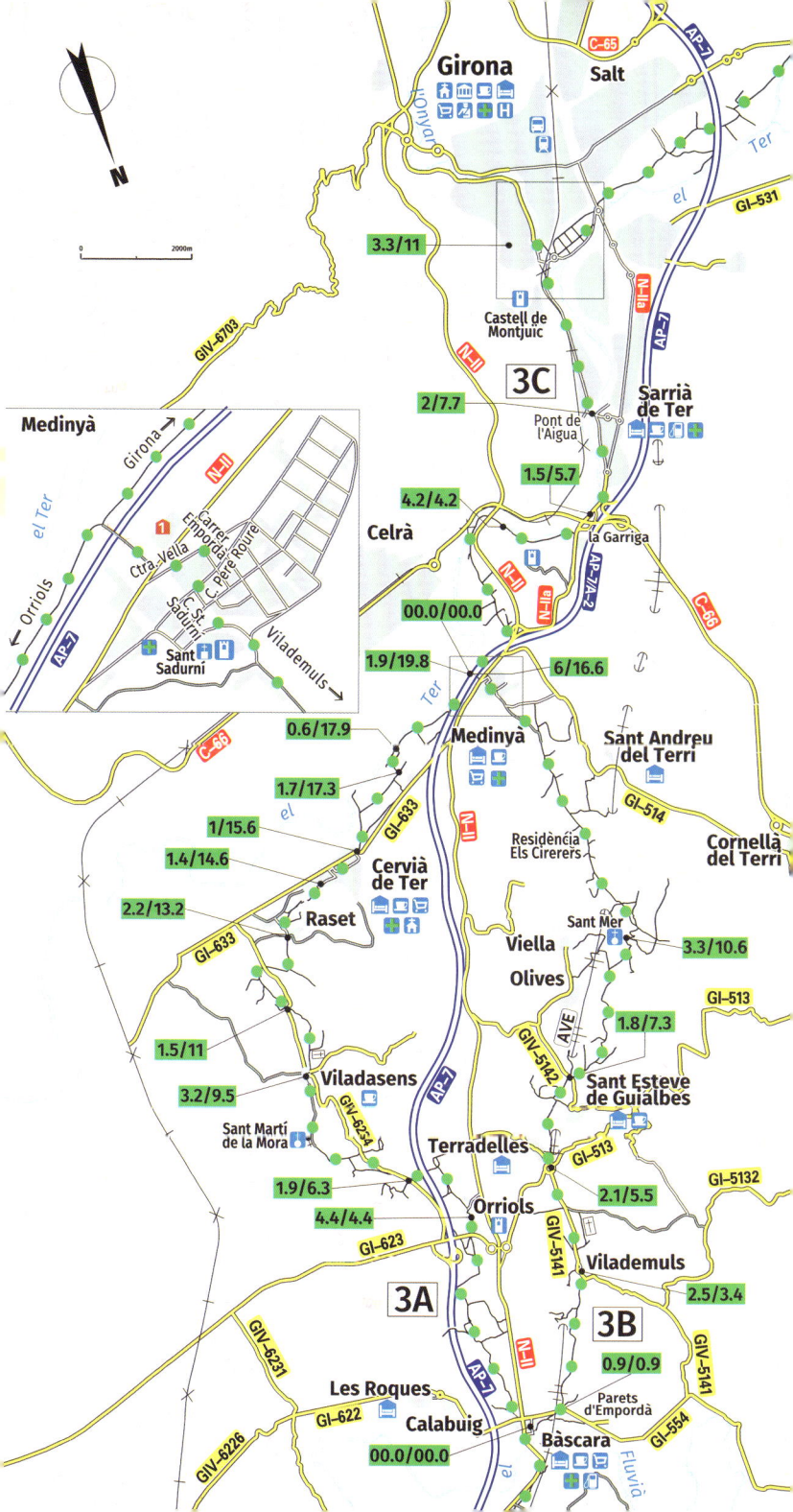

1.9km/19.8km Bridge AP-7. Continue straight on parallel to the AP-7 leaving Medinyà to your right. Upon reaching the N-II, take the track on the left (Cami del Congost), between the fields and poplar groves.

Cervià de Ter

Cervià de Ter
🟢 **Mas Borrell** 💰💰   Tel. 972 496 724 - 678 661 839

Orriols Castle. Whilst the present building is a fortified palace from the C16th-C18th, this large rectangular residence has its origins in the Middle Ages.
Chapel of Sant Martí de la Móra. Chapel serving several 'Masias' (farmhouses), possibly dating from the C11th or C12th.

Santa Maria Monastery, Cervià de Ter. Romanesque settlement with church and cloister. Founded by Silvi Llobet in 1053, it housed a Benedictine community.
Torre de les Hores, Cervià de Ter. Tower that once defended one of the gates of the medieval wall, it currently holds the large public clock.

3B. BÀSCARA - MEDINYÀ via VILADEMULS: 16.6km

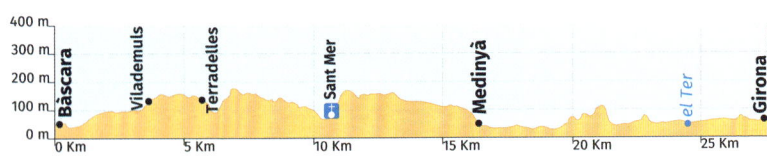

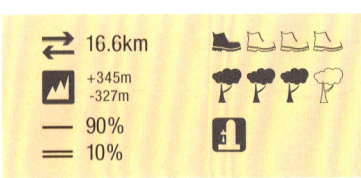

- 16.6km
- +345m / -327m
- 90%
- 10%

This option through Vilademuls is somewhat shorter than the one through Orriols. The gradients are more pronounced but it enjoys more shade.
0km Bàscara. From the old town you connect with the GI-554 road in the direction of Esponellà.

0.9km/0.9km Road on Left. After passing under the Ave rail line, turn left on a country lane towards 'Veïnat de Monells'.
2.5km/3.4km Vilademuls. From the village continue uphill on the GIV-5141.
2.1km/5.5km Roundabout GI-513. Continue straight on towards Terradelles and after about 200m, turn right onto a gravel track.
1.8km/7.3km Road to Sant Esteve de Guialbes. On reaching the road, turn right, then after 50m turn left onto an asphalted track towards Sant Mer, soon becoming a gravel track.
3.3km/10.6km Sant Mer Chapel. Continue uphill some 500m through woodland and join a wider track turning left. Continue across a plateau with magnificent views towards the interior of the Empordà region. Descend abruptly into Medinyà. Halfway down the hill take the steps on the right hand side down into the town. Emerge at the N-II by a traffic light. Cross the N-II here (with care), to pick up a dirt lane opposite. A few metres along, cross a bridge over the AP-7 to exit the town.
6km/16.6km Bridge AP-7. Over the bridge

Vilademuls

you rejoin the Camino coming from Orriols. Turn right to continue parallel to the AP-7 and then to the N-II, between fields and poplar groves on the Camí del Congost.

 Terradelles
🏠 **Mas Alba** 🪙🪙🪙
Tel. 972 560 488
Sant Esteve de Guialbes
🏠 **Mas Vidal** 🪙
Tel. 636 490 992

Sant Andreu del Terri
🏠 **Can Portell B&B** 🪙🪙🪙
Tel. 972 594412
Medinyà
🏨 **Hotel Restaurante Medinyà** 🪙
Tel. 972 498 000

🏛 **Hermitage of Sant Mer.** Charming C17th chapel.

Medinyà Castle. Ancient medieval castle now a stately home.

3C. MEDINYÀ - GIRONA: 11km

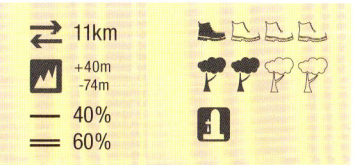

From Medinyà the Camino follows the river Ter, first by the Camí de Congost and then through the outskirts of the city into Girona.
0km Bridge AP-7. Meeting point of the two routes from Bàscara.
4.2km/4.2km Sant Vicenç. Country house with a chapel on the banks of the Ter. The

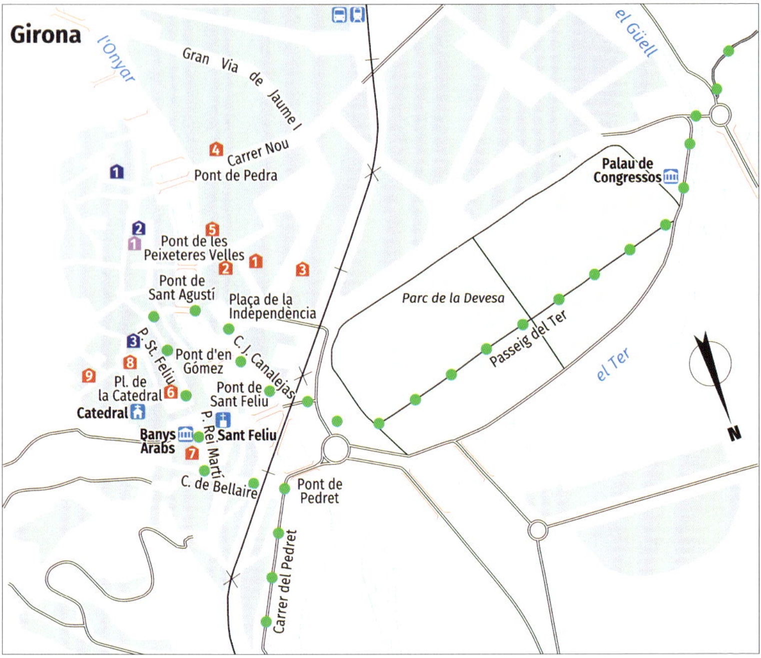

Camino approaches the N-IIa, to meet a road junction. Turn left, along the asphalt verge with care.

1.5km/5.7km La Garriga. Cross the Garriga stream just before entering Sarrià de Ter. When you reach a roundabout take the C. Vora el Ter, which then becomes C. Major de Sarrià.
2km/7.7km L'Aigua Bridge. Cross the Ter and continue to the right, along the C. del Pont Major. Reaching the Pedret bridge look for C. Bellaire on the left. Enter the old town climbing the Pujada del Rei Martí.
3.3km/11km Girona Cathedral.
Girona - pop. 98.000. Capital del Gironès. An impressive city that preserves a large historic centre with medieval walls.

Girona

- **1 Alberg Cerverí**
  Tel. 972 218 003
- **1 Pensió Borràs**
  Tel. 972 224 008
- **2 Pensió Viladomat**
  Tel. 972 203 176
- **3 Pensió Bellmirall**
  Tel. 972 204 009

- **1 B&B Bed in Girona**
  Tel. 872 026 543
- **2 Hotel Nord 1901**
  Tel. 972 203 850
- **3 Hotel Ultònia**
  Tel. 972 203 850
- **4 Hotel Peninsular**
  Tel. 972 203 80
- **5 Hotel Ciutat de Girona**
  Tel. 972 483 03

- **6 Hotel Casa Cundaro**
  Tel. 972 223 583
- **7 Hotel Rei Martí**
  Tel. 676 635 530
- **8 Hotel Històric**
  Tel. 972 223 583
- **9 AS Palau dels Alemanys**
  Tel. 618 536 852

Girona (©ACT. Oriol Clavera)

Cathedral, Girona. Built on top of a Roman temple, most of the Cathedral is Gothic. The bell tower and cloister are Romanesque and the main façade is Baroque. It has the broadest Gothic nave in the world spanning some 22m.

The Tower of Sant Feliu, Girona. A remarkable Gothic spire which belongs to the main temple of the city built prior to the construction of the cathedral. It too presents the different architectural styles of Romanesque, Gothic and Baroque.

Arab Baths, Girona. Public building from the C11th imitating North African Arab baths though the style is Romanesque.

The Bridges, Girona. Linking the two banks of the river Onyar and the old city to the Mercadal neighborhood. Roman, medieval, wooden or metal bridges have been replaced in turn by today's bridges. Les Peixateries Velles (1876), features iron work by Gustave Eiffel.

4. Girona - Amer: 26.6km

This extremely well marked cycle route from Girona to Amer follows the 'Via Verde del Carrilet', an off-road, former narrow gauge railway that linked Girona with Olot. This earthen track combines stretches along the Ter and Brugent rivers amongst woodland and waterfalls, with other sections that pass through a valley dotted with villages and fields. Passing through oak groves and pastures, occasional small ravines are crossed by bridges.

0km Girona. From the Cathedral, make your way down through the old town to enter the Parc de la Devesa, crossing its impressive urban woodland.

2.1km/2.1km Start of the Via Verde. At the end of the Park, after crossing a roundabout (next to the Palau de Congressos), the Via Verde del Carrilet to Olot begins.

5.4km/7.5km Aigües Braves la Pilastra Park. The banks of the river are filled with poplars and ash trees. Reach the height of the N-141e road (without joining it) and continue along the Via Verde.

1.2km/8.7km Bescanó Station. From this former station the landscape broadens, giving attractive views.

6.5km/15.2km Vilanna Station. Situated just after the Bonmatí road junction and the bridge over the Ter. Later, on entering Anglès, cross the road by a gas station and continue along the other side of the N-141e following the Via Verde.

4km/19.2km Anglès Station. The Way continues along the Ter river valley. Bypass the village of Cellera de Ter, then pass under the C-63.4.

3.8km/23km El Pasteral Station. The Via Verde descends and crosses over the river Ter. Ignore the arrows directing you left along a longer option to the Susqueda reservoir.

0.6km/23.6km Road C-63. Caution is needed when crossing.

3km/26.6km Amer. The track makes its way to the highest part of Amer, where the station is located.

Amer - pop. 2200. Most populated municipality in the Brugent river valley.

Anglès
1 Hostal Tarrès
Tel. 972 421 314
2 Hostal Can Massot
Tel. 972 420 007

Pasteral
1 Hotel Pasteral
Tel. 687 639 057
Amer
1 Restaurant Fonda Giralt
Tel. 972 430 045

1 Restaurant Hotel Sant Marçal
Tel. 678 403 326
1 Hotel Rural Masia d'Amer
Tel. 972 431 051

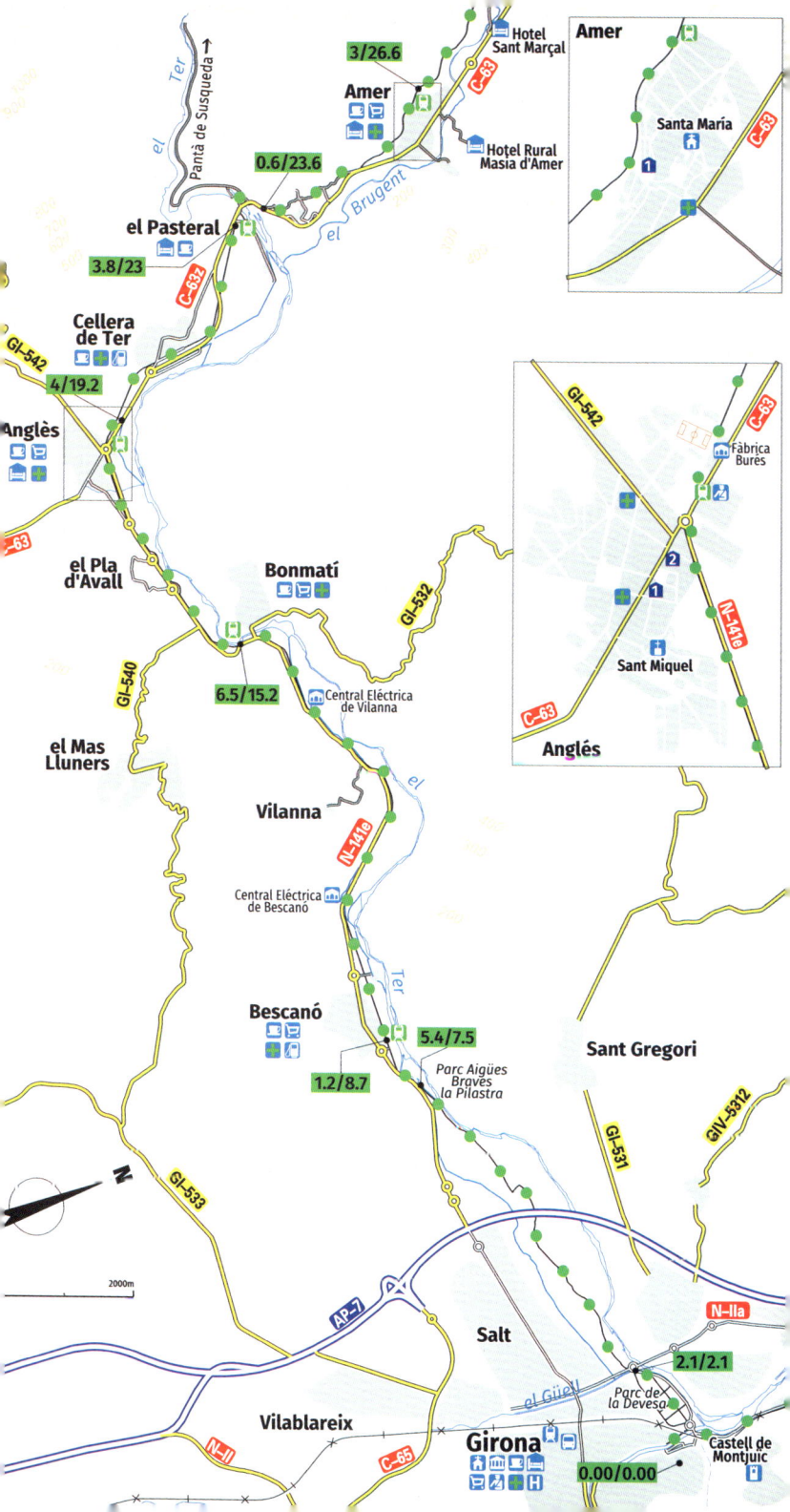

Amer (©Julián López-Arenas González)

La Devesa, Girona. This 40 hectare urban park is the largest in Catalonia. Built in the 19th century some of its Plane trees were established in 1850 and reach a height of 60 m.
The Trainline from Girona to Olot. Built in 28 years it came into operation in 1911 connecting the lowlands around Girona with the mountains of La Garrotxa. The railway service was shut down in 1969 and converted into the 'Via Verde de Carrilet' in the 1990s.
Power Plant, Bescanó. Established in the early 20th century, it consists of a guard house and two floors for machinery. In the lower part, two bridges regulate the passage of water.
Power Plant, Vilanna. Industrial building from the early C20th. Whilst functional, it also has some aesthetic value, together with its striking irrigation canal.

Vila Vella, Anglès. The old town streets of C. Major, C. Molí, C. del Castell and C. Avall, along with their surroundings, form an interesting urban network of medieval origin housing a Jewish neighbourhood. The castle of Los Cabrera and the church of Sant Miquel are also of interest.
Santa Maria de Sales, La Cellera. The oldest remains of this church are from the C12th, when the building suffered the effects of an earthquake. The Tower of les Bruixes is the most impressive part of the present C17th building.
Old Town, Amer. The Plaza Mayor. This grand arcaded square is considered to be the second largest in Catalonia.

5. AMER - SANT ESTEVE D'EN BAS: 23.1KM

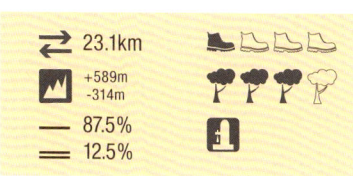

This leafy section of the Camino continues to follow the former train route through mixed oak woodland, interspersed with lush green fields. The Brugent valley is dominated by the Far mountains. If you choose to continue on to Olot, the Way travels through a valley with superb views towards the Pyrenean peaks.

0km Amer. Continue from the former station.
8.1km/8.1km Les Planes d'Hostoles Station. The Via Verde crosses the C-63 to continue opposite, along the Passeig de l'Estació.
5.3km/13.4km Sant Feliu de Pallerols Station. The Via Verde now becomes a street that goes under a railway bridge and passes by the former station, now a bar.
4.9km/18.3km C-152a. Turn left upon reaching the junction with the C-152a, leaving the Via Verde to climb to the Coll d'en Bas.
1.5km/19.8km La Casilla. Rejoin the Via Verde, turning right and passing a former railway building, now a restaurant.
1.9km/21.7km Road C63z. Turn right onto a local road and pass under the C-63 to reach the C-63z road. Once over the zebra crossing, after a few metres turn right onto the Via Verde.
1.4km/23.1km Sant Esteve d'en Bas. Follow the path along the Ridaura stream to reach the end of this stage in the town. Carrer l'Andana and the parallel Carrer Sant Josep take you to C.del Agutzil Ramón Martí, where the option to continue on towards Olot on the Via Verde begins.
Sant Esteve d'en Bas - pop. 1500. Main town of the Vall d'en Bas municipal area, which includes the hamlets of Sant Privat and Joanetes i Pinya.

Les Planes d'Hostoles
🟢 **Mas Vedruna** ⌒⌒
Tel. 625 522 864
🟢 **El Llober** ⌒⌒
Tel. 646 612 714
🟠 **Hotel Can Garay** ⌒⌒⌒
Tel. 972 448 253

Sant Feliu de Pallarols
🔵 **Fonda Finet** ⌒⌒
Tel. 972 444 024
🟢 **La Rectoria** ⌒⌒⌒
Tel. 691 353 111

Sant Esteve d'en Bas
🟠 **Alberg Vall d'en Bas** ⌒
Tel. 972 690 794
Veïnat de Can Trones
🟠 **Hotel Vall d'en Bas** ⌒⌒⌒
Tel. 972 690 10

 Church of Sant Feliu de Pallerols. C16th church with an imposing bell tower, an interesting wooden pulpit in the nave and an alabaster image of the Virgen de Gracia.
Sant Miquel de la Pineda, Sant Feliu de Pallerols. Romanesque chapel in the hamlet of Sant Miquel de la Pineda which suffered great damage during the earthquakes of the C15th.
Church of Sant Esteve d'en Bas. Built in Romanesque style this church has undergone transformation after the earthquakes of the C15th and the Spanish civil war.

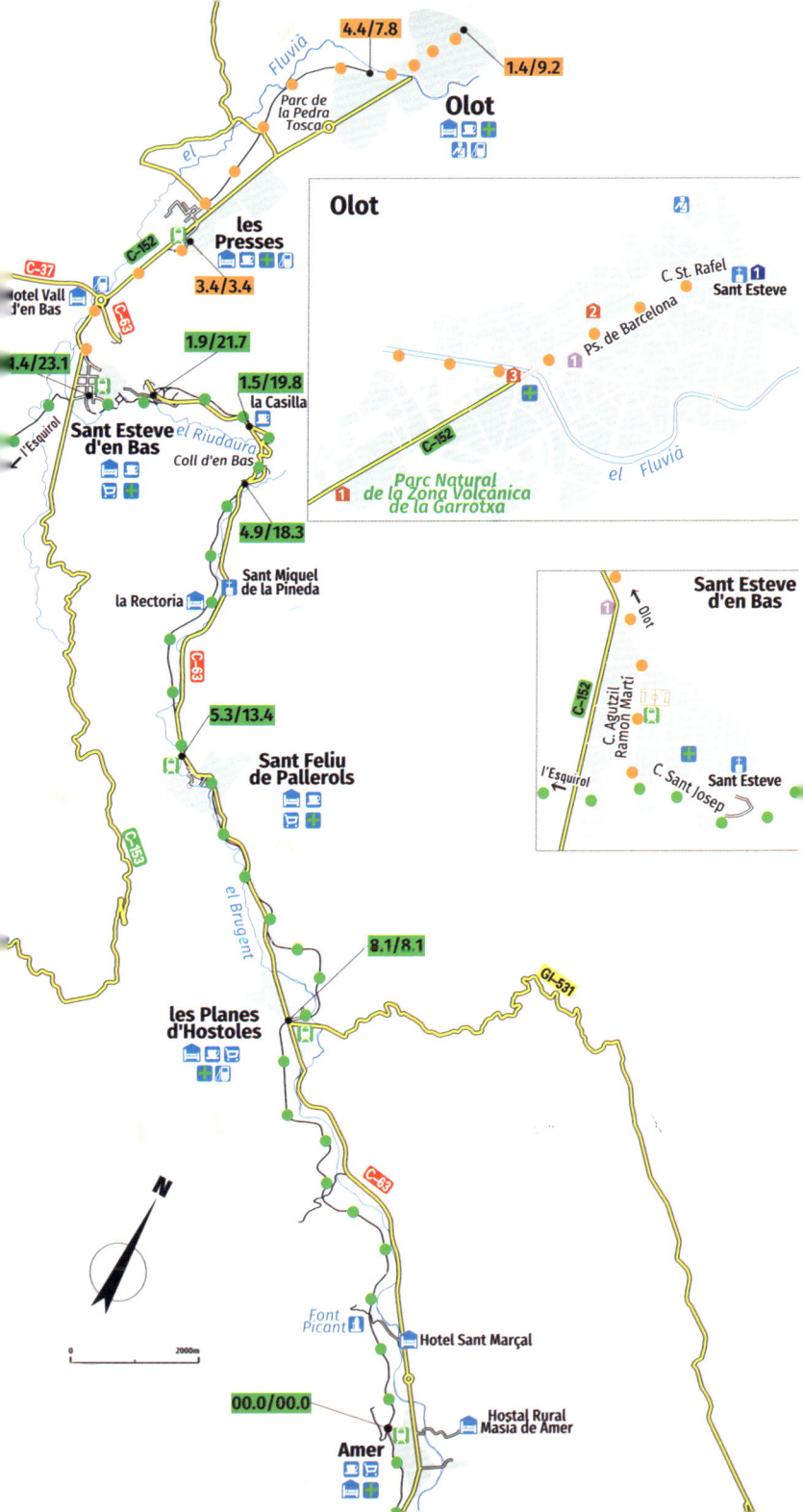

Falgars d'en Bas (©ACT. Kim Castells)

SANT ESTEVE - OLOT: 9.2km

Sant Esteve - Olot (Via Verde del Carrilet)
0km Sant Esteve d'en Bas. From C. de l'Agutzil Ramón Martí, take the Via Verde towards Olot.
3.4km/3.4km Les Preses Station. Cross the main street (C-152) and continue ahead on C. Pintor Pascual. Enter Olot following the course of the river Fluvià to a bridge
4.4km/7.8km Bridge of Sant Roc, Olot. Cross the river and continue straight on to the church.
1.4km/9.2km Church of Sant Esteve.

Les Preses
- Hostal Ventijol
  Tel. 972 692 148

Olot
- Alberg Xanascat
  Tel. 972 264 200
- Hostal la Vila
  Tel. 972 269 807
- Hotel la Perla
  Tel. 972 262 326
- Hotel Borrell
  Tel. 972 276 161
- Hotel l'Estació
  Tel. 972 261 007

Olot Volcanos. Some 40 extinct conical volcanoes and more than twenty lava flows with an age ranging from 350,000 to 10,000 years.

6. Sant Esteve d'en Bas - L'Esquirol: 21.4km

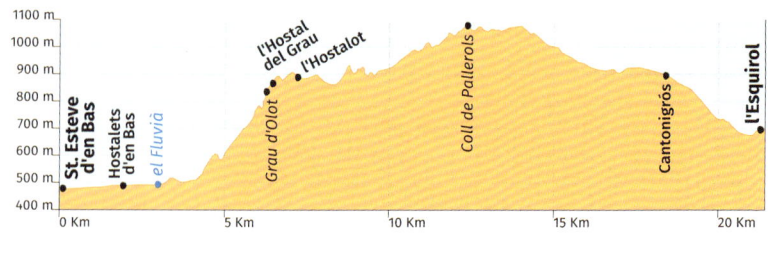

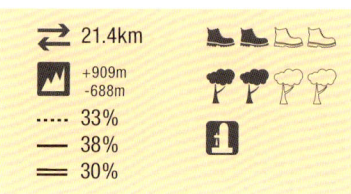

- 21.4km
- +909m / -688m
- ····· 33%
- — 38%
- ═ 30%

This is one of the most attractive stages of the Camino in the Girona region. With a considerable climb, it takes you from the valley d'en Bas up over a beautifully secluded highland in the heart of Collsacabra. The journey on the Camí Ral de Olot to Vic begins on the fertile plain of the river Fluvià. From a cobblestone way in the Cingle del Grau, it rises through woodlands of beech and oaks, dotted with meadows and pastures. For a good part of this walk, the imposing Cingle d'Aiats, with its vertical walls, will be the visual reference. Descending from Cantonigrós to l'Esquirol you follow another historical track.

0km Sant Esteve d'en Bas. Continue along the C. de Sant Josep until it joins the C-153, crossing to continue along an asphalted lane. After 200m, take the first track on the left that crosses the river Fluvià over a small stone bridge. Eventually, turn left onto an

Els Hostalets d'en Bas

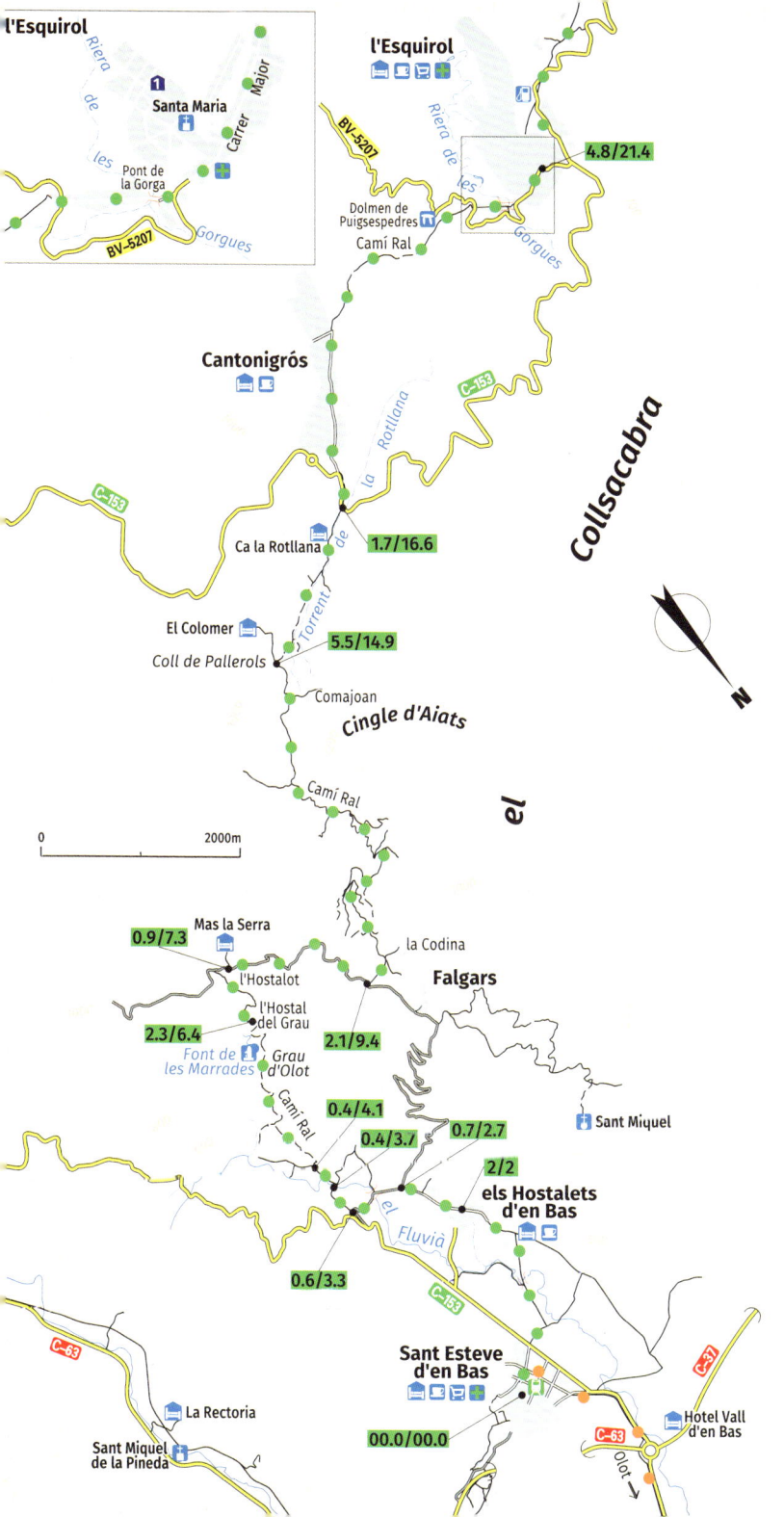

asphalted lane.
2km/2km Els Hostalets d'en Bas. Passing the church, continue along the C. de Vic.
0.7km/2.7km Track to Falgars. Ignore a signed track on your right (it is a new zigzagged asphalt way via Falgars, considered neither attractive nor historical). Continue straight on (left), crossing the Fluvià again.
0.6km/3.3km Track Right. A few metres before a house, take a dirt track on the right.
0.4km/3.7km Bridge. After 400m cross the Fluvià again and immediately turn left at a fork in the track.
0.4km/4.1km Camí Ral. Upon reaching the woods, take the right hand track and begin the gradual ascent along the Camino Ral de Vic, passing through areas of exceptional beauty such as the Font de les Marrades.
2.3km/6.4km L'Hostal del Grau. After climbing to the Grau d'Olot and reaching a cattle meadow, you cross a wood, the abandoned hostel building now behind you.
0.9km/7.3km L'Hostalot. Reaching an asphalted track, turn right to pass by the driveway to Mas de la Serra and after 1km pass the entrance to another farmhouse next to the road.
2.1km/9.4km Track Left. 1km further on, an asphalted track to a cattle farm appears on the left. Take this track and 100m before a farmhouse take a minor earthen track on the left. The Camino now follows a series of tracks climbing between woods and meadows. The Cami Ral de Vic enjoys excellent views of the surrounding flat topped outcrops. Eventually you join an asphalted track, walk 400m across the pass known as Coll de Pallerols.
5.5km/14.9km El Colomer. About 200m before reaching the El Colomer farmhouse, turn right onto a path that descends between pastures and fences following the course of the Rotllada stream. The path ends at Creu and joins a track where you head left downhill.
1.7km/16.6km Road C-153. Reaching the C-153, cross and walk parallel to the road. On reaching the first houses of Cantonigròs, walk along Camí Ral, C. Major and then C. de l'Esquirol which leads into the beginning of a rough track. The Way continues downhill through an old cobbled section of Camí Ral.
4.8km/21.4km L'Esquirol. Enter the town by the C. del Pont and shortly after the bridge over the Gorgues river, climb to the town centre.
L'Esquirol - pop. 2150. Main town of a larger municipal area that includes the hamlets of Cantonigròs, Sant Julià de Cabrera and Sant Martí Sescorts.

Els Hostalets d'en Bas
● **Ca La Remei**
Tel. 620 587976
Folgars d'en Bas
● **Mas la Serra**
Tel. 648 778 128

Rupit i Pruit
● **El Colomer**
Tel. 636 48 05 83
Cantonigròs
● **Ca la Rotllada**
Tel. 93 856 50 24
● **Hostal Cabrerès**
Tel. 93 856 50 22

● **Casa de Colònies Santa Maria del Roure**
Tel. 93 856 50 59
L'Esquirol
● **Hostal Collsacabra**
Tel. 93 856 80 33

Camí Ral Hostalries, Vall d'en Bas. L'Hostalot and l'Hostal del Grau are part of this road engineering heritage. The town of Hostalets originates from providing lodging for knights and was a well known stop-over on the route. The historic Hostal de Can Llonga is still standing.
Dolmen of Puigsespedres, L'Esquirol. This megalithic monument lies hidden just off the Camí Ral.
La Gorga Bridge, L'Esquirol. C14th Stone bridge with two unequal arches, its pillars have breakwaters.
Santa Maria Church, L'Esquirol. Baroque church that suffered major damage to its nave during the Civil War.

7. L'ESQUIROL - VIC: 18.7KM

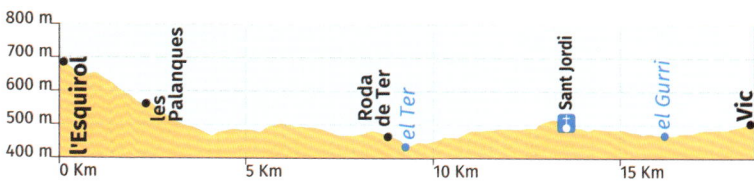

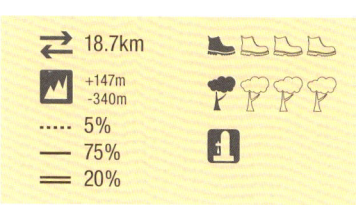

The descent from Collsacabra to the plain surrounding Vic continues along the historic Camí Ral enjoying some short cobbled sections. The Way leads you gently down through a tranquil landscape of fields and farmhouses. The town of Vic has an impressive, well-preserved medieval quarter.

0km L'Esquirol. Starting from C. Nou, continue on C. Francesc Macià and C. Major to leave the town, reaching the C-153 at the petrol station. Cross the road and turn left, briefly following the old road that brings you back to the C-153. Cross the road and turn right onto the Camí Ral which winds though fields between farm buildings.

2.3km/2.3km Les Palanques. At this farmhouse (next to the C-153) continue left, parallel to the road, for 200m. At the Km13 road post, turn left down an asphalted track that eventually reaches the Sant Martí Bridge. Passing by a factory (walking between industrial buildings), you come to the C-153. At the road, turn left onto a parallel track and after 400m turn left onto a well defined asphalted track. Going downhill, turn right at the first fork onto a rough earthen track which gently descends passing through woodland, then open fields.

5.1km/7.4km Les Cases Noves. At the entrance to this neighbourhood you come to a fork with 2 alternative signs for the Camino. Take the officially marked route to the left along the Còdol Dret road.

0.6km/8.0km Cobbled Track. A few metres after the last house, take a cobbled track to the right, uphill. Continue straight on towards the outskirts of Roda de Ter and enter along C. Balmes and C. Ramón Martí.

1.2km/9.2km Pont Vell. Crossing the 'Old Bridge', immediately turn left by the Chapel of the Verge del Sol del Pont. Walk along the narrow C. Verge del Sol del Pont, eventually turning left into C. del General Carbó then right into C. del Puig to leave the town. The Camino returns to the Camí Ral.

2.6km/11.8km Road BV-5213. Cross and continue south though farmland, passing close to the chapel of Sant Jordi de Puigseslloses.

2.3km/14.1km Bridge over C-25. After crossing over the bridge, turn left and walk parallel to the C-25 for 400m. At a fork in the track, turn right leading you to an unfinished industrial park. Take a track to the left that skirts the asphalt layout, soon reaching the delightful setting of the Gurri river.

2.1km/16.2km Pont d'en Bruguer. Cross this spectacular medieval bridge and 400m further on reach the outskirts of Vic. At a fork in the asphalt, turn right along C. de Josep Vicenç Foix then left onto the urban section of the C-153. After 200m you pass the roundabout of Pl. de Catalunya and continue straight on along Ctra. de Roda reaching the Pl. de la Divina Pastora. Keep straight

Vic (©Gen-Lock. Germen Coll)

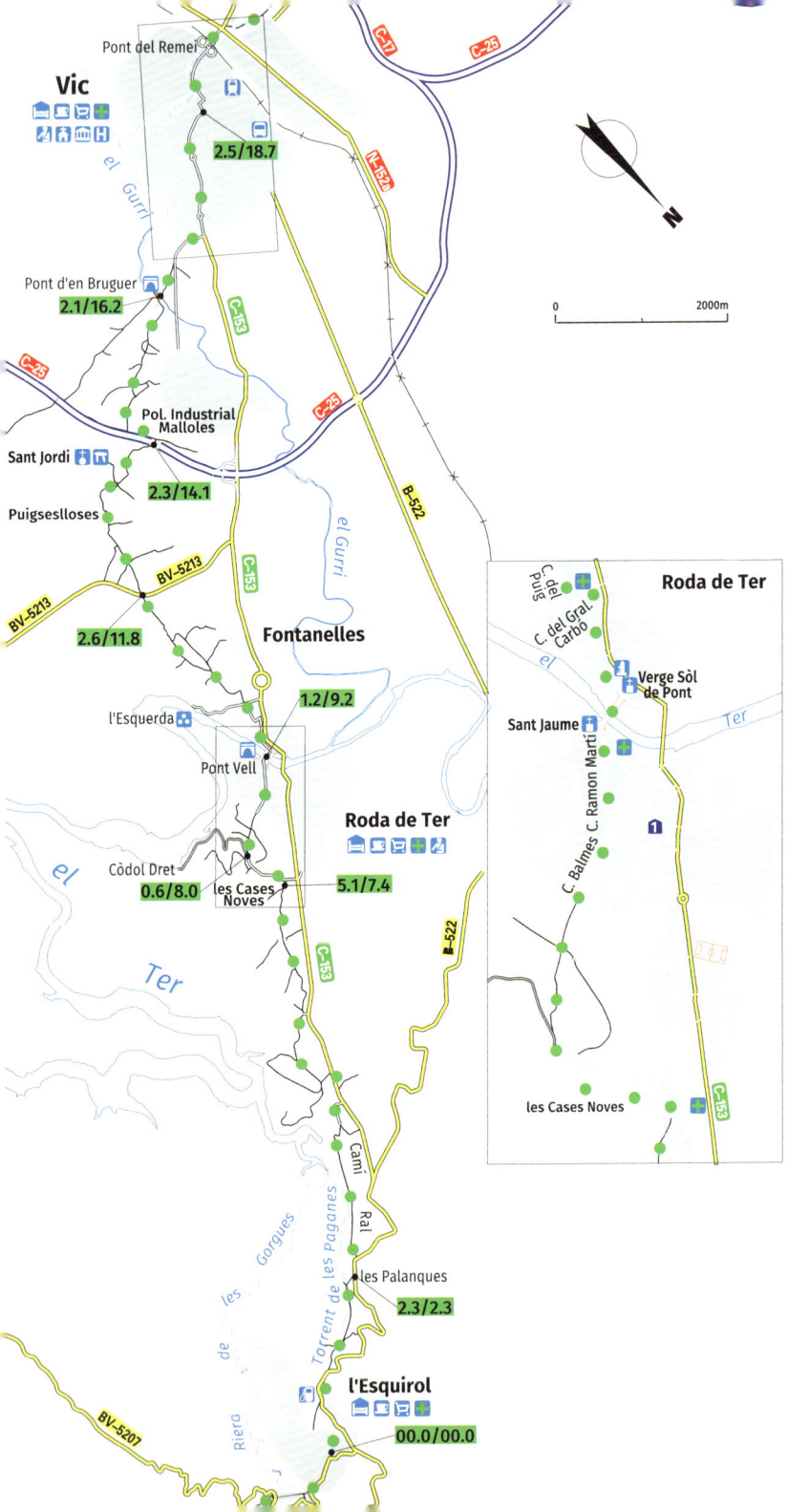

on, taking the narrow C. de Santa Joaquima de Vedruna which becomes the C. de Dues Soles. At the Pl. de la Pietat you find the Roman temple and the Cathedral.
2.5km/18.7km Vic Cathedral.

Vic - pop. 48.000. This historical town is one of the economic and social axes of the interior of Catalonia. It is the main town of the Osona region.

Roda de Ter
🏠 **Fonda Urgell**
Tel. 93 850 00 82
Vic
🏠 **Alberg Canonge Collell**
Tel. 93 889 49 38
🏠 **Seminari de Vic**
Tel. 93 886 15 55
🏠 **Hotel Balmes**
Tel. 93 889 12 72
🏠 **Hotel Estació del Nord**
Tel. 93 516 62 92
🏠 **Hotel Can Pamplona**
Tel. 93 883 31 12
🏠 **Hotel Ups Room Vic**
Tel. 93 889 25 51
🏠 **Hotel les Clarisses**
Tel. 93 660 60 00

Pont Vell, Roda de Ter. C16th bridge over the river Ter.
L'Esquerda, Roda de Ter. Archaeological site, occupied since the Bronze Age by various cultures. Now housed in a museum.
Sant Jordi de Puigseslloses, Folgueroles. C16th rectangular chapel with a small semi-circular apse. Next to it are the remains of a dolmen.
Pont d'en Bruguer, Vic. Medieval bridge from the C14th-C15th. Its magnificent 40 metre span consists of five arches.

Roman Temple, Vic. An impressive rectangular temple with columns and a portico.
Plaça Major, Vic. Also known as the Mercadal, this beautiful porticoed square holds the weekly market. It houses various historical buildings, including the gothic styled town hall.
Sant Pere Cathedral, Vic. The Cathedral combines a mixture of architectural styles ranging from the Romanesque bell tower to the later neoclassical extension. It features a gothic style cloister and the baroque Sant Bernat chapel.

8. VIC - L'ESTANY: 20.1KM

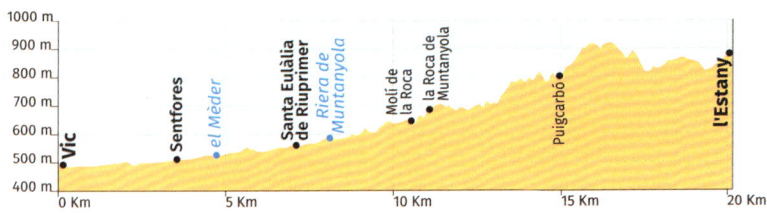

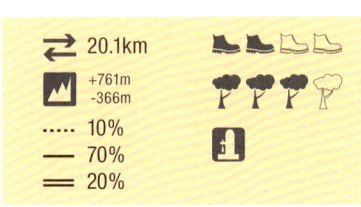

- 20.1km
- +761m / -366m
- ···· 10%
- — 70%
- ═ 20%

The first section enjoys the riverside woodland with its dams and fords, waterfalls and old mills. The Way then climbs the wooded slopes of the Serra de Can Postius leading to l'Estany.

Observations: Attention crossing the fords if it has rained.

0km Vic. From the Cathedral take the C. de Santa María which leads to the river Mèder. Without crossing, turn right and reach the Pont del Remei, with its six arches. Cross and turn right following the course of the river and passing under the railway line. Under the N-152a road turn right onto a track following the Mèder and past an ice well. Turn left on an asphalt track and after 100m take the first track on the left.

2.3km/2.3km C-17. Just after passing under the C-17 motorway, do not cross the small bridge but continue alongside the river. Leaving Sentfores village to the left, the Camino continues along the banks of the Mèder and before reaching the BV-4316 you cross the stream. If the water covers the ford you can reach the road by taking a track on the right and crossing a bridge.

2.5km/4.8km La Riera. Cross the road following a wide gravel track ahead.

2.3km/7.1km Football Ground. Reaching the outskirts of Santa Eulàlia you cross the Muntanyola river and follow its course on a dirt track parallel to the main road. Pass a large green warehouse before returning onto a narrow dirt track. Eventually rejoin the main road.

2.5km/9.6km Road BV-4317. Turn left to walk with care along the roadside.

1km/10.6km Molí de la Roca. 100m after this farmhouse, turn right to leave the BV-4317 taking the asphalt track to La Roca on the right, going uphill.

4.2km/14.8km Puigcarbó. Farmhouse on the left of the track, slightly hidden by oak and pine trees. Continue, climbing up through the woods.

5.3km/20.1km L'Estany. Pass by the 'mina' at the entrance of the town.

L'Estany - pop. 400. Village of the Moianès.

Santa Maria de L'Estany

  L'Estany
 Cal Sabata
Tel. 93 830 31 20
 Monestir de Santa Maria
Tel. 93 830 30 40

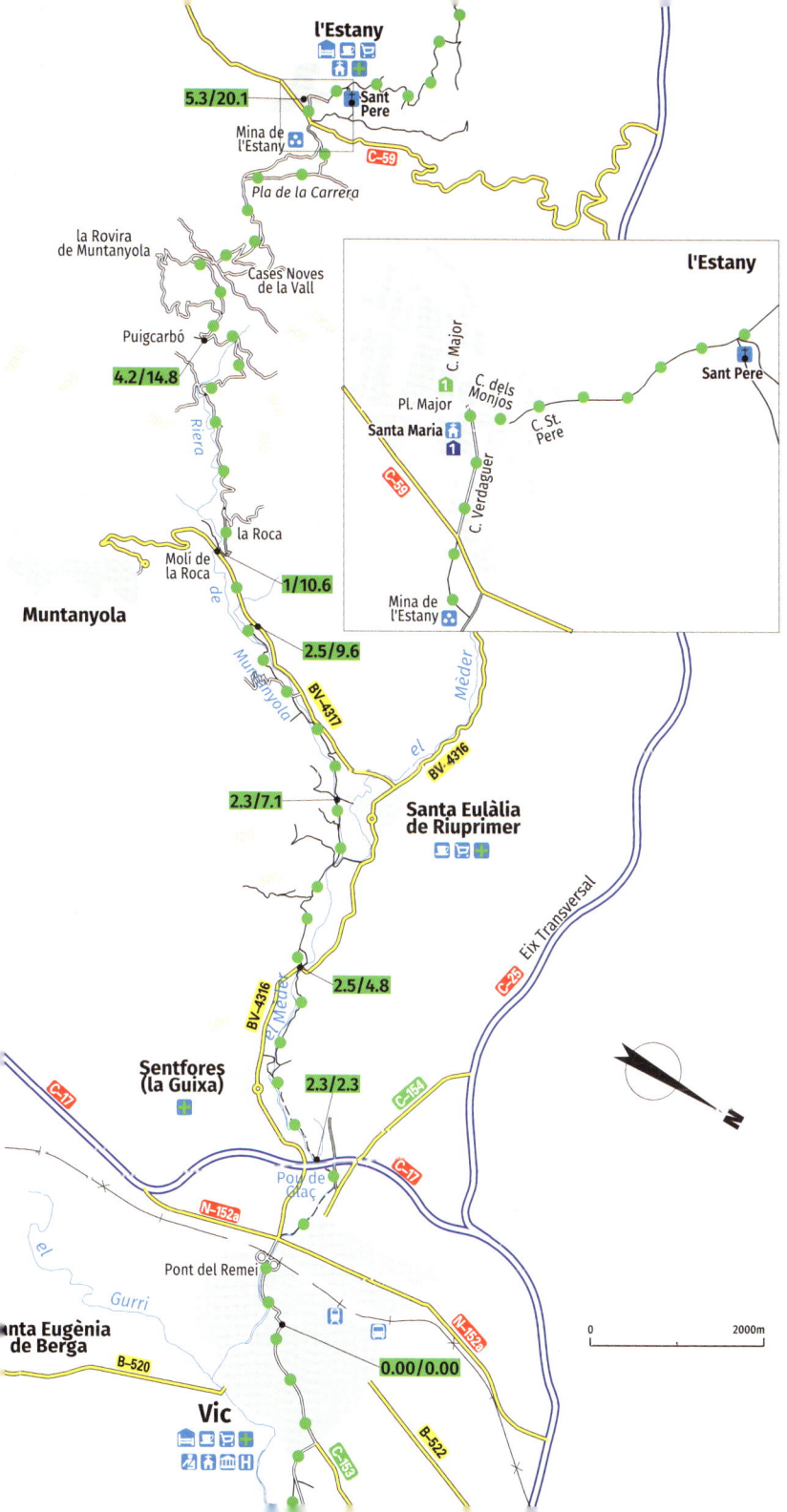

Santa Maria de l'Estany (©ACT. Georama)

The Mina of l'Estany. Most of the valley of l'Estany used to be a lake. In the C16th it was drained using underground stone built channels ('minas').

Monastery of Santa Maria de L'Estany. Currently the parish church, this large complex was a monastery for the canons of San Agustín. It preserves one of the most important cloisters in Catalan Romanesque style.

9. L'ESTANY - ARTÉS: 23.5KM

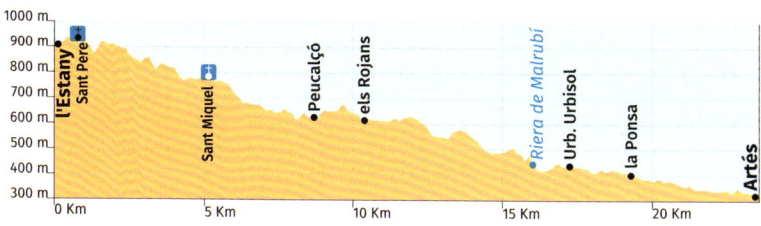

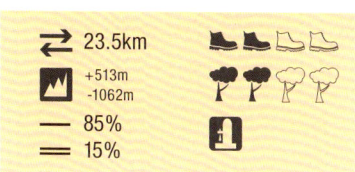

- 23.5km
- +513m / -1062m
- 85%
- 15%

From the Ter river basin to that of the Llobregat, the Way crosses the beautiful Moianès region, encountering the silence of its forest. Oak groves, pine woods and some cultivated land separate the few isolated farmhouses that inhabit this wonderful plateau.

Observations: The Camino coincides with several GR trails. At the time of publication, there is no accommodation available in Artés.

0km L'Estany. Starting from the Plaça Major, climb C. Sant Pere where you pick up the GR 177. After 400m you pass the remains of the chapel of Sant Pere on the right.

5km/5km Chapel of Sant Miquel. Located by the farmhouse and vineyard of the same name.

2.9km/7.9km Fork at Santa Maria d'Oló. Continue left along an asphalt road, with the road to this town to your right.

1km/8.9km Fork Left. After passing the large farm of Peucalçó, take a track on the left, leaving the road.

1.3km/10.2km Els Rojans. About 200m after passing this large group of farm buildings, continue straight on (GR 117.1), ignoring the detour to Sant Vicenç de Vilarassau on the left (GR 177).

6.5km/16.7km Urbisol. Modern housing estate with uneven streets.

2.4km/19.1km Fork. Take the well maintained track straight on. Ignore the left turn to Calders.

4.4km/23.5km Artés. Walk a few fairly flat kms between vineyards and cereal fields to enter the town.

Artés - pop. 5600. Village important for wine production.

Sant Miquel

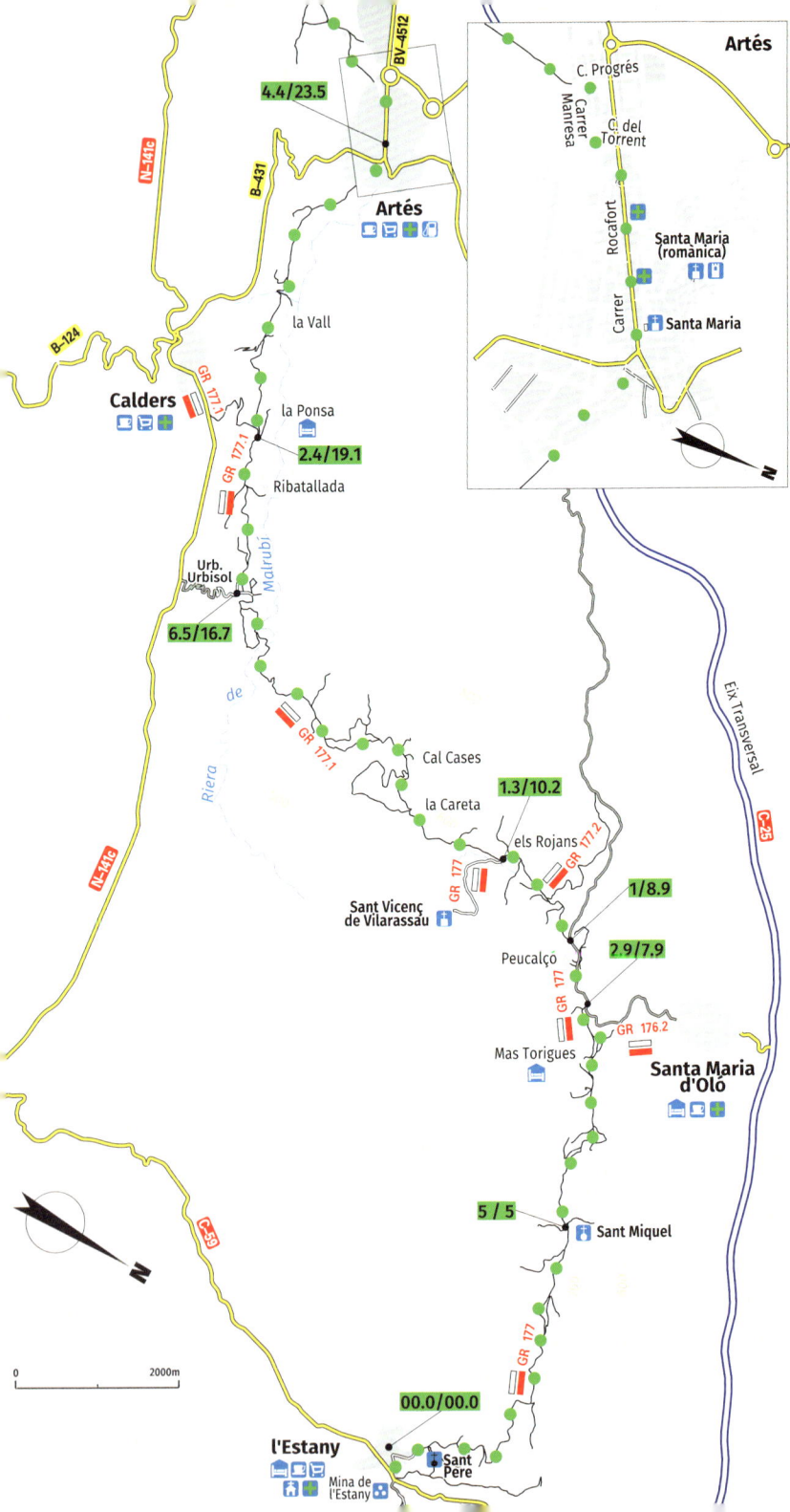

©Callum Christie

Santa Maria d'Oló
- **Hostal Santa Maria**
  Tel. 93 838 50 01
- **Cau del Segimon**
  Tel. 673 956 805
- **Mas Torigues**
  Tel. 676 048 897
- **La Ponsa**
  Tel. 609 929 089

Artés
Taxi Ramon Pascual
Tel. 608 740 719

 Chapel of Sant Miquel, Santa Maria d'Oló. Chapel of Romanesque origin renovated during the C18th. Destroyed during the civil war, then abandoned, it has been rehabilitated in recent years.
Romanesque Church of Santa Maria, Artés. Romanesque church, of which only the tower, apse and part of the nave remain. Remodelled over the years, it suffered serious damage in 1914 when the square was rebuilt.
Church of Santa Maria, Artés. Eclectic style church that was begun in 1892 and consecrated ten years later.

10. ARTÉS - MANRESA: 21.7KM

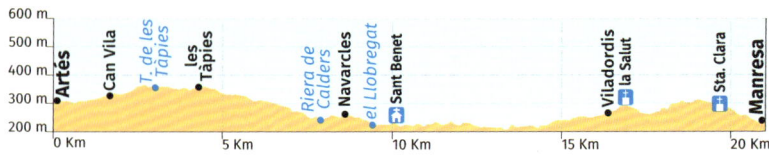

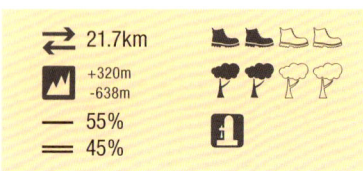

- ⇄ 21.7km
- +320m / -638m
- — 55%
- = 45%

The Way reaches Navarcles and the impressive monastery of Sant Benet. Manresa is the main town of the Bages region where the main focus of the economic and industrial activity is found along the river Llobregat.

0km Artés. From Casa de la Vila town hall, turn right, then left towards Manresa along C. Rocafort.

0.8km/0.8km Gas Station. Turn left onto C. Batlle, then right onto C. Manresa and then left into C. Progrès, soon crossing fields.

0.9km/1.7km Can Vila. Continue to the left, keeping the Masía Can Vila on your left. After 200m, go right at a fork then uphill between vineyards and pines. At a crossroads after 300m, continue straight on, along the main track that crosses the Serra de Can Vila through pine woods. The descent continues along the same main track, crossing the Torrent de les Tàpies.

1.4km/3.1km Fork: Forn de Calç. Turn right, then after 250m take the right hand track at a fork. At the next intersection, continue straight on along the main track towards the Masía de les Tàpies.

1.1km/4.2km Les Tàpies. After 500m reach a crossroads where you turn left. Shortly, you pass under an electricity line and then turn right at an intersection along a farm track.

1.8km/6km Riding School. Cross a road and go straight on past the Riding School. After 300m take a path through a field reaching the N-141 road.

0.6km/6.6km N-141 Road. Cross and follow a track in front, going under another power line. On reaching an asphalted street, turn left.

1.8km/8.4km Navarcles. Descend to the town, crossing the Calders stream. Cross the Sant Benet Bridge over the Llobregat river on leaving the town.

1.6km/10km Sant Benet. Reaching the monastery, follow the river Llobregat without ever crossing it.

2.8km/12.8km Dam. Continue on between a canal and the river.

1.5km/14.3km Fork. Take the first track on the right, leaving the river. Passing under the C-16, turn left at the first intersection and walk through the small village of Viladordis, along the C. de la Salut. 200m after the last house is the Santuari de la Salut.

2.6km/16.9km Fork. 100m from the Sanctuary, at the first intersection, the Camino forks. Continuing straight on avoids Manresa (*see Bypass note below*). Our path turns right, towards Cal Pep. After 200m take the first track on the left crossing fields and orchards until you pass under the C-55 ring road where an overhead electricity line also crosses it.

1.5km/18.4km Retail Commercial Park. Turn left onto C. Agustí Coll (just below the power line). At the junction with Av. Dels Països Catalans, turn left and reach a large roundabout. Turn right onto C. Alvar Aalto then at the next roundabout turn left onto Pont de Vilomara road, taking the first street on the right; C. de Sant Joan de Déu.

1.1km/19.5km Hospital. Passing Sant Joan de Deu hospital, continue left at a roundabout along the C. Nou de Santa Clara which becomes C. de Sant Bertomeu. Next to an old brick chimney, take a pedestrian street to the left which crosses a pedestrian bridge connecting to C. Galzeran d'Andreu. Turn left at the end into C. Baixada de la Seu.

2.2km/21.7km La Seu de Manresa.

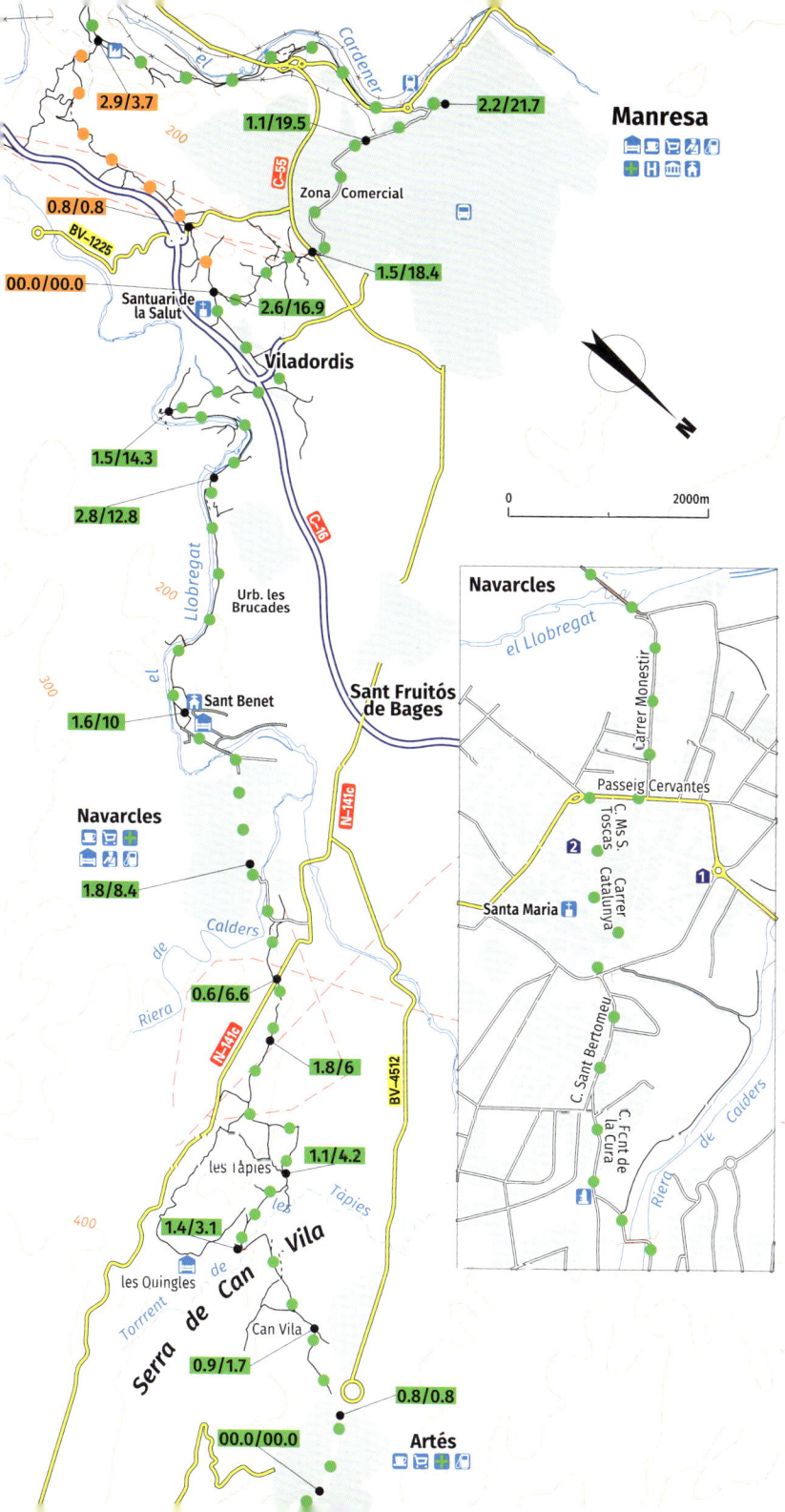

Manresa (©ACT. Inmedia Solutions)

BYPASS MANRESA

0km Fork. 200m after the Santuari de la Salut continue straight on.
0.8km/0.8km BV-1225. Cross this road and keep straight ahead.
2.9km/3.7km Waste Plant. Arrive at a junction near a large processing plant warehouse. Turn left. (see stage 11).
Manresa - pop. 76.000. Main town of the Bages region.

Manresa (©ACT. M.A.S.)

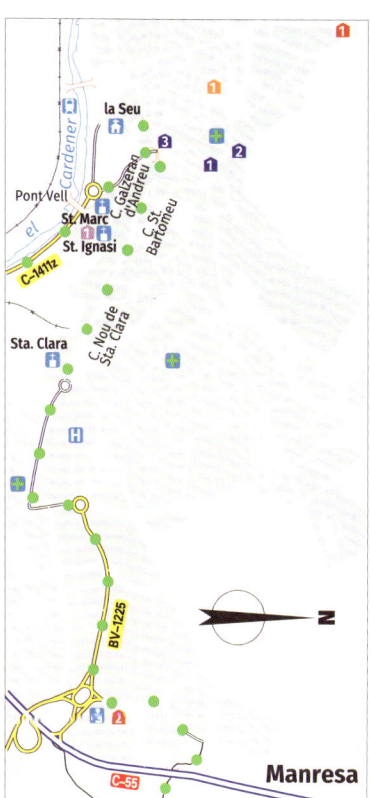

 Masia les Quingles
Tel. 649 993 839
Navarcles
1 Hostal Baviera
Tel. 605 702 116
2 Hostal Muntané
Tel. 93 831 04 40
Sant Fruitós de Bages
Monestir de Sant Benet
Tel. 93 875 94 04
Manresa
1 Alberg del Carme Xanascat
Tel. 93 875 03 96
1 Alberg Lluís Espina
Tel. 93 872 04 22
1 Hostal la Masia
Tel. 93 872 42 37
2 Hostal Roser Manila
Tel. 93 875 55 90
3 Apartaments Urbi
Tel. 93 876 82 41
Hostal Turó de la Torre
Tel. 93 873 32 86
1 Hotel Casa Padró
Tel. 683 599 522
2 Hotel els Noguers
Tel. 93 874 32 58
Hotel 1948
Tel. 93 874 82 16

Santa Maria Church, Navarcles. Late C17th church with a large nave and an impressive bell tower.

Sant Benet de Bages Monastery. One of the best preserved medieval architectural ensembles in the region. This Benedictine abbey is of Romanesque origin and features Baroque and Modernist additions, amongst others.

Santuari de la Mare de Déu de la Salut, Viladordis. C12th - C13th sanctuary church with an impressive wooden carving of Mary.

La Seu, Manresa. Collegiate Basilica dedicated to Santa María. This Gothic style church maintains the Portal dels Claustres from one of the previous Romanesque constructions.

Cave of Sant Ignasi, Manresa. Group of buildings built for the veneration of Saint Ignatius of Loyola, who secluded himself here, in a cave, for one year during his pilgrimage to Jerusalem. He founded the Company of Jesus. The Ignatian Way coincides with much of the Camino de Santiago, but in the opposite direction.

11. Manresa - Montserrat: 25.5km

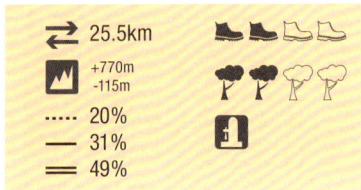

- 25.5km
- +770m / -115m
- 20%
- 31%
- 49%

The Montserrat mountain range with its imposing rocky spires dominates the horizon.
Observations: The final part of this stage uses stretches of the access roads to Montserrat that are usually quite busy, especially during weekends and holidays.
0km Manresa. From the cathedral, descend to the C. de Sant Marc (under the C. Galzeran pedestrian bridge) and turn right downhill to reach the church of Sant Marc.
0.4km/0.4km Pont Vell. Cross the road and pass under the Pont Vell following a track, parallel to the C-141z road and later along the banks of the Cardener River.
1.3km/1.7km Canal. Reaching a small canal, turn left and follow it for a few metres, then turn right onto a gravel lane.
0.2km/1.9km Fabrica Blanca. With this factory on your right, continue straight ahead then, turning right between two blocks of flats, follow a track towards the C-55 bridge. Passing under, follow a narrow track beside the river which climbs up to join a wider track. Turn right.
0.7km/2.6km Fork. After 100m at a fork, take the track on the left, uphill. After the crest of a hill, it zigzags down, passing a composting centre on your left.
1.8km/4.4km Compost Plant. Turn right and continue straight on.
1.8km/6.2km Train Track. Cross over and continue on a road, ignoring a track on your right.
0.7km/6.9km Bridge over C-55. After crossing the river you reach an overpass across the C-55. Cross it using the walkway protected from traffic by a railing and continue along and up Av. Montserrat.
1.3km/8.2km Roundabout to Castellgalí. Turn right and after 100m turn left into C. Camí de Montserrat continuing straight on.
1km/9.2km Fork. At C. Til·lers fork right and after 200m turn right onto a concrete track going into woodland. Follow a dirt road that enters an agricultural area of vineyards and scrubland. Fork left after 250m and left again 250m further on. After 800m turn left to go around the head of the Riera de Castellet ravine.
1.5km/10.7km Riera de Castellet. Climbing slightly, after 800m you come to an asphalt road and turn right, then pass some large farm buildings on your right.
2.1km/12.8km BV-1123. Turn right along the BV-1123 crossing the Riera de Marganell then take a left on the BV-1122 towards Sant Cristòfol. After 100m turn right onto a track that passes by the chapel of Sant Jaume. The Camino passes by the side of a house and winds up through woods and out into a flat agricultural area.
1.2km/14km Masroig Plain. Continue to the left, around this huge field, reaching the far end where the track reaches some fenced plots and ends on a street where you turn left. After 400m take a left then 100m further on turn right onto a gravel track reaching the BV-1122.
1.8km/15.8km BV-1122. Turn right and follow the road slightly uphill.
2.2km/18km La Calsina. Continue straight (to the left) passing La Calsina and walking on the road for some time until you reach an

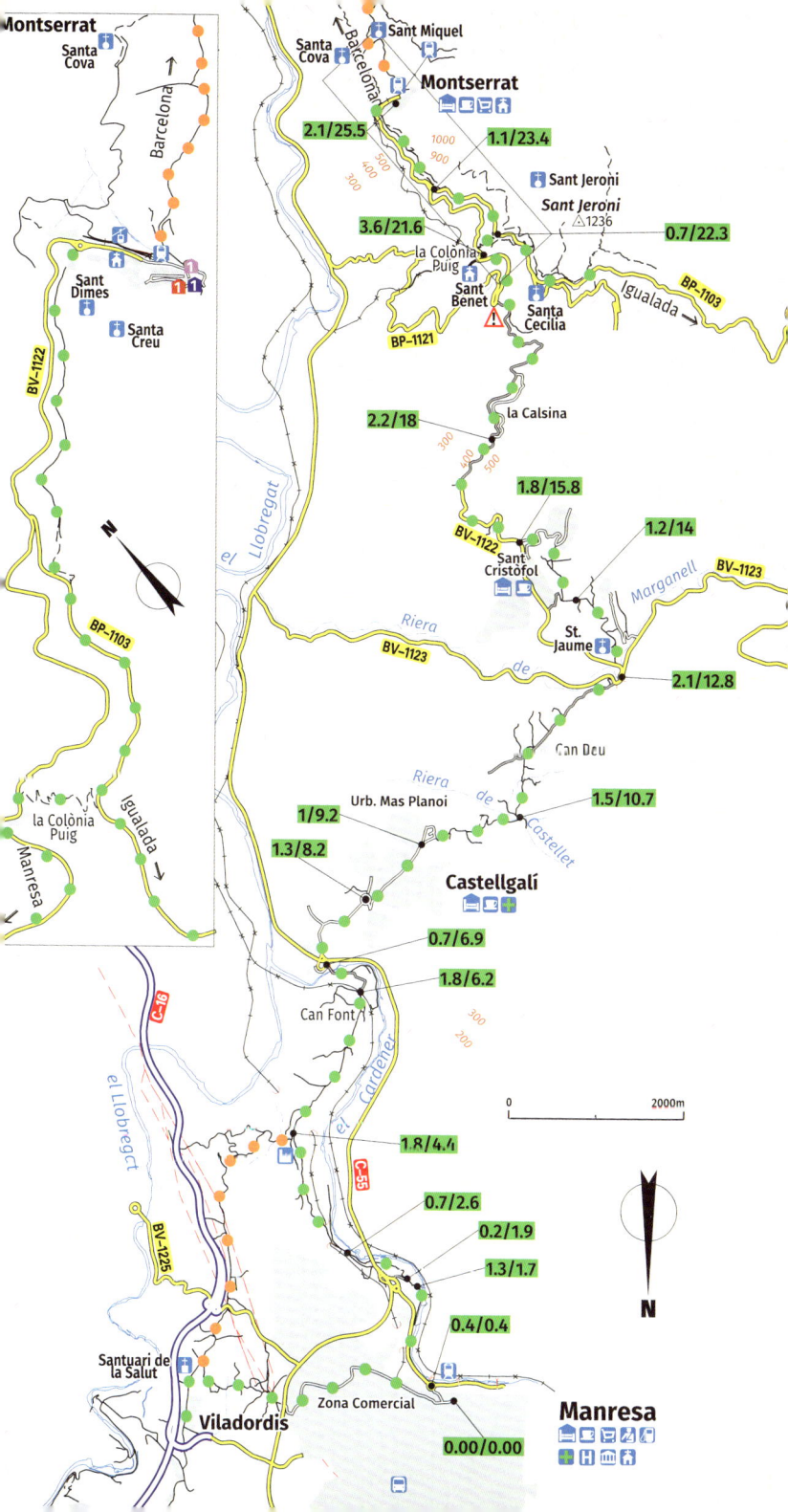

Montserrat (©Maria Remei Estrada)

intersection with the B-1121. ATTENTION to traffic: Turn right, uphill on the side of the road.
3.6km/21.6km La Colònia Puig. After this abandoned building, take a path on the right that zig zags steeply to the BP-1103. Turn left
0.7km/22.3km BP-1103. ATTENTION to traffic: Keep left along the side of this road until the start of the Degotalls track, which is on the right.
1.1km/23.4km Camí dels Degotalls. Climb up some steps.
2.1km/25.5km Monestir de Montserrat. A small community of monks. Benedictine abbey founded, around 880. It constitutes one of the most important spiritual centers in Catalonia and one of its identity icons.

Castellgalí
 Refugi de Pelegrins Masia del Pla
Tel. 93 833 1975 - 689 008 359
Sant Cristòfol de Castellbell
 Ca la Ramona
Tel. 93 835 72 72

Monestir de Montserrat
 Hotel Hostal Abat Cisneros
Tel. 93 877 77 01
 Alberg Abat Oliba
Tel. 93 877 77 01
 Cel·les Abat Marcet
Tel. 93 877 77 01

Chapel of Sant Marc, Manresa. C15th chapel. The only remains of a leper hospital.
Sant Jaume de Castellbell. C12th chapel.

Monastery of Sant Benet, Marganell. Benedictine convent.
Monastery of Montserrat. Benedictine Abbey with origins in the C9th.

12. Montserrat - Igualada: 26.4km

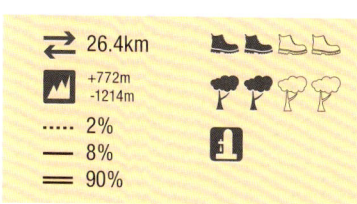

- 26.4km
- +772m / -1214m
- 2%
- 8%
- 90%

The Montserrat mountain range is an icon of pilgrimage in Catalonia and also an important geographical and spiritual reference point. The Way begins at the Montserrat monastery and runs along the north face of the mountain, gradually descending to the plain of Conca de Òdena.

0km Montserrat Monastery. Follow the Degotalls track that leads to the RP-1103 road. Cross over and turn left, following a path by the side of the road.

3.6km/3.6km Santa Cecília. Past the abbey, the path ends and you continue along the BP-1103 road with care.

5.6km/9.2km Can Maçana Crossroads. Turn left onto the BP-1101 and continue on the road for 30m. Leave the parking lot behind you and 20m further on, take a track on the right that is partially hidden by vegetation. The Camino is now marked with GR 172 signposts. After 1km turn right and after a small cemetery continue straight on.

2.1km/11.3km Sant Pau de la Guàrdia. After 300m you immediately enter the Montserrat Parc urbanization. Continue straight on, along the flat C. Verge de Montserrat. At the first fork turn right, downhill. Continue and ignore street junctions for about 800m until the intersection with C. Castellolí where you turn sharply to the right, up a steep hill leaving the urbanization via a track. After 250m you join a wider track, going left, then leaving the GR 172 at the next intersection by taking a lesser used track to the right.

2.5km/13.8km Coll del Bruc. Rejoin the N-II, turn right on a curve. After 100m take a lane to the right that ends again by the road. Turn right and on reaching a fork, continue to the left to go over the A-2.

1.6km/15.4km Bridge over A-2. Over the bridge take an asphalt track on the left running parallel to the highway.

0.8km/16.2km Junction. Reaching another access road to the A-2, turn left onto it and continue downhill.

1.0km/17.2km Castellolí. Continue straight on, through the town along the Av. de la Unió. Follow a pedestrian track that runs parallel to the highway.

1.5km/18.7km Stop Sign. Continue downhill coming to a stop sign. ATTENTION. Turn left and after 50m, cross with care and take a road to the right uphill reaching a roundabout where you continue straight on.

0.7km/19.4km Intersection. Turn right and cross above the A-2. At a small junction, continue straight on, passing some houses, then continue under the A-2 (the Camino proceeds to the right of the road). The asphalt track passes under the C-37 where, on reaching a roundabout, you turn right, towards Igualada. Using the left hand slip lane of this technology park, continue straight towards the town centre.

4.8km/24.2km Roundabout. ATTENTION. Just before reaching a large roundabout, take a small path on the left that leads to a road. Cross carefully and turn right taking an asphalt track, then a narrow track, parallel to the road towards Igualada Centro (C-244). Continue to a T-junction with traffic lights, where you turn left.

0.8km/25km Train Line. Cross the railway line and continue along Av. De Montserrat.

1.4km/26.4km Igualada. After a petrol station, continue straight on, along Av. De

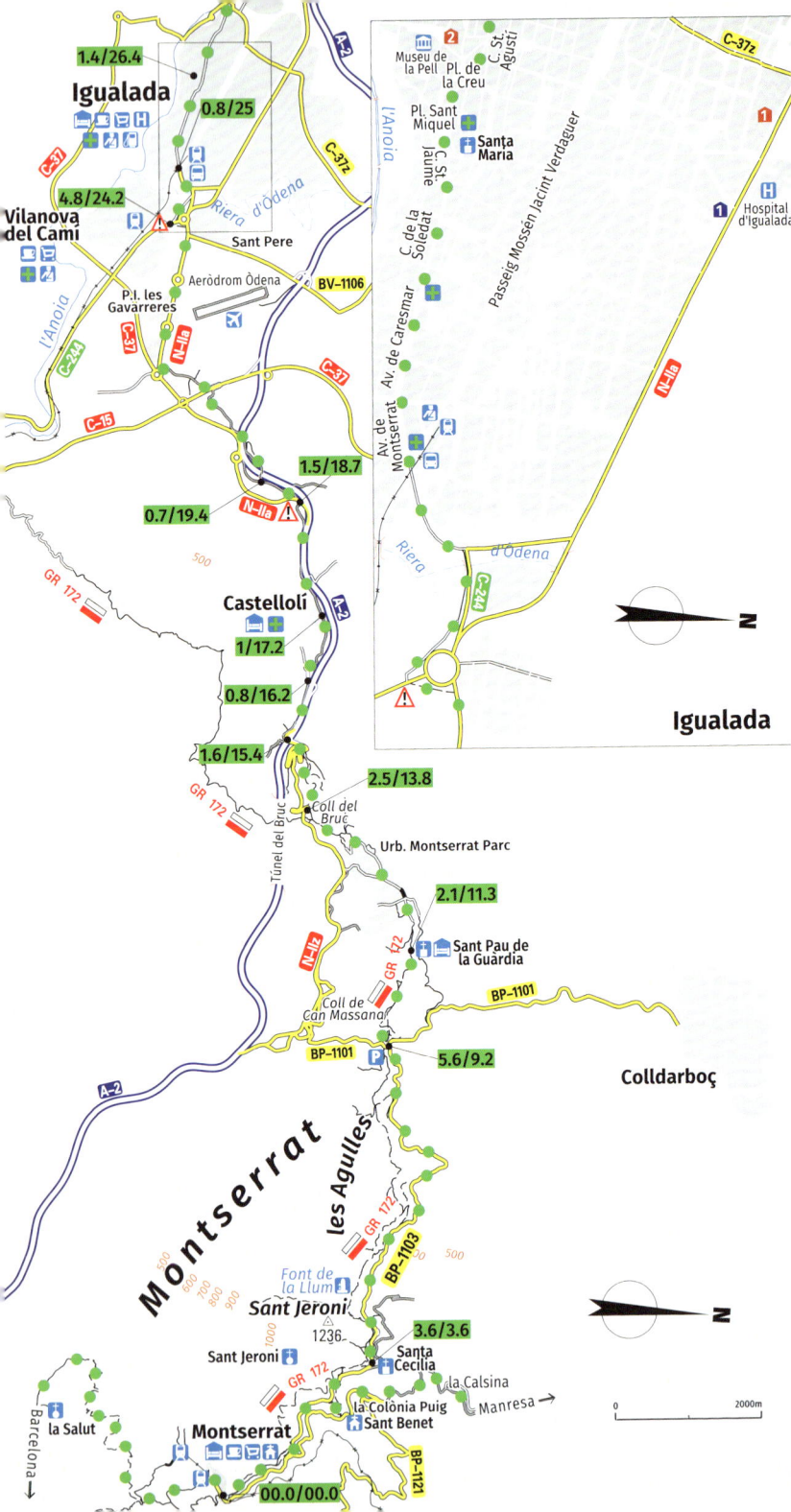

Monestir de Montserrat (©Abadia de Montserrat)

Caresmar reaching Plaça del Rei. Turn right onto C. Roser, leading to the Basilica of Santa Maria and the Town Hall.
Igualada - pop. 50.000. Capital of the Anoia area. This historic town developed at a strategic ford of the river Anoia. It has an industrious heritage specialising in textile and leather products.

Sant Pau de la Guàrdia
- **Hotel El Celler de la Guàrdia**
Tel. 93 771 03 23

Castellolí
- **El Centre. Allotjament de Pelegrins**
Tel. 93 808 40 00

Igualada
- **Refugi de Pelegrins**
Tel. 93 804 55 15
(Map 13 Igualada-La Panadella)
- **Alberg Mare de Déu de la Mercè**
Tel. 627 429 773
(Map 13 Igualada-La Panadella)
- **Hostal Canaletas**
Tel. 93 803 27 50
- **Hotel Amèrica**
Tel. 93 803 10 00
- **Hotel Somiatruites**
Tel. 93 803 66 26

Santa Cecília de Montserrat. C11th Benedictine abbey in Romanesque style. The most notable element is the three-body apse, with Lombard-style arches.
Sant Pau de la Guàrdia. Guàrdia castle was the origin of a medieval hamlet which exists to the present day. It preserves ruins of the castle and the old church.
Old town, Igualada. Walled town centre featuring the Portal d'en Vives and the Portal Font Major, along with the Plaza Major and the baroque church of Santa María.

13. Igualada - La Panadella: 22.5km

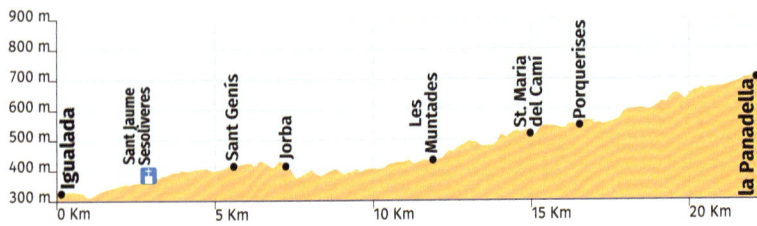

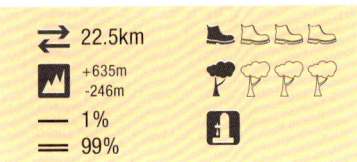

- 22.5km
- +635m / -246m
- 1%
- 99%

A strategic stage as the pilgrim climbs alongside the historic way that links Barcelona to the rest of the Iberian peninsula. Numerous small villages, with charming churches and stone built farmhouses, dot a landscape of alternating arable fields and a gently rising narrow valley.

0km Igualada. From the town hall continue onto Pl. de la Creu, and follow C. del Sant Simplici and C. Sant Agustí. Continue straight on past Escola Pía (a school), and then turn left along Av. Angel Guimera. At a roundabout carry straight on.

2.9km/2.9k Junction. After 200m veer right up onto Av. Emili Vallès and follow it to the end where you turn left by the Pere Vives school. Continue straight along C. Trulls Algué to reach a small roundabout where you keep straight on along C. Jordana i Puig and Empordà. After a bend in the street, turn left onto C. de l'Ermita. The chapel of Sant Jaume Sesoliveres is on your left. At the next street junction turn right, along C. del Bages and then immediately veer left C. Alt Camp. At Av. Sant Jaume Sesoliveres turn right and then left onto C. Penedès. At C. del Solsonès turn right. After 100m turn left on an asphalt road leading to a modern convent.

0.8km/3.7km Convent of Barefoot Carmelites. Pass by the front of the convent then head for a small gap between this and the neighbouring house. Emerge onto a farm track that passes a walled corral. The track descends to the B-222.

0.4km/4.1km B-222. Turn right, then, at a roundabout, keep straight on, to cross the A-2. At the next roundabout choose a country road to your left. It has a cycle lane for your use and runs parallel to the A-2.

1.6km/5.7km Sant Genís. After this small village the Camino continues along the cycle lane towards Jorba.

1.6km/7.3km Jorba. Continue along the cycle lane to the far side of the town, then turn left to follow the cycle lane as it meanders under the motorway and up to a large roundabout. Take the first road on your left, still on the protected cycle lane. At a mini roundabout, veer left and pass behind a gas station, soon

Jorba

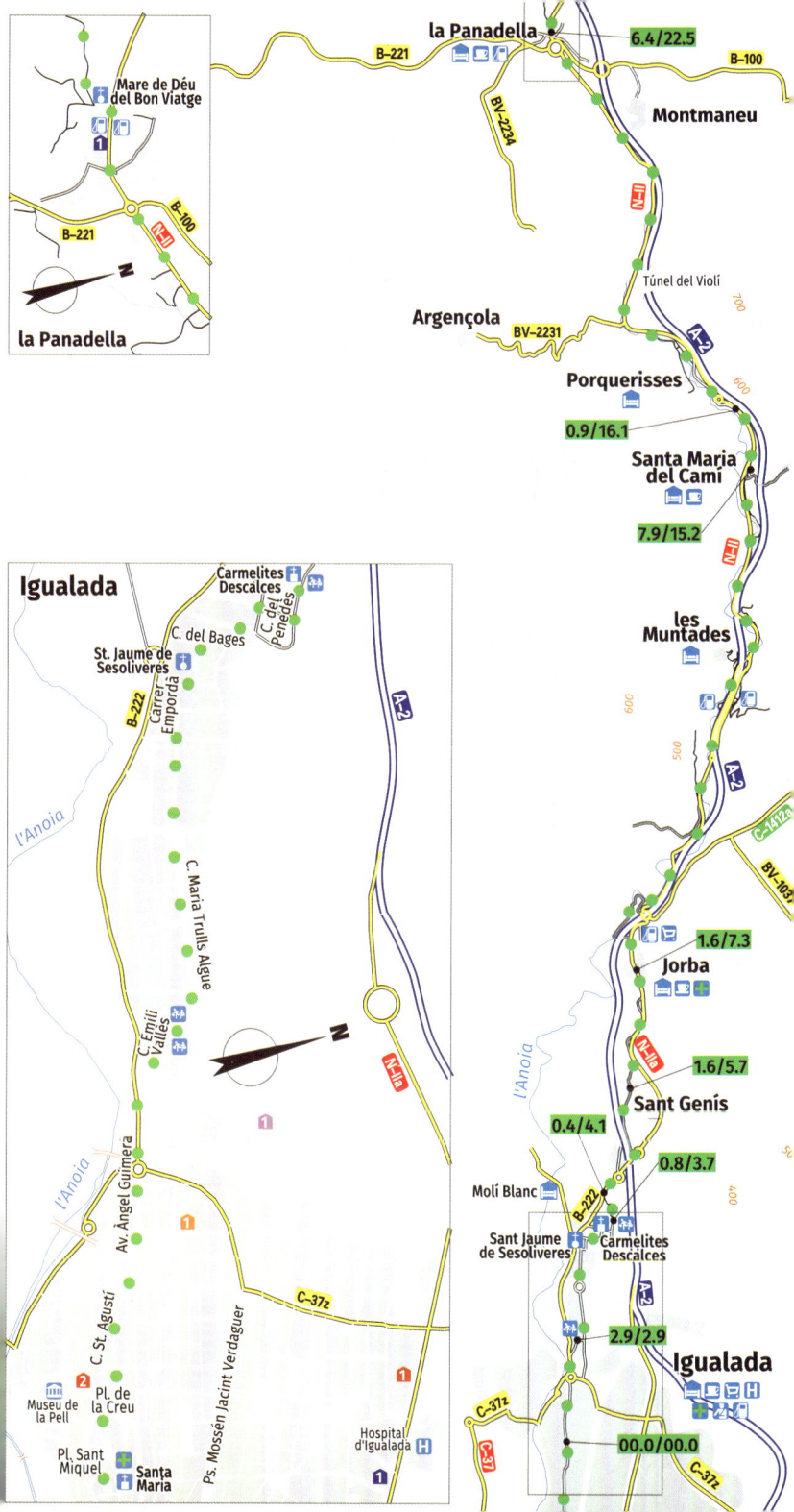

crossing under the A-2, and later over it.
7.9km/15.2km Santa María del Camí. A tiny village that is traversed swiftly. After 150m the cycle lane ends and you will have to walk on the roadside.
0.9km/16.1km Asphalt Lane. Take a narrow lane on your left to access the small village of Porquerisses. After leaving the village and just before regaining the N-II, take a shady asphalt lane on your left. It rejoins the main road where you turn left along the side of the road with care. At a roundabout continue straight on into La Panadella.
6.4km/22.5km La Panadella. A traditional stopping place for weary travellers.
La Panadella - pop. 41.

Igualada (©ACT. Oriol Llauradó)

Igualada
- Hotel
Molí Blanc ☺☺☺
Tel. 93 801 91 79

Jorba
- Alberg Sant Jaume ☺
Tel. 93 809 81 80

Les Muntades
- Hotel
les Muntades ☺☺☺
Tel. 620 204 772

Porquerisses
- Allotjament Rural
Porquerisses ☺☺☺
Tel. 620 775 283

Santa Maria del Cami
- Can Llobet ☺
Tel. 616 722 311

La Panadella-Montmaneu
- Hotel Bayona ☺
93 809 20 11

Hermitage of Sant Jaume Sesoliveres, Igualada. C11th Romanesque temple. Also known as Sant Jaume of the Camino, it succoured pilgrims throughout centuries.
Chapel of Saint Sebastian, Jorba. Situated on the royal road between Barcelona and Lleida since the C17th.
Parochial Church of Sant Pere, Jorba. Built in the C16th.
Municipal Boundary Cross, Jorba. 1604.
Church of Santa Maria del Camí. Romanesque C13th construction, formerly part of a Benedictine monastery.

14. LA PANADELLA - TÀRREGA: 27.7KM

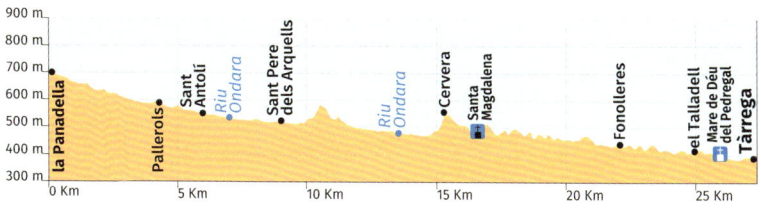

- 27.7km
- +377m / -669m
- 85%
- 15%

A stage with a gentle descent from the Segarra region towards flatlands of the Urgell area. An intensely farmed area with arable fields and irrigation canals that make fruit production possible. The medieval centre of Cervera is well worth exploring.

0km La Panadella. As you leave the village, turn left to pass by the modern chapel dedicated to 'Mother of God of the Good Journey'. At its rear, choose a track to the right that crosses an area of arable fields dotted with small woodlands.

3.3km/3.3km Country Road. Turn right to join the LV-2032. Upon reaching Pallerols village, continue on C. Sant Jaume and onwards until Sant Antolí.

2.6km/5.9km Sant Antolí. Cross this village to reach a roundabout and continue ahead on the left hand side of the road. A street between houses brings you to a stone cross.

0.5km/6.4km Stone Cross. Veer left on C. dels Amics to leave the village and reach the L-203 road. Turn left and, after 200m, cross a bridge over the river Ondara. Now turn right on an asphalt country lane alongside the river. After 1km turn right onto another lane.

2.7km/9.1km Sant Pere dels Arquells. Turn right to enter the village and keep straight on to exit by a fountain and a metal cross. *Here, there is signed an alternative route to Cervera along the N-II but we do not recommend it.* Carry straight on along a dirt track.

0.7km/9.8km Fork. After a bend in the track, take the left option which soon peters out. Turn 90 degrees to your right to follow a path through scrub and pines. After 700m reach a track and turn right downhill to arable fields. At a fork, turn right on the widest track and after 600m continue straight on, passing a farmhouse on your right.

After a further 800m, continue on a path between fields and the hillside.

3.7km/13.5km Río Ondara Bridge. Cross the river and then the Font Fiol spring. Follow the main track parallel to the river. After 1km take an asphalt track to the right. Climb and then turn left onto Costa Sant Francesc d'Assís. At the end of this slope, continue straight on into the old town of Cervera by way of C. Sant Cristòfol. Turn left and pass by the church of Sant Cristòfol up to the Pl. Major.

2km/15.5km Church of Santa Maria de Cervera. Continue downhill to Pl. Sant Domingo and turn right, downhill to the end of C. Sant Magí. Turn left onto a country road leading out of town to a ruined roadside church.

1km/16.5km Ruins of Santa Magdalena. Turn right onto a good earthen track. The Camino now proceeds in a straight line towards Tàrrega, gently downhill between arable fields along the river Ondarra valley.

5.6km/22.1km Fonolleres Crossroad. Continue straight on along an asphalt lane, then after 900m keep straight ahead through a crossing of lanes.

3km/25.1km El Talladell. Cross the village on the C. Major and continue straight on. After 800m pass by the chapel of Mare de Déu del Pedregal.

2.6km/27.7km Tàrrega. Entering by Av. Generalitat, continue along to the end of C. Jacint Verdaguer. Cross C. Joan Margall to climb a few steps and turn left into the small square of Pl. d'Anselm Clavé. Continue ahead on the narrow C. d'Agoders to the Pl. Major, the church of Santa María de l'Alba and the town hall.

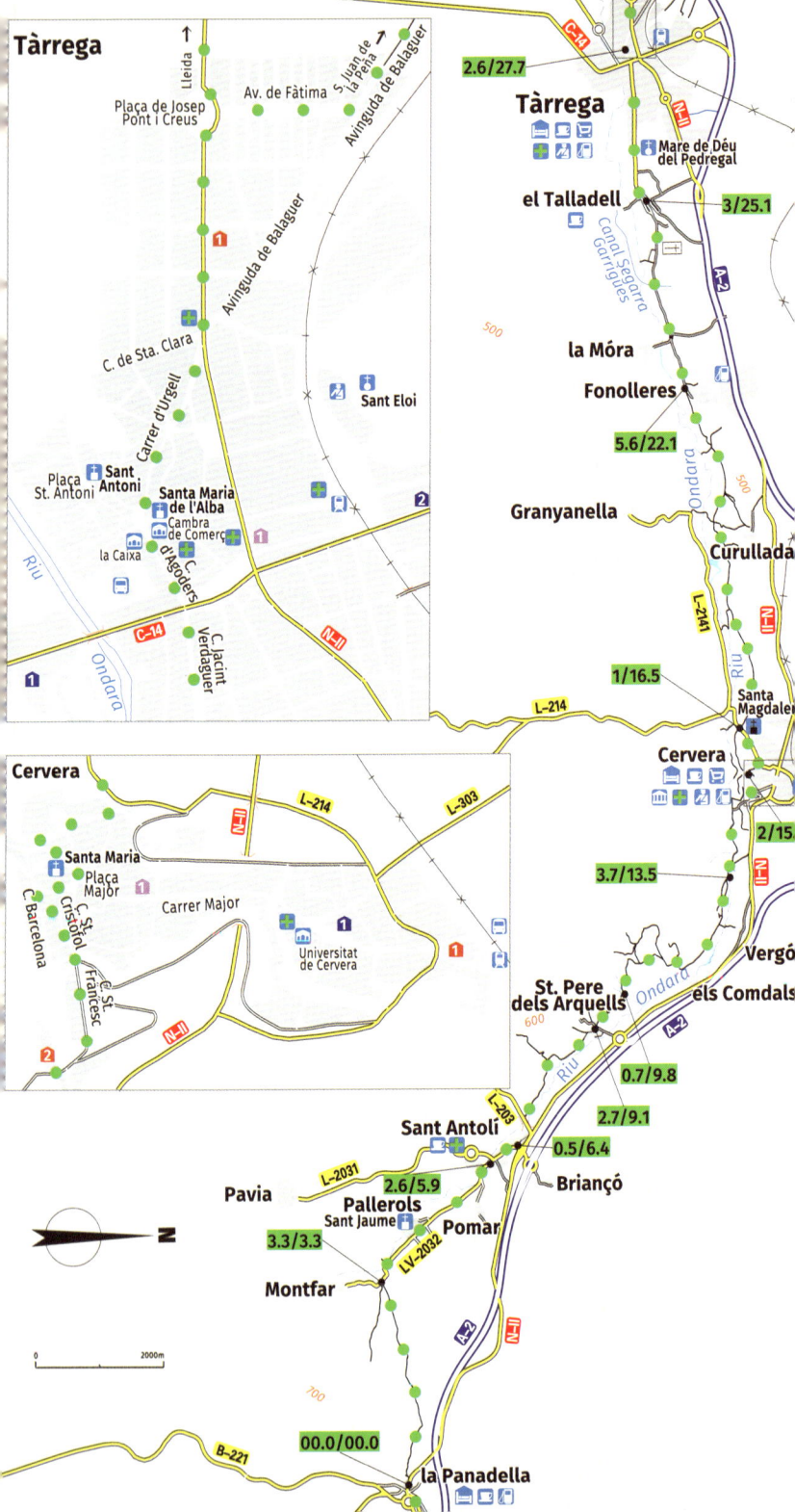

Cervera - pop. 9400. Capital of the Segarra area. A town filled with notable historic buildings.
Tàrrega - pop. 16.500. Capital of the Urgell region. A town situated at an historic crossroads. Today it's a bustling commercial town.

Cervera

🟧 Camino towards Puente la Reina - p. 84
🟥 Camino towards Pina de Ebro - p. 130

Cervera
1 Alberg Sagrada Família ⊙
Tel. 641 860 940
1 Hostal Universitat ⊙⊙
Tel. 973 10394
1 Hotel Bonavista ⊙⊙
Tel. 973 53 00 27

2 Hotel la Savina ⊙⊙
Tel. 973 53 13 93

Tàrrega
1 Residència Ca l'Aleix ⊙
Tel. 973 314 635
1 Habitacions Sant Pere Claver ⊙⊙
Tel. 973 31 31 35

2 Hostal Ciutat de Tàrrega ⊙⊙
Tel. 973 31 47 37
1 Hotel Pintor Marsà ⊙⊙
Tel. 973 31 10 00

Sant Jaume Church, Pallerols. Originally Romanesque, it was reformed and decorated in Gothic style.
Sant Isidre Church, Sant Antolí. A C11th-12th Romanesque temple.
Church of Sant Pere dels Arquells. Medieval in origin with subsequent modifications.
Cervera University. C18th Baroque building with impressive dimensions. A seat of learning from 1717 until 1842.
Cervera Old Town. A significant amount of the medieval walls remain intact. The Paeria town hall, churches and the porticoed calle Major with its palatial villas are all worthy of mention.
Santa Maria Church, Cervera. C14th. An outstanding example of Catalan Gothic design.
Coptic Orthodox Church, Cervera. The former C18th church of Dolors, recently transformed in use. Cervera has one of the largest coptic communities in Spain.
Pedregal Chapel, El Talladell. Romanesque in origin with varying styles of restoration.
Santa María de l'Alba, Tàrrega. A C17th-18th Baroque church with a single barrel vault and side chapels.
Chapel of Sant Eloi, Tàrrega. Romanesque hermitage situated upon a hill with magnificent views over the town.
Sant Antoni Church, Tàrrega. Gothic style with an outstanding belltower.

BARCELONA - MONTSERRAT

The shortest section in this book crosses the vibrant Catalan capital city and ends with a climb to the impressive serrated mountain that holds the sacred image of Our Lady of Montserrat, one of the two patron saints of Catalonia. The monastery is home to the Escolania, one of Europe's oldest boy choirs.

Historically, the city of Barcelona was a very popular starting point for the Camino. Pilgrims arrived by sea from Mediterranean territories and departed from the church of Sant Jaume, which originally stood on the site of the Roman forum. Traditionally they would follow the easier river Llobregat route, but an alternative via Sant Cugat is more direct despite first having to climb the Collserola hills. The ascent to the monastery of Montserrat was a celebrated part of the Way of St.James and was also a site of pilgrimage in its own right. Today It still attracts the devotion of thousands of local and foreign visitors.

Barcelona - pop. 1.600.000. Capital of Catalonia.

Barcelona nestles on a small coastal plain between the Collserola hills and Montjuic. One of the impressive features of the city is the vast and fascinating 'Gothic Quarter' which dates from its medieval golden age as the principal port city of the Crown of Aragón. During this period the Catalan government was formed. The Gothic style Palau de la Generalitat de Catalunya in Pl. Sant Jaume is still the headquarters of the Catalan government today. The nearby church of Sant Jaume is slightly hidden, with only its facade visible from the street. It was originally built in Gothic style along with many other splendid churches throughout the Quarter.

An important Mediterranean power, the world's first book on maritime law was written in Barcelona and the oldest extant gothic style shipyards in the world can still be viewed along with the merchant palaces of Carrer Montcada. The 'Gothic Quarter' in turn contains the remains of the old Roman city of *Barcino*. Remains of its C3rd-C4th walls can still be seen today along with an underground museum of its streets. It centred around Mons Taber where today we find the Cathedral of Santa Creu. Built between C13-C15th, it is dedicated to Santa Eulàlia, a Christian martyr (whose remains rest in the crypt) and co-patron of the city. It replaced the Romanesque, as well as the earlier paleochristian church. Its façade is Neo Gothic from the C19th and the cloister has a team of feathered guardians. A thriving Jewish community existed in the nearby quarter of 'El Call'. The Black Death of the C14th decimated Europe and claimed a third of Barcelona's inhabitants.

During the C16th-C17th the Crown of Aragón's fortunes began to wane. War with the Ottoman Empire, along with incursions from Barbary corsairs led to an economic decline. The union of the Castilian and Aragonese crowns would generate a series of political tensions causing two long wars with Castille in the C17th and C18th. These caused the loss of Rousillon to France, and loss of Catalonia's independent institutions of power to Castille. The results were catastrophic for the city, above all with the siege of 1714.

From the mid C18th the fortunes of Barcelona's

La Verge de Montserrat
(©ACT. Juan José Pascual)

port improved with the opening of trade routes to the American colonies, bringing to an end the commercial monopoly enjoyed by the ports of Seville and Cádiz. The city was finally allowed to expand outside its medieval walls in 1854, creating the modern iconic grid pattern of the 'Eixample' district so recognised by visitors today. The first factories and railway of the Spanish Industrial Revolution were built in Barcelona and the resulting wealth of its entrepreneurs was expressed with the *art nouveau* architectural style we now call 'Catalan Modernisme'. Hundreds of examples of this unique style still line the streets of the 'Eixample'. A renaissance of the Catalan language and traditions during the C19th reached a peak with the hosting of the International Exhibition in 1885.

The city suffered great damage during the Spanish civil war and post war persecutions, causing an economic, political and cultural downturn. The international isolation and cultural oppression during General Franco's dictatorship were not reversed until the transition and return to democracy. Since the reinstatement of the Catalan government in 1977 a new golden age has led to Barcelona being once again one of the most dynamic cities in the Mediterranean. This exciting city of culture, art, design and commerce emerged onto the world stage in 1992 with its eye-catching and successful Olympic games.

Sagrada Família (©ACT. Edgar De Puy Fuentes)

La Boqueria (©ACT. Lluís Carro)

1A. Barcelona - Sant Cugat del Vallès: 17.2km

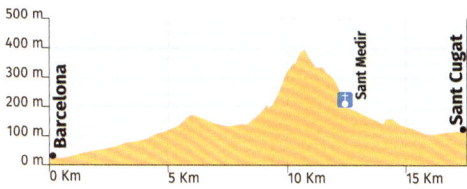

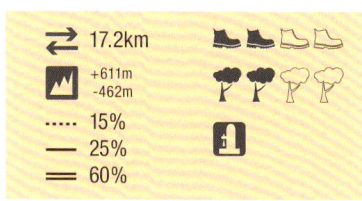

- 17.2km
- +611m / -462m
- 15%
- 25%
- 60%

A short stage that traverses Barcelona from its historic centre through the districts of Eixample, Gràcia and finally Horta, with its impressive vistas over the city. From there the Camino crosses the Collserola range through dense woodland and affords panoramic views both towards the sea as well as the interior of Catalonia, before descending to the town of Sant Cugat del Vallès.

Observations: From the Labyrinth in Horta to Sant Cugat, the Camino follows the red and white markings of the GR 6.

0km Church of Sant Jaume. With your back to the door of the church in C. Ferran, turn right to access Pl. Sant Jaume. Take C. del Bisbe to the left up to C. de Santa Llúcia and round to the steps of the cathedral. With your back to the cathedral door, cross the Pl. Nova to its far left corner and follow C. dels Arcs and continue in a straight line along Av. del Portal de l'Àngel, reaching Pl. de Catalunya. Keep straight on up the right hand side of the square to continue along Passeig de Gràcia.

2.4km/2.4km Avinguda Diagonal. At the confluence with this major urban thoroughfare at the Pl. Cinc d'Oros with its obelisk, turn left for a few metres and cross over to follow C. Riera de Sant Miquel next to the church of Virgen de Pompeya. The pilgrim enters the Gràcia district. At the Placeta de Sant Miquel the route forks right along C. Vic and continues in a straight line, passing the Llibertat indoor market, now on C. Berga. At the end of this street turn left along Rambla de Prat. In a few metres turn right along Av. de la Riera de Cassoles for a short distance. Take the first street to the right, after C. Bretón de los Herreros and then the first street to the left which is C. d'Aulèstia y Pijoan. The Gaudí designed Casa Vicens awaits at the end of this street. Turn right along C. de les Carolines until you meet the wide C. Gran de Gràcia, where you turn left.

1.9km/4.3km Plaça Lesseps. Cross over and proceed past the sculpture of a giant cube. Continue along the tree lined Av. de Vallcarca to its end.

1.8km/6.1km Ronda de Dalt. Cross Pl. de la Vall d'Hebron to continue along the right hand pedestrian walkway of the Ronda de Dalt, an urban motorway.

1.6km/7.7km Mundet Metro. Some 200m after this station, pass in front of the red brick façade of the Horta Salesian school. Descend a flight of steps and pass under the Ronda de Dalt. Once on the other side turn left away from the motorway and walk up a narrow wooded street.

0.4km/8.1km C. Germans Desvalls. Continue along this street past the Horta Velodrome and continue uphill past the entrance to the Labyrinth Park of Horta. The last building on the right is the Can Llupià school. Here, the Way becomes an earthen track continuing uphill. Soon leave the main track to turn sharply to the left and ascend to the ruins of the Fortí castle. Proceed on a path along the ridge until you meet a broad dirt track.

1.8km/9.9km Track. Continue to the left and in 300m take the left fork. After a further 300m take a path to the right, climbing through thick woodland to the highest point of the day. The path reaches a dirt track where you turn right. After 200m, ignore a track to the right and immediately take a

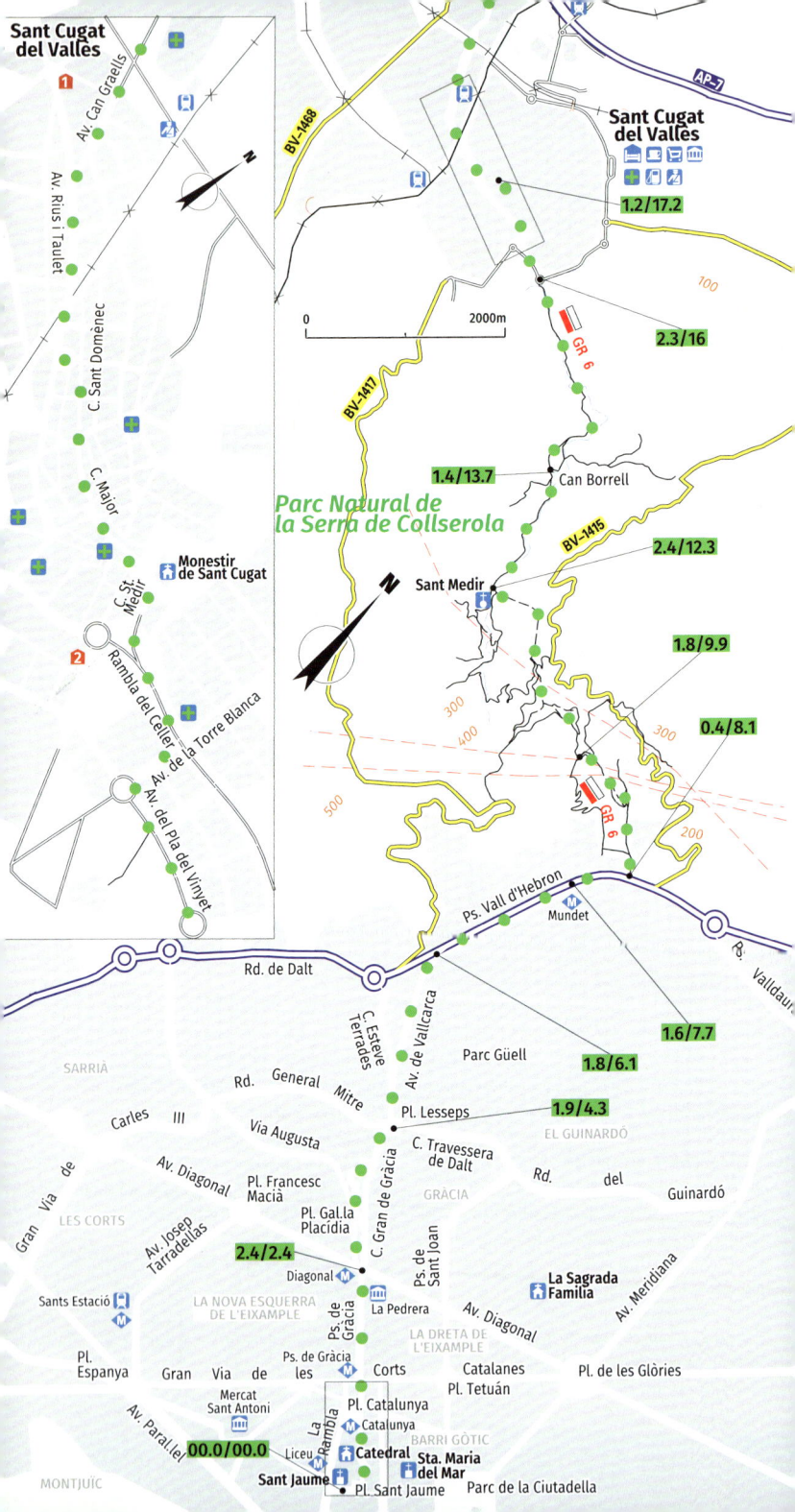

Casa Vicens (©ACT. Gemma Miralda)

path to the right, re-entering the woods and starting a continual descent.
2.4km/12.3km Junction. Join another earthen track and turn left, then after a few metres turn right. The Sant Medir chapel is a short distance away in the opposite direction.
1.4km/13.7km Can Borrell. Take a dirt track to the left to bypass this farmhouse and its terraced fields.
2.3km/16km Roundabout. On the outskirts of the town take the first exit to the left along Av. del Pla del Vinyet. At the next roundabout turn right along Av. de la Torre Blanca. At the next major junction turn left to follow the central pedestrian walkway along the middle of C. Puig i Cadalfalch/la Rambla del Celler. After 250m turn right to climb Passeig de Francesc Macià along the bicycle and pedestrian lane. After 200m turn left to skirt the medieval towers to arrive at Pl. d'Octavia.
1.2km/17.2km Monastery of Sant Cugat.
Sant Cugat del Vallès - pop. 91.000. A town of the Vallès Occidental region. The town grew up around the most important medieval monastery of the ancient 'County' of Barcelona. The present size of the town owes much to its proximity to Barcelona city.

Laberint d'Horta (©ACT. Nano Cañas)

Barcelona
www.visitbarcelona.com
Sant Cugat
① Hotel Venture ⊜⊜⊜
Tel. 93 589 06 05

② Hotel Sant Cugat ⊜⊜⊜
Tel. 93 544 26 70
Holiday Inn ⊜⊜⊜
Tel. 93 561 25 00

AC Hotel ⊜⊜⊜
Tel. 93 589 41 41
QGAT Hotel ⊜⊜⊜
Tel. 93 544 19 22

Passeig de Gràcia, Barcelona. One of the most well known and popular avenues in the city, as well as being a bustling commercial artery. Built along the route that connected the city to the outlying village of Gracia it is one of the most important showcases of Modernism architecture in Catalonia.

Church of Verge de Pompeia, Barcelona. Designed in the Historicism style by Enric Sagnier i Villavecchia and built between 1908-1915 to form part of a convent.

Mercat de la Llibertat, Barcelona. One of the indoor wet and dry markets of Gracia with attractive wrought iron façades. Built towards the end of the C19th when the outdoor market squares were sanitised.

Casa Vicens, Barcelona. The first house designed by Antoni Guadí in the Catalan Modernisme style. Built between 1883 and 1885, now a museum.

Parc del Laberint d'Horta, Barcelona. The oldest neoclassical formal garden in Barcelona dating from 1794 with a later C19th Romantic layout. The maze attracts visitors from all over the world.

Chapel of Sant Medir. A humble Romanesque design built on the former Roman road between Barcelona and Sant Cugat, this chapel, of humble Romanesque design, first appears in records from 1046.

Sant Cugat Monastery. A Benedictine abbey, built between C9th-C14th with an outstanding cloister.

Municipal Indoor Market, Sant Cugat. A Modernist design from the early C20th.

1B. Sant Cugat del Vallès - Esparreguera: 30.9km

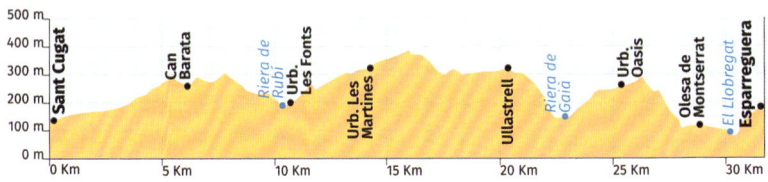

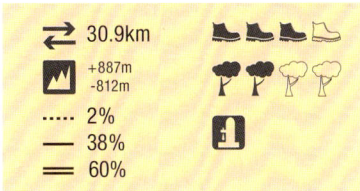

- 30.9km
- +887m / -812m
- 2%
- 38%
- 60%

The approach to the base of the Montserrat mountain is through a landscape of continual climbs and descents, dotted with small towns and sprawls of rural urbanisations that cling to the hillsides. The panorama widens as the walker continues to gain height, with the reward of stunning all around views.

Observations: This stage coincides fully with the red and white stripes that mark the GR6. After very heavy rain the confluence of the Gaià and Sant Jaume streams may be impassable.

0km C. Sant Cugat Monastery. Take C. Major towards Pl. de Sant Pere. Continue along C. de Sant Domènec and Passeig de la Creu. Upon reaching the small square of Pl. Rafael de Casanova, turn left to cross through its park and then veer right onto Av. Rius i Taulet. Shortly cross over the railway line.

1.2km/1.2km Avinguda Can Graells. At the first major fork veers right until you meet a small roundabout. Turn right along Av. de la Clota to cross a further three roundabouts on the same avenue. ATTENTION Cross a bridge over the AP-7 motorway along the right hand verge. At the next roundabout continue counter clockwise with care, taking the third exit to follow the left hand side of Camí de Can Graells. Continue on past a modern business park.

2.5km/3.7km Track. Fork to the right along the main earthen track past fields and woods, ignoring all minor turnings.

1.6km/5.3km Junction of GRs. Turn sharply to the left, following the GR6 and soon enter the Can Barata urbanisation. Continue to the right along an asphalt street in a straight line until the C-1413a road. Cross straight over to follow a dirt track uphill. Climb the track through woods following the GR6 markings. After a couple of left turns the track continues upwards along the crest of a ridge within a firebreak.

2.2km/7.5km Tracks Junction. At the summit of the ridge turn left. After 400m fork right along an earthen track to descend along the crest of another ridge towards les Fonts urbanisation. Upon reaching the asphalt turn right uphill on C. Camí de Can Corbera and after a few metres, fork left downhill on the same street. At the end of the street at a roundabout, turn left along C. Verge de Fàtima. About 50m before its end, take a short cut to the right through a car parking area and emerge onto a main road.

2.5km/10km C. Mossèn Parramon. Cross straight over to follow this street. After a short distance, pass the church of Mare de Deu del Roser, then cross over the Rubí stream and soon after, the trainline. At a roundabout by the train station of les Fonts, take the third exit clockwise uphill on Passeig de la Muntanya. Eventually turn right onto C. Esperanto and left onto C. del Fornot. Leave the urbanisation behind to follow a wide earthen track, at times also asphalted. It crosses a bridge over the busy C-16 highway. Follow the main track steeply uphill for 1km through a landscape of scrub and young pines.

2.6km/12.6km Junction of Tracks. Continue to the left on a gentler slope uphill to enter the Martines urbanisation. Keep straight on, along the asphalt of Camí de les Martines, a very long street that skirts the edge of the urbanisation, ignoring all turnings to the left. The end of this street meets a very busy road which passes over the highest area of this stage.

2.9 km/15.5km C-243a Road. ATTENTION. Turn left towards Martorell following the

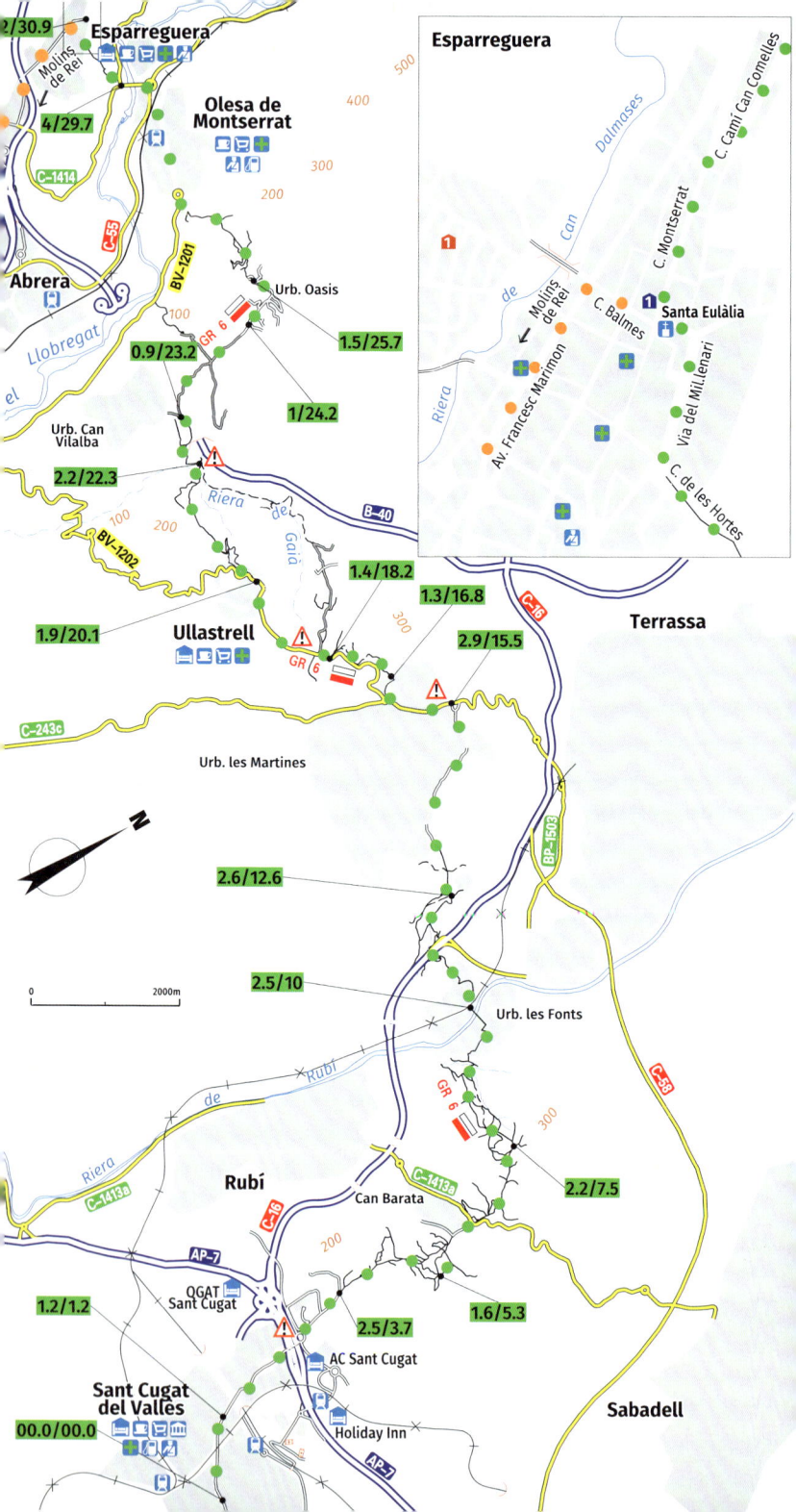

Sant Cugat (©ACT. M.A.S.)

left hand verge. Just after passing a petrol station, cross the road with care and continue along C. Falciot, parallel to the main road. At the end of the street, continue straight ahead, downhill on C. Xot. From here, the views inland open up to take in the jagged outline of the Montserrat mountain. Continue 300m ignoring two left hand turns.

1.3km/16.8km Path. Take a path to the left between house plots, leaving the street behind to enter woodland. Cross over a dirt track and go straight ahead on a path through more woods. Turn left onto a track and continue for 200m.

1.4km/18.2km BV-1203 Road. ATTENTION. Turn right taking care as you walk along the verge. Ignore all junctions to reach the village of Ullastrell. Continue along the road until you fork right along the flat part of C. Serra.

1.9km/20.1km Ajuntament d'Ullastrell. Pass the town hall to climb C. Serra until you find Pujada de Ponent street on the right. Here take a track downhill to leave the village and after 200m turn to the left to continue on a track steeply downhill ignoring all turnings. Pass a couple of country houses and a farm before reaching the valley bottom along a zig zag narrower track.

2.2km/22.3km Confluence of Gullies. ATTENTION. After heavy rains the Gaià stream crossing may be impractical. There are a number of paths and tracks here. Look to the left to pick out the GR markings that lead to a track uphill.

0.9km/23.2km Asphalt Track. Join and turn to the right.

1km/24.2km Oasis Urb. Continue straight on along the asphalt into the urbanization, ignoring markings that attempt to detour the Camino along side tracks. Continue to a roundabout and keep straight on following the main street past all turnings.

1.5km/25.7km Hairpin Bend. Leave the asphalt and continue straight on along an earthen track. Descend a steep slope towards Olesa de Montserrat. Upon reaching the outskirts take the first street downhill to the right. At its end turn left and in a few metres turn right towards a roundabout. Continue straight on along Av. Francesc Macià, then straight on again at the next large roundabout. At the following small roundabout turn left, crossing the road to follow the right hand verge. Continue under the railway line and at an enormous roundabout continue counter clockwise to take the fifth opening towards Esparreguera. Cross a bridge over the river Llobregat and take the first street on the right.

4km/29.7km Track. After 50m take a narrow track to the left between vegetable plots. Climb past more plots until you reach an asphalt street. Turn right to enter the town of Esparreguera, taking the second street to the right, C. Via del Mil·lenari. Turn left at the end of this street.

1.2km/30.9km Santa Eulàlia Church.

Monestir de Sant Cugat (©ACT. M.A.S.)

Ullastrell
 Hostalatge Jordi Sans
Tel. 93 788 72 62

Esparreguera
 Hostal Can Duran
Tel. 696 530 913

 Hollidays
Domus Iano
Tel. 617 235 873

Church of Santa Maria, Ullastrell. Built in the C20th. It has an attractive façade and belltower.

La Torre del Rellotge, Olesa de Montserrat. Once a tower in the defensive walls of Olesa, it was converted into a clock tower and for a time, used as the local prison.

2A. Barcelona - Molins de Rei: 21km

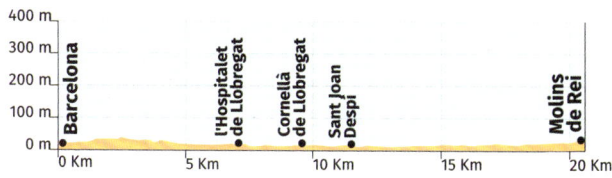

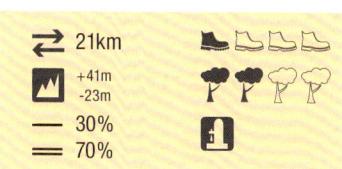

The urban landscape of Barcelona forms a built up corridor to the surrounding towns. It contrasts with the second stretch of this stage that follows the banks of the river Llobregat. This green corridor with its protected nature areas provides a welcome respite from the hustle and bustle of the modern industrial surrounds.

0km Church of Sant Jaume. From the door of the church in C. Ferran turn right to reach Pl. Sant Jaume. Veer left up C. del Bisbe to C. de Santa Llúcia to arrive at the steps of the cathedral. From the door of the cathedral continue to the far left side of the Pl. Nova square to take the narrow C. de la Palla that leads to the front door of the Basilica de Santa Maria del Pi. Continue along C. Cardenal Casañas which quickly reaches the wide tree lined Rambla.

0.9km/0.9km La Rambla. Cross straight over to head into C. Hospital. At Pl. del Pedró, continue along C. de Sant Antoni Abat. Skirt around the opposite corner of Mercado de Sant Antoni indoor market and continue along C. Tamarit. At the first junction continue ahead and fork to the right along Av. Mistral. On meeting Av Paral·lel turn right.

2.1km/3km Plaça Espanya. Proceed clockwise around this huge open space passing the venetian towers that mark the entrance to Montjuic. At the corner of the grandiose Fira de Barcelona building and the Gran Via de les Corts Catalanes, cross the road and turn left. In a few metres fork right along C. de la Bordeta. Now follow a long straight line that continues along C. Gavà, C. Constitució, and C. Santa Eulàlia. Eventually pass under the elevated railway tracks and arrive at a roundabout. Continue straight on along C. Prat de la Riba and then C. Major.

4.8km/7.8km Church of Santa Eulàlia de Mérida. Proceed straight along C. Major and then the Carretera de l'Hospitalet road. On entering the town of Cornellà de Llobregat, keep straight ahead on C. Joaquim Rubió i Ors. At the end of this street cross straight over a wide avenue to continue, parallel to the tramlines on the Carretera Sant Joan Despí. At a roundabout, go straight on.

4.2km/12km Sant Joan Despí. At the next roundabout, at the tramlines, veer right, the Camino turns left along Av. de Barcelona. At the first roundabout turn right along the Rambla Josep Maria Jujol. At the first junction turn left along C. Montjuic. At the end of this street, cross over C. Maria Tarrida by the traffic lights to continue straight ahead on a narrow asphalt lane between market garden

Catedral de Barcelona (©ACT. Georama)

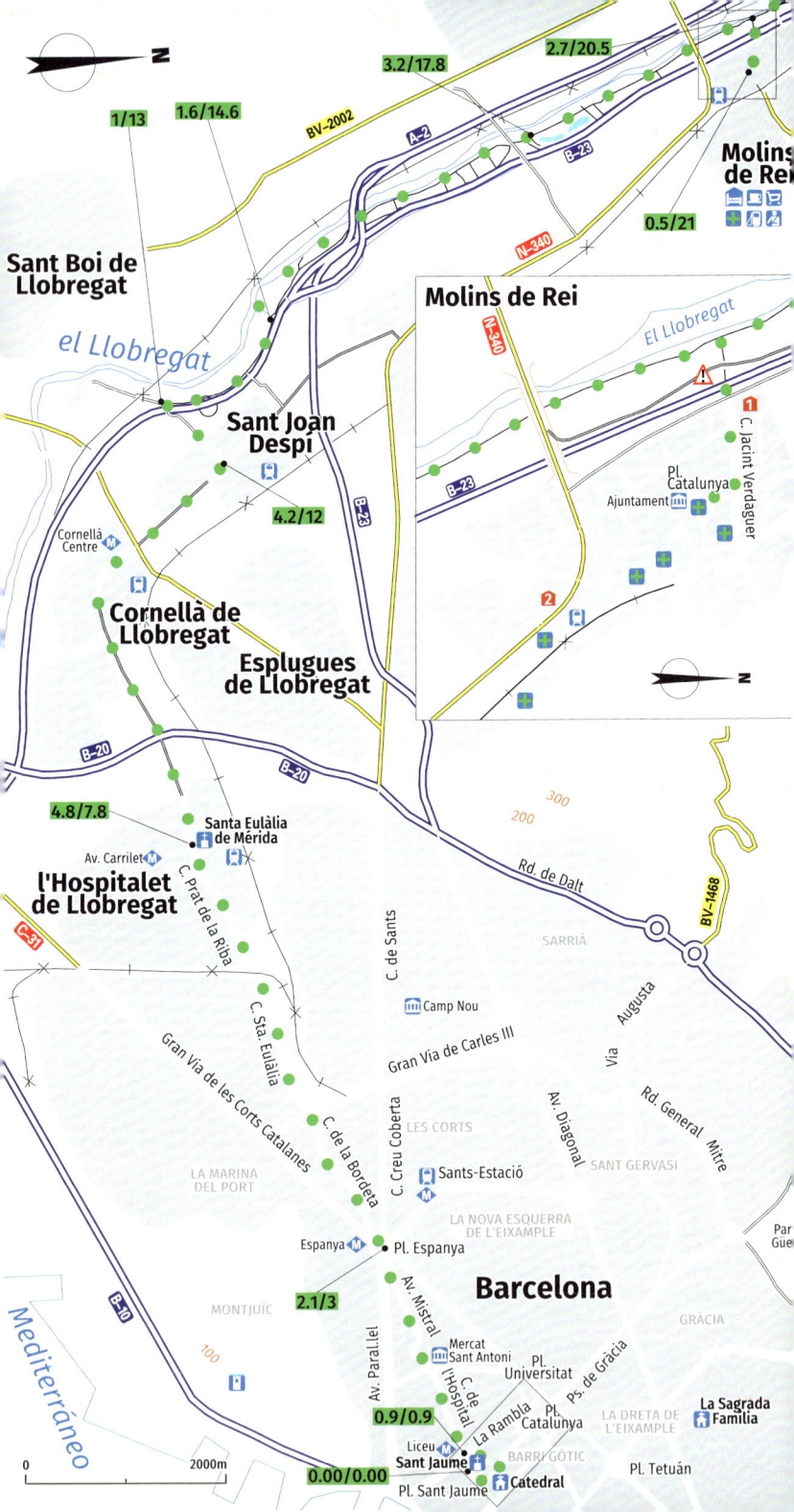

plots. At a junction of lanes continue ahead to cross a bridge over the A-2 motorway. On the other side fork to the right.
1km/13km Junction. After a few metres, turn sharp right onto an asphalt track which continues on between the river Llobregat and the motorway.
1.6km/14.6km Riera d'en Paissa. Cross a bridge over this stream. Here the Camino splits briefly into two. The more pleasant route turns to the left along a narrow track towards the river. It then veers right to follow the river course along a earthen track surrounded by reeds and elephant grass. After 700m, keep straight on under a double viaduct of motorways. Keep straight on at all junctions.
3.2km/17.8km Variants Meetup. After passing under a metal road bridge with four arches the two Camino routes rejoin. Continue straight on alongside the river, passing under the concrete bridge that carries the N-340, to continue between reeds and market garden plots.
2.7km/20.5km Junction. At the first junction after the bridge turn right, leaving the Camino and the river behind, to enter Molins de Rei. ATTENTION. At the traffic lights on the outskirts of the town. Cross the road with care to proceed through a couple of tunnels under the urban motorway. Continue straight along C. Verdaguer to the corner of Pl. de Catalunya. Turn right to reach the town hall.
0.5km/21km Pl. Ajuntament de Molins de Rei.
Molins de Rei - pop. 25.000. A town of the Baix Llobregat. Situated on the left bank of the river Llobregat, its origins date back to the construction of watermills built by order of Alfonso II in the C12th. Today, light industry forms the principal economic activity of the area.

Molins de Rei
1 Hotel Ibis Barcelona Molins de Rei
Tel. 93 680 44 14

2 Hotel Calasanz
Tel. 93 668 16 39

Basilica of Santa Maria del Pi, Barcelona. Built on the site of a C5th church, this C14th Gothic structure has an impressive single nave. It was damaged by artillery fire during the siege of Barcelona in 1714.
La Boqueria Market, Barcelona. Opened as the Mercat Sant Josep in 1836. Today it is a popular tourist attraction, but still excites the senses with its visual and gastronomic flair.
Santa Eulàlia de Mèrida Church, L'Hospitalet de Llobregat. Built in the 1940's after the C16th church was destroyed during the Spanish Civil War. It is a stunning example of Romanesque Revival with a towering bell tower and a delicate facade of triple arches.
Chapel of Santa Maria del Bon Viatge, Sant Joan Despí. C13th of modest design. It has long been a custom for travellers to stop and ask for the blessing and protection from the patron.
Castellciuró, Molins de Rei. A ruined medieval Templar castle atop a low hill that overlooks the Llobregat.
Sant Pere de Romaní hermitage, Molins de Rei. Romanesque C11th-12th. Its 12m high watchtower was added in C15th.

2B. Molins de Rei - Esparreguera: 24.8km

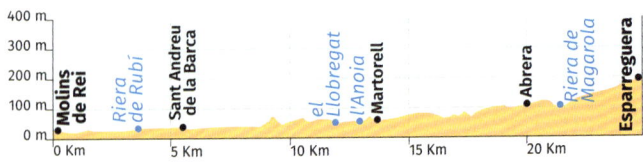

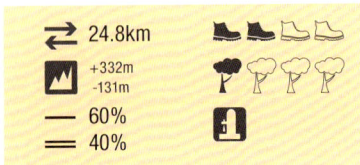

24.8km
+332m
-131m
— 60%
= 40%

The course of the river is the main reference for the first half of this stage as you follow the Camí del Llobregat. After crossing the town of Martorell, the Camino begins a gradual ascent before joining the alternative route from Barcelona on the outskirts of Esparreguera.

Observations: After heavy rains, caution should be taken when crossing the Rubí and Magarola gullies.

0km Molins de Rei. To regain the Camino, proceed from the Pl. de Catalunya along C. Verdaguer. At the crossroads by the traffic lights, continue straight on to pass under a road bridge. Then take a track straight ahead after crossing the main road with care. Continue a short distance to a junction of tracks.

0.6km/0.6km Junction. Turn right and after 500m ford a stream and continue straight on to pass a picnic area on the right.

1.4km/2km AVE Viaduct. Pass under and fork left to follow the bank of the Llobregat river along a mix of dirt tracks and paths.

1.7km/3.7km The Rubí Gulley. ATTENTION. Cross the wide floor of this water course (normally dry unless heavy rainfall) via the ford and veer to the left. Cross under the viaduct of a highway and continue along an earthen track next to the river. Pass under a pedestrian bridge that grants access to the town of Sant Andreu de la Barca. Follow the signed Camí del Llobregat on an earthen track alongside the winding river, passing under a series of motorway viaducts, road and pedestrian bridges, always following the Camí del Llobregat signed way. Eventually the Camino climbs to the same height as the railway line.

8.1km/11.8km Pont del Diable. Cross over this outstanding Roman bridge to enter Martorell. Proceed in a continuous straight line to Pl. de la Creu, then along C. Pere Puig, and C. Anselm Clavé, to Pl. de la Vila. Continue straight along C. Francesc Santacana to its end by the river Anoia. Turn right for a short distance towards a ford over the river.

1km/12.8km River Anoia Crossing. Once across the river turn left to follow a cycle lane. Curve round to meet a roundabout and fork right onto the long and winding C. Montserrat.

0.8km/13.6km Martorell Central Station. After the railway station, continue straight on at a roundabout to enter the industrial outskirts of the town. At the next roundabout veer left to cross the railway line, still on C. Montserrat.

1.7km/15.3km Junction. Turn right to follow an overhead electric pylon line. At the next junction, turn left towards Can Bros still following the electricity lines past more industrial units.

0.6km/15.9km Can Bros Roundabout. Turn right at this roundabout, then left at the next one. Pass under the A-2 motorway.

0.5km/16.4km Track. Immediately take the earthen track to the left. Follow the main track and soon cross the railway line. The track meets the motorway and follows it parallel, up to an ironworks unit. After a short distance fork right, leaving the motorway behind. The track winds into Abrera entering along C. Nou, then continues along C. Major and Passeig de l'Església.

3.5km/19.9km Abrera Church. Fork left past the church of Sant Pere. Continue along Av. de la Generalitat, passing under the C-55 flyover, to the roundabout at Pl. Regato. Take the first exit to the right and then the first left turn onto C. Sant Jaume. At its end continue straight on along a dirt track to access an underpass below the B-40 highway.

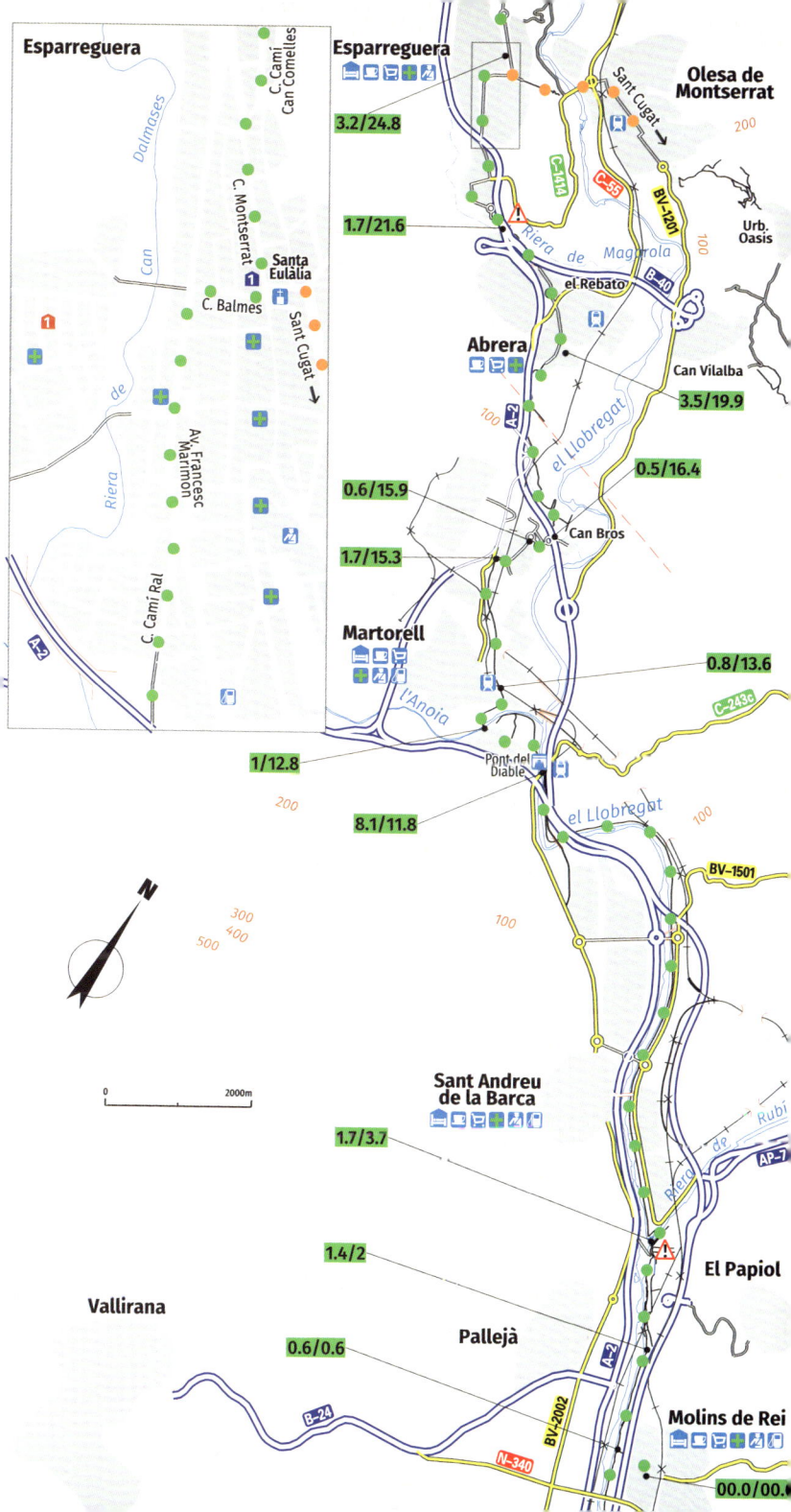

Pont del Diable (©ACT. Georama)

1.7km/21.6km The Magarola Gulley. ATTENTION. Cross the wide water course (normally dry unless heavy rainfall) and veer left under the A-2 motorway viaducts to enter an area of industrial units. Continue along the asphalt to a roundabout and veer left. At the next junction turn right. Take the next turn to the left along C. Camí Ral and soon cross over the A-2 motorway to enter Esparreguera. Continue straight on ignoring all junctions until you reach the Av. Francesc Marimon. Turn left and after approximately 500m turn right along the narrow C. Balmes.
3.2km/24.8km Esparreguera Church.
Martorell - pop. 27.000. A town of the Baix Llobregat. An industrial town and a place of strategic importance throughout the centuries due to its location; the confluence of the Anoia and Llobregat rivers and proximity to Barcelona.
Esparreguera - pop. 22.000. A town of the Baix Llobregat. A town with a thousand years of history. Well known for its ceramic and textile industries during the C19th. It is famous for the Esparreguera Passion Play, a theatrical representation staged by the townsfolk over 10 Sundays between March and May, featuring over 300 players.

Martorell
- **Hotel Sant Joan**
Tel. 93 774 21 73
- **Hotel Ciutat de Martorell**
Tel. 93 774 51 60
- **Hotel Manel**
Tel. 93 775 23 87

Sant Andreu de la Barca
- **Hotel Catalonia Bristol**
Tel. 93 682 11 77
- **Ibis Budget Barcelona**
Tel. 93 653 54 70

Esparreguera
- **Hostal Can Duran**
Tel. 696 530 913
- **Holidays Domus Iano**
Tel. 617 235 873

Chapel of Sant Joan, Martorell. First referenced in 1313, as a Gothic style chapel to a hospice.
Pont del Diable, Martorell. The 'Devil's Bridge' of Roman origin, by which the Via Augusta crossed the river Llobregat.
Santa Maria Church, Martorell. C16th. Rebuilt after the Spanish Civil War.

Sant Pere Church, Abrera. Of Romanesque design with a single nave, first referenced in the C12th.
Church of Santa Eulàlia, Esparreguera. A variation of styles from the Gothic to the Baroque. The single large nave along with the 63m high belltower are outstanding.

3. ESPARREGUERA - MONTSERRAT: 12.1KM

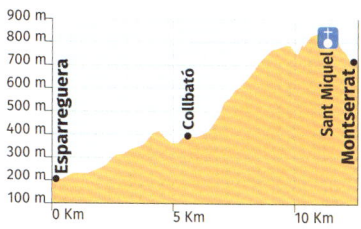

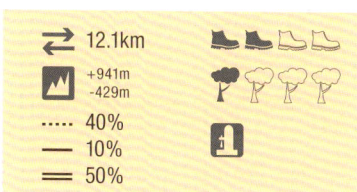

The ascent to the monastery of Montserrat through its emblematic sierra follows historic tracks that have been trodden since time immemorial. Multitudes of pilgrims, drawn by the spirituality attached to the setting of this unique 'serrated mountain' landscape, make the climb in order to venerate the Virgin of Montserrat.

Observations: A short but demanding stage with some steep paths up the slopes of the Sierra de Montserrat.

0km Esparreguera. From the church take C. Montserrat as far as Pl. Sant Magi and continue straight on along C. Bruc. Turn to the right along Can Comelles and very soon at a roundabout veer left. Follow this road to the outskirts of the town to pick up the Camí Veïnal de Can Roca. Continue on in a straight line, passing the junction with C. Tallaferro.

2km/2km Clearing. At a junction of tracks in a woodland clearing, take an earthen track to the right marked by the red and white stripes of the GR long distance route. After 600m turn to the left and at the next junction, keep straight on.

1.3km/3.3km Crossroads. Take the path straight ahead through a pine wood until a junction with a track where you turn left. Continue along this dirt track following the GR markings.

1.5km/4.8km B-112 Road. ATTENTION. This road can be busy especially at weekends. Turn to the left and after 150m leave the asphalt to take a path to the right that climbs to the village of Collbató. At the first street turn right. Continue straight on along C. Amadeu Vives to the Pl. de l'Església. Now follow C. Pau Bertran and look for a flight of steps to climb to C. Pujolet. Keep straight on to rejoin C. Pau Bertran and leave the village on an earthen track through olive groves.

1.4km/6.2km Junction. At this first junction turn right. The track narrows to a path and starts to climb in a zig zag through pines and scrub.

4.4km/10.6km Cement Track. Follow it to the right, reaching the chapel of Sant Miquel. Continue along a cement track along the mountainside.

1.5km/12.1km Montserrat Monastery. A small community of monks. Benedictine abbey founded around 880. It constitutes one of the most important spiritual centers in Catalonia and one of its cultural icons.

> **Camino towards Tàrrega - p. 55**

Montserrat (©ACT. José Luís Rodríguez)

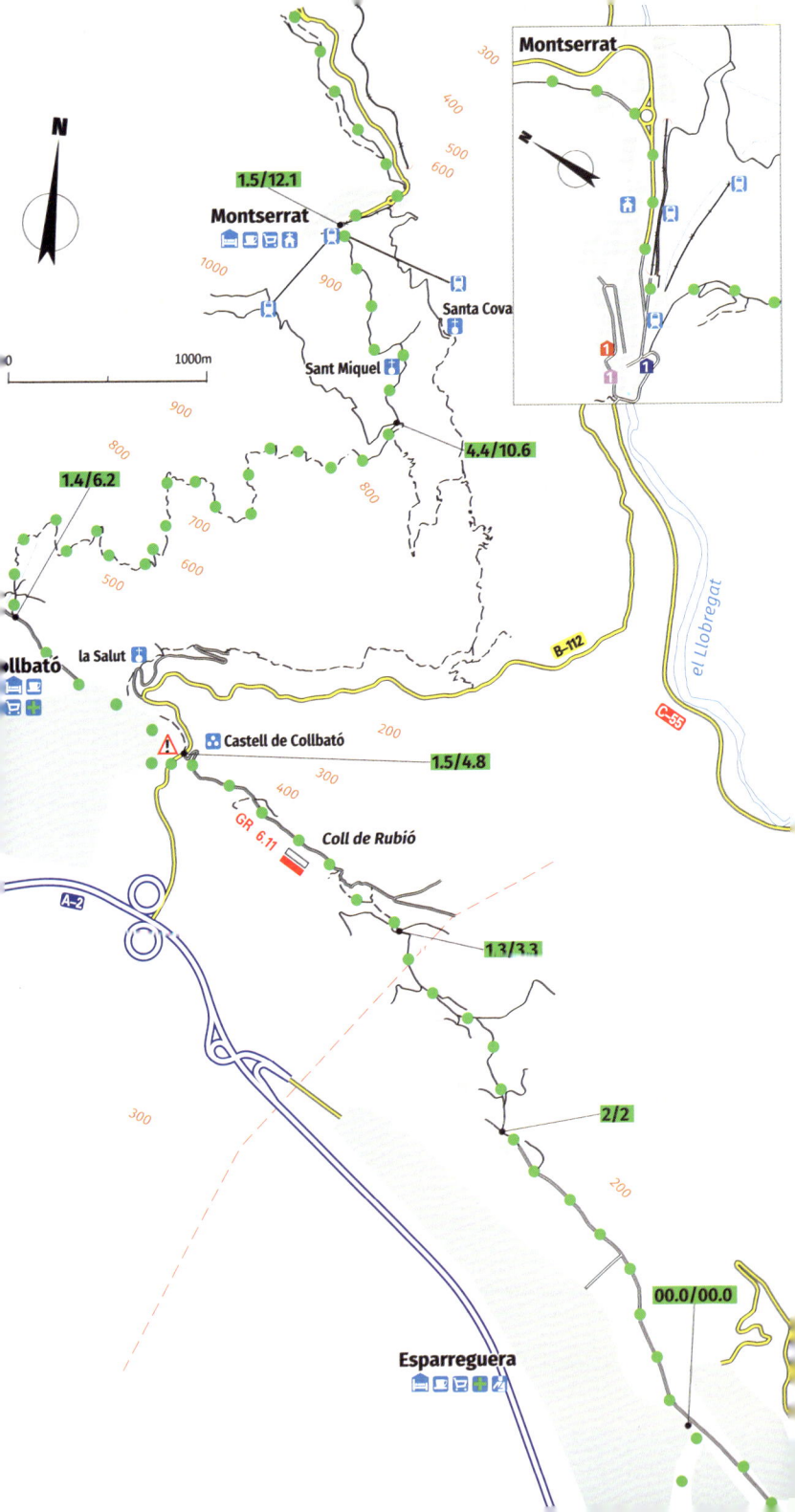

Monestir de Montserrat (©ACT. José Luís Rodríguez)

Church of Sant Corneli, Collbató. An attractive rural Baroque design with an attractive simple façade. Little remains of the original C11th church.
Chapel of Sant Miquel, Montserrat. Legend tells how the Archangel Michael destroyed a temple dedicated to Venus in order to erect the first Christian chapel of Montserrat.
Monastery of Montserrat. Benedictine Abbey with origins in the C9th. It has two groups of buildings; the Abbey, which includes the monks' accommodation, and the annexes that welcome pilgrims. Surrounding these are numerous shrines and chapels, dotted around the mountain.

Collbató
Hostal Can Missé
Tel. 93 777 90 61
Monestir de Montserrat
Alberg Abat Oliba
Tel. 93 877 77 01
Cel·les Abat Marcet
Tel. 93 877 77 01
Hotel Hostal Abat Cisneros
Tel. 93 877 77 01

TÀRREGA - PUENTE LA REINA

The first stretch crosses fairly desolate and dry terrain. This was once cultivated land and contrasts greatly with the ensuing large tracts of orchards and fields of maize, irrigated today by the canals and rivers that criss cross the land. This whole section is accompanied by views of the distant Pyrenean mountain chain and its rugged foothills.

Monzón, with its hilltop Templar castle and the mudejar style tower of the Romanesque cathedral, guards the Way as it enters the fertile cereal plains of the 'Hoya de Huesca'. Leaving the watchful eye of Loarre castle behind, the route embarks on the most dramatic and rugged stages within this book. The Camino climbs through pine forests to reach a wild terrain of towering cliffs and broken ridges patrolled by vultures. Footpaths connect remote half hidden villages where tales of witches still abound. Crossing densely wooded hillsides, they follow narrow valleys with streams of pure icy water.

The earliest pilgrims kept close to these foothills of the Pyrenees along this older northern route within the relative safety of these Christian lands until reaching the wider, more secure, Aragón river valley. This secluded valley hides the striking monastery of San Juan de la Peña. Perched within a sheer cliff face it is considered by many to be the birthplace of the kingdom of Aragón. The modern Camino has, perhaps rightly, been rerouted via this monastery, and soon links up with the pilgrim route from Somport. The enigmatic octagonal chapel of Santa Maria de Eunate welcomed pilgrims prior to their safe arrival in Puente la Reina on the well established Camino Frances.

Huesca - This small provincial capital sits on the plain known as La Hoya de Huesca. It is bordered to the north by the Guara mountains and the eye catching rocky outcrops of Roland's Leap. Once an important Iberian settlement, the strategic importance of this hilltop by the river Isuela was also recognised by the Romans, and *Osca* formed the base for the rebellious Quintus Sertorius.

During Moorish times *Wasqah* stood firm as the northern bastion for just over three centuries, first ruled by the Emirate of Cordoba and later the Taifa of Zaragoza. Just a single tower, of the original ninety-nine, and some of the defensive walls still remain from this period. The city was briefly the capital of Aragón after its conquest by Pedro I in 1096. The compact old quarter with its gardens and squares centres around the graceful Huesca Cathedral, the Plaza del Mercado and nearby Abbey of San Pedro el Viejo, one of the best examples of Aragonese Romanesque architecture.

©Callum Christie

1. TÀRREGA - LINYOLA: 23.9KM

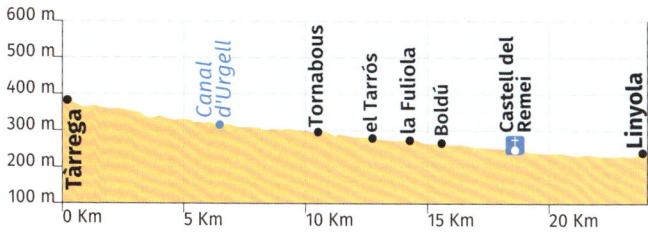

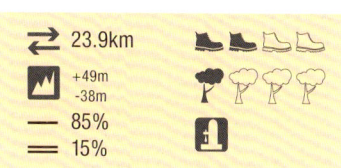

23.9km
+49m / -38m
85%
15%

The Camino crosses an arid, rain dependent plain, traditionally used for grazing and cereal production. It has now been transformed by C20th irrigation projects. Fields of maize and fruit farms extend between the small villages along the route.

0km Tàrrega. From Pl. Major take C. Urgell until Av. de Catalunya and veer left. At a large roundabout in Pl. de Josep Pons turn right along Av. de Fàtima. At its end, turn left onto Av. de Balaguer which soon becomes an earthen track. Cross over the railway and continue straight on.

2.4km/2.4km A-2 Tunnel. Pass under the motorway and at the next junction turn right. Over the next couple of kilometres at each fork turn left until you reach a wayside farm. After these brick built buildings, keep straight on at a junction and cross over an irrigation canal.

4km/6.4km Canal d'Urgell. Turn right and after 300m choose the left fork, leaving the canal behind. Continue straight on until a junction by a large farm warehouse. Turn left onto an asphalt lane for 200m. At the first

Castell del Remei (©Callum Christie)

fork, turn right onto a dirt farm track. Continue straight on until Tornabous.
4.3km/10.7km Tornabous. Cross this small village along C. Llibertat. Turn right at the church and then first left to exit the village passing a small park, out onto a country lane.
1.9km/12.6km El Tarròs. The Camino skirts this small village to continue along a lane.
1.7km/14.3km La Fuliola. Enter by the first street to the left, crossing straight through the attractive old village centre. A lane continues to the nearby village of Boldú which you traverse, on C. Major. Continue straight, on by a dirt track. Cross the country road LV-3344 and go straight on along an asphalt lane between vines to Castell del Remei.
4km/18.3km Castell del Remei. Continue past the chapel, on a dusty compact earthen track. After a long straight stretch bordered by trees and a drainage ditch, turn right at a junction. After 100m turn left and continue straight on. At a roundabout on the outskirts of the village keep straight on.
5.6km/23.9km Linyola. Enter by C. Pau Claris and turn right on C. Calderón de la Barca. At its end, turn left to the church, its square and the C. Major.
Linyola - pop. 2600. A village of the Pla d'Urgell area.

©Callum Christie

Tornahous
🛏 **Cal Modest**
Tel. 662 50 50 66

Linyola
🛏 **La Teulerla**
Tel. 609 930 663

🛏 **Apartaments Perebep**
Tel. 679 183 943

 Santa Llúcia Church, La Fuliola. C18th. Attractive Baroque construction.
Castell del Remei. A 'noucentista' style grand country house, with chapel and vineyard.

Old Town, Linyola. C16th-18th buildings and arcades including numerous 'palaces' and the church of Santa Maria.

2. LINYOLA - ALGERRI: 30.2KM

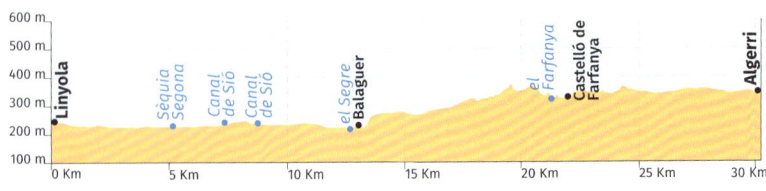

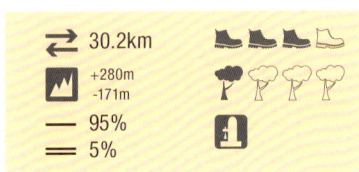

- 30.2km
- +280m / -171m
- 95%
- 5%

The Camino crosses a fertile plain of dry and irrigated fields that has helped feed the surrounding villages. Balaguer, a historic town, is situated by a strategic ford of the river Segre.

0km Linyola. Leave the old town along C. Major and turn right at its end. After 100m leave the road and continue straight on along C. Ramon Formiguera. Turn left at its end, passing the cemetery to leave the village.

1.9km/1.9km Fork. Just after passing a couple of new farm warehouses on the right, at a fork, take the left option. After 200m at the next fork turn right to keep straight on. In a further 150m at the next fork choose the left hand track. Ignore all further turnings and continue straight on until meeting a water channel.

3.3km/5.2km Sèquia Segona del Canal d'Urgell. Cross the bridge and go straight on, leaving the channel behind. Continue straight on ignoring all turnings until you cross the Sió Canal. Keep straight on through all the crossings of tracks until you recross the same canal. Now continue straight on by the main track until you meet a road and flyover.

5.6km/10.8km Cross the C-13. ATTENTION. Cross the road under the flyover and then turn left onto an asphalt lane towards the outskirts of Balaguer. Upon reaching a main road, turn left and cross the Canal de Balaguer. Continue straight on to cross the river Sègre.

2.1km/12.9km River Segre Bridge. On reaching the far bank, turn left to follow the river downstream to the next bridge. Turn away from the water and continue along C. Sant Jaume to the Pl. Mercadal.

Balaguer (©ACT. Georama)

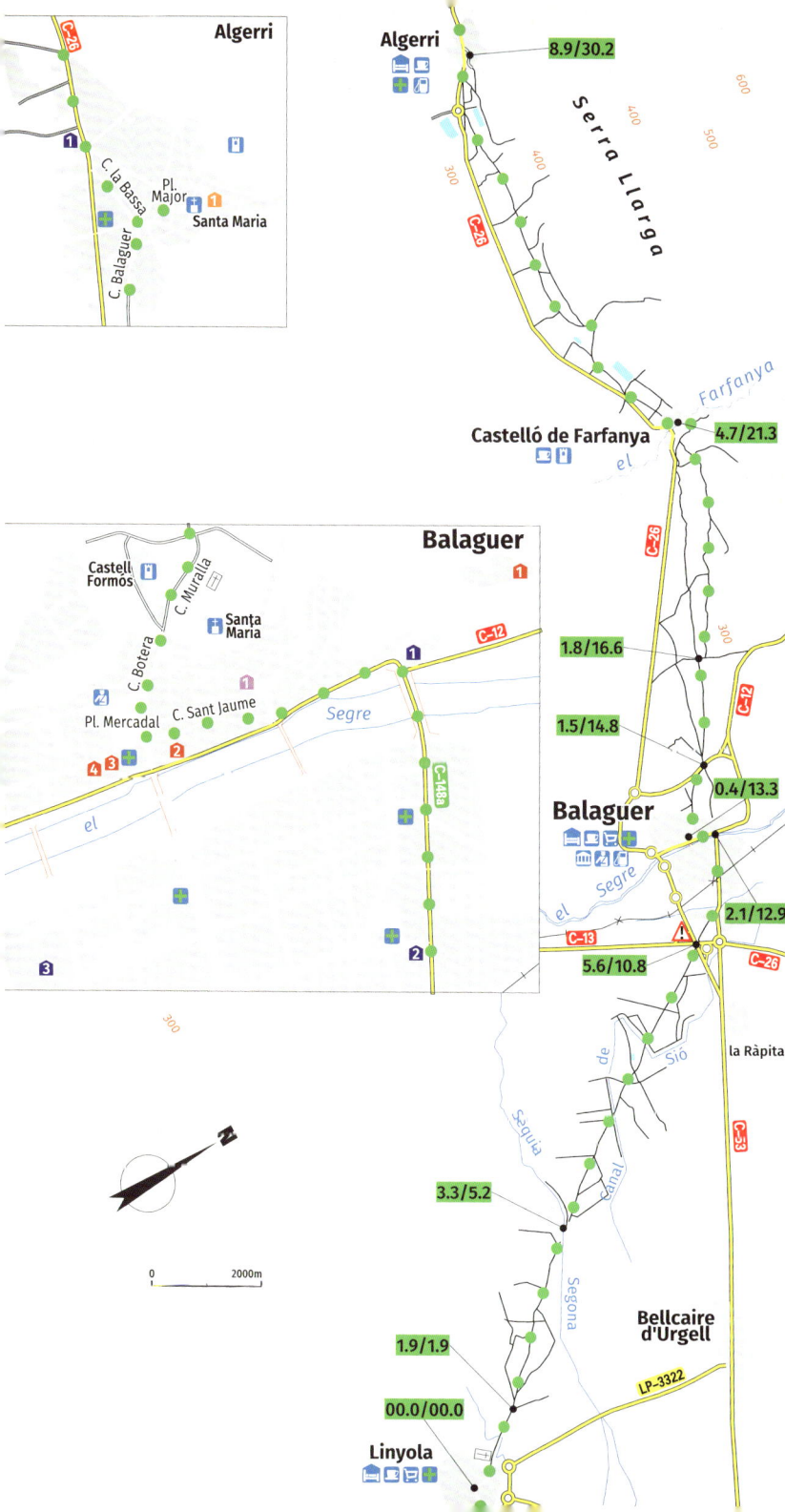

0.4km/13.3km Balaguer. Turn right, going uphill on C. Botera to pass under the arch of a gateway through the ancient defensive walls. At the top of the rise, at a crossroads, keep straight on along an asphalt lane, leaving the town.
1.5km/14.8km C-12 Tunnel. By an ancient boundary marker column (it has lost its cross), pass under a new road. In 100m at a fork, turn right along a track.
1.8km/16.6km Crossing of Tracks. By a modern irrigation pipeline installation, turn right and in 200m take an earthen track to the left, that rises through an area of holm oaks and arable fields. Follow the main track until you meet an asphalt lane. Cross straight over to continue downhill. In 400m turn right to follow an asphalt track.
4.7km/21.3km Castelló de Farfanya. Cross the old bridge to enter the village by an archway. Turn right, climbing to the centre. From the Pl. Major take a narrow street exit that joins C. Hospital and then C. Sant Roc. The street widens to meet Av. Catalunya and after 50m, take the first street on the right, C. Algerri. As you leave the village, cross a road and follow an earthen track straight ahead. After 500m, continue to the right to avoid joining the main road (C-26). Follow the main earthen track, parallel to the road, ignoring all turnings, and with the Llarga hills to your right.
8.9km/30.2km Algerri. Between pine woods and farms, you soon enter the village with its Pl. Major and the Church of Santa Maria.
Balaguer - pop. 16.600. Capital of la Noguera region.
Algerri - pop. 478. A village of la Noguera region.

Balaguer
Alberg de Pelegrins Teresa Pàmies
Tel. 973 451 555
      973 445 200
Hostal Sant Miquel
Tel. 615 459 77
Hostal Urgell
Tel. 973 445 348

Dpass pel Segre
Tel. 667 886 930
Hotel Santuari
Tel. 973 449 617
Hotel Balaguer
Tel. 973 445 750
Cal Comabella
Tel. 676 680 135

El Palauet de la Muralla
Tel. 667 248 299
Algerri
Hostal Terraferma
Tel. 973 426 004
Alberg de Pelegrins
Tel. 973 426 013

Fortifications, Balaguer. The Formós castle and town walls confirm the strategic importance of this historic town. Built during Moorish times. it has undergone numerous changes throughout the ages.
Mercadal Square Porticos, Balaguer. A medieval quadrangle of porticoed shop fronts.
Castelló de Farfanya. An attractive medieval village complete with bridge, walls, towers, gateways and arches. Originally C13th, the church of Sant Miquel was largely rebuilt during the C18th.
Farfanya Castle. Moorish in origin, noteworthy for its flanking watchtower.
Church of Santa Maria, Algerri. Possesses one of the largest Baroque facades in Catalonia.
Algerri Castle. Moorish in origin, sadly now in ruins upon an adjacent hilltop.

3. ALGERRI - TAMARITE DE LITERA: 21.5KM

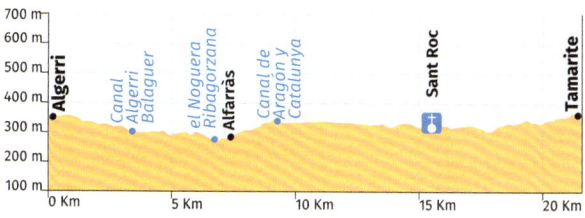

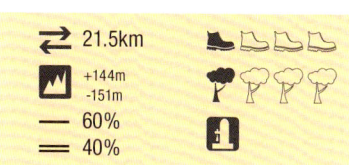

- 21.5km
- +144m / -151m
- — 60%
- = 40%

The Camino enters Aragón, crossing the river Noguera Ribagorçana to continue through the Litera region. Irrigation canals carry water to the green fields and orchards that are surrounded by dry and rough hillsides.

0km Algerri. Follow C. de la Bassa to the main road and turn right towards Alfarràs. Upon leaving the village follow the asphalt for 300m.

0.8km/0.8km Almenar Track. Turn left onto a farm track between olive groves and arable fields. Continue straight on ignoring side turnings, descending gently until you meet an irrigation canal.

2.6km/3.4km Algerri - Balaguer Canal. Turn right, after crossing a small bridge, to follow the canal.

2.1km/5.5km C-26 Road. ATTENTION. Turn left alongside the C-26, going downhill (preferably walking at first within the fruit orchard instead of the hard shoulder of the road), to-

Sant Roc

wards Alfarràs. At a roundabout by the river Noguera Ribagorçana, turn to your right towards Ivars de Noguera. After 100m, drop down from the left verge, on a lane towards the river and a footbridge.

1.2km/6.7km Old Bridge of Alfarràs. Cross this metal bridge, built on the remains of the medieval bridge.

0.9km/7.6km Alfarràs. Rejoin the main road (C-26) up into the small town, the last in Catalonia on this route. Follow Av. de Balmes uphill to a roundabout. Leave Alfarràs on the C-26 towards Tamarite de Litera. ATTENTION. Take care, due to the traffic, as you walk nearly 2km uphill on the hard shoulder of the road.

1.7km/9.3km Junction A-2219. The Camino enters Aragón by the impressive aqueduct of the Aragón - Catalonia Canal. Just after it, at a junction, turn left along the A-2219 towards Almacelles. After only 20m take a farm track to the right. From this point, keep straight on at all forks or junctions, following a farm track between fruit orchards and fields of maize or cereal crops.

3km/12.3km Asphalt Crossing. Cross over an asphalt track and continue straight on.

1.7km/14km Double Junction. The Camino turns right and after 100m, veers back to the left to go straight on.

2.7km/16.7km Sant Roc Chapel. Situated at a crossing of tracks. Keep straight on.

4.8km/21.5km Tamarite de Litera. Cross the Aragón - Catalonia Canal to enter the village.

Tamarite de Litera - pop. 3500. Village of the Aragonese area of Litera.

©Callum Christie

Alfarràs
🛏 Pensió Florida
Tel. 675 083 653

Tamarite
🛏 Casa Galindo
Tel. 974 420 724

🛏 **Alberg Municipal de Pelegrins**
Tel. 974 420 075

 Pont Vell, Alfarràs. A bridge originally spanning eight round arches, of which only three survive, having suffered during various wars.

Torre del Molí, Alfarràs. Moorish mill tower, also used as an electricity power station in more modern times.

Old Church of Sant Pere, Alfarràs. C12th with numerous changes over the centuries.

Sant Roc Chapel, Tamarite. Baroque style, with a single nave and walls of sandstone blocks.

Church of Santa María la Mayor, Tamarite. Romanesque build with gothic remodelling.

4. TAMARITE DE LITERA - MONZÓN: 21KM

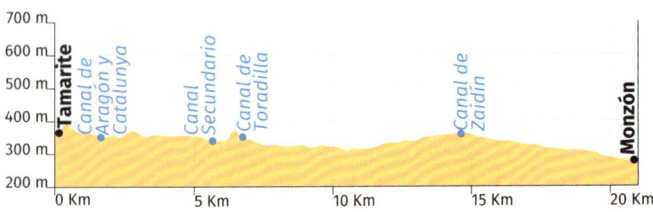

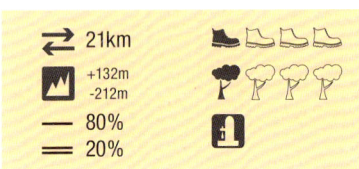

- 21km
- +132m / -212m
- 80%
- 20%

The impressive castle of Monzón is visible from the hills and irrigated fields that line the Camino. Numerous irrigation canals cross the route, bringing water from the foothills of the Pyrenees.

0km Tamarite de Litera. From the town hall take C. San Miguel and then climb a long set of steps. At the end of an upslope look for a short flight of steps up to the right and cross a road to continue, on C. Patrocinio. Keep straight on to leave the town. Cross a small industrial zone in a straight line via a couple of roundabouts. At the end of the units turn right to join an earthen track to the left, downhill to an irrigation canal.

1.6km/1.6km Canal. Cross the Aragón and Catalonia Canal and go straight on ignoring turnings to either side. At another bridge on the left hand side, recross the canal. Continue to the right, straight on until another bridge (with a large reservoir to the right), and once across it, turn right to follow the canal. Ignore the next two bridges and then, at a third one (which also remains uncrossed, you encounter a fork in the track.

3.4km/5km Fork. Take the track to the left and continue to go straight on, ignoring any junctions. After a farm storage unit, the pilgrim is faced with a short steep slope on a rougher section of track. At the crest, cross over another track to go straight on, downhill to the Toradilla canal and a bridge. Cross over and continue straight on.

The country track takes a straight line through fields of irrigated crops, small reservoirs and small farm sheds. The track converts to asphalt.

5.4km/10.4km A-133. Cross this asphalt road and go straight on gently uphill. The asphalted Camino continues ahead. In 300m at a fork, keep straight on, to the left, following the main track.

1.5km/11.9km Fork by a Hut. At a three way fork, take the second earthen track to the right (with a hut on the left). Continue straight on past more irrigated fields and reservoirs to the Zaidín canal. Turn left to follow the canal until you reach a bridge.

2.7km/14.6km Bridge over Canal. Turn right to cross the bridge and right again onto a track. Keep straight on, the track then turns to asphalt.

3.5km/18.1km A-22 Bridge. Pass under the motorway. Continue straight on to a junction by a railway line. Turn left and cross a bridge over the rails and immediately veer right on an asphalt track. Keep straight on until a roundabout on the Av. Lérida at the entrance to Monzón. Continue directly ahead on the narrow C. Joaquin Costa, that leads you to the cathedral.

2.9km/21km Monzón Cathedral.

Monzón - pop. 17.100. Capital of the Cinca Medio. The second most populated city in Huesca province, and of historic note. Once a royal seat of Aragón it has also hosted the Catalan Courts.

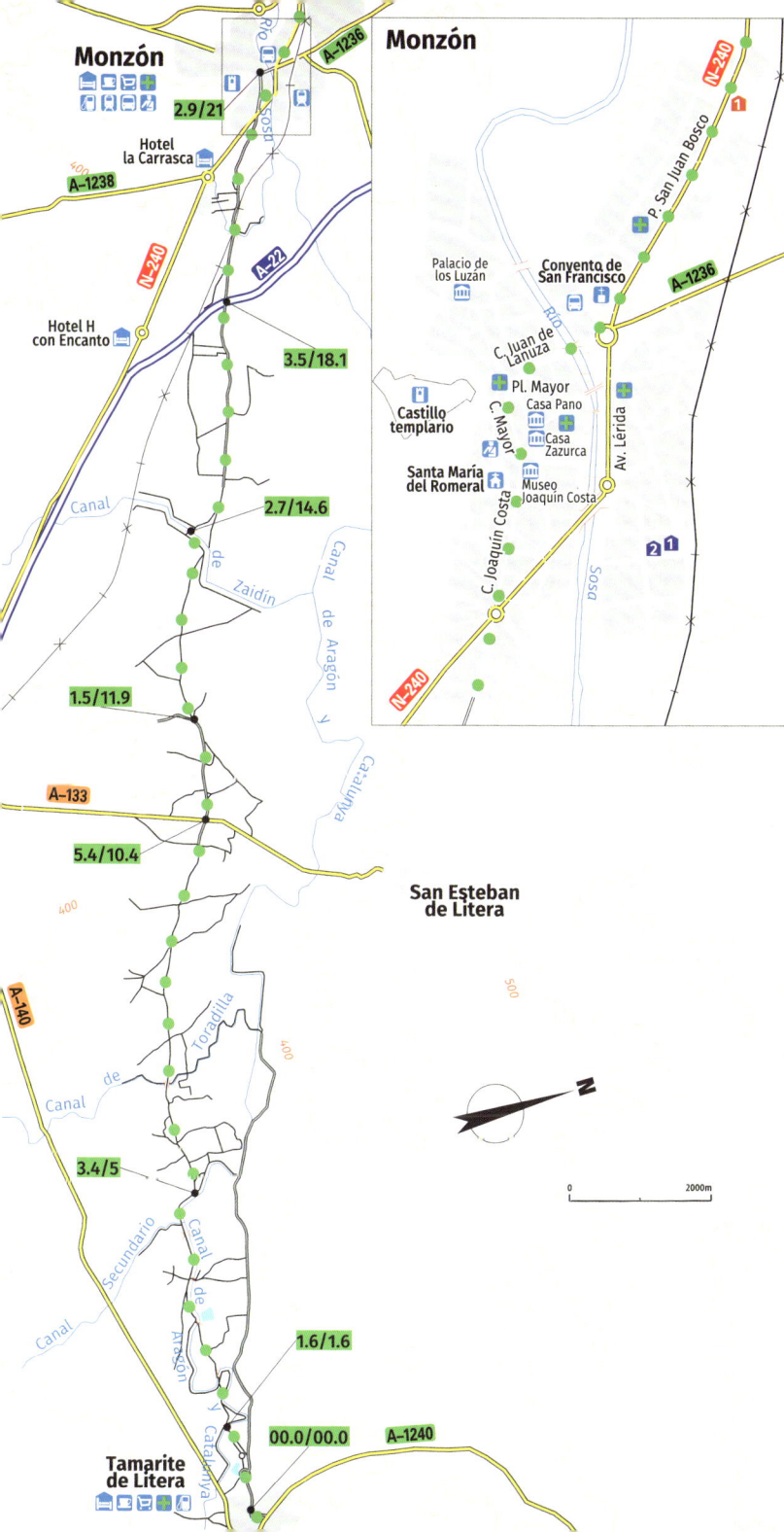

Monzón (©Teresa Mumbiela)

Monzón

- **1** Hostal Venecia I
  Tel. 974 403 699
- **2** Hostal Venecia II
  Tel. 974 403 699
- **1** Hotel Masmonzón
  Tel. 974 404 322
- **Hotel La Carrasca**
  Tel. 974 401 627
- **Hotel H con Encanto**
  Tel. 974 400 506

Monzón Castle. A large fortress of Moorish origin but remodelled by the Knights Templar. The walls were adapted to seat artillery of the C17th-18th. The Chapter hall and the Moorish tower of Homage are worthy of note.
Cathedral of Nuestra Señora del Romeral, Monzón. C12th Romanesque temple that shares the bishopric with Bobastro. The crenellated 'mudéjar' tower is a unique feature.

The Old Quarter, Monzón. Casa Pano, the Town Hall, the Palace de los Luzán, Casa Zazurca as well as the museum of Joaquín Costa are all worthy of further investigation.
Convent of San Francisco, Monzón. Founded by Saint Francisco of Assisi, in the C13th, on his pilgrimage to Santiago. Today it houses a music conservatory.

5. MONZÓN - BERBEGAL: 20.1KM

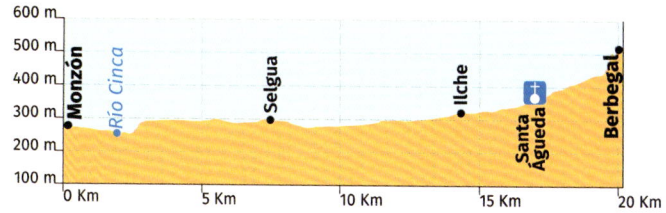

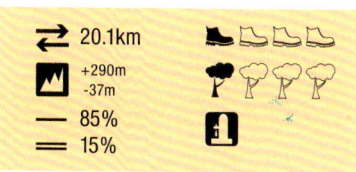

- 20.1km
- +290m / -37m
- 85%
- 15%

The quiet Way crosses an area of irrigated fields from the Cinca Medio to the area of Somontano. The village of Berbegal perches atop a low ridge with outstanding all around views from the Pyrenees to the plains around Huesca.

0km Monzón. From the cathedral, continue along C. Major. Cross the Pl. Major, with its town hall, to descend along C. Juan de Lanuza and cross the river Sosa, coming to a large roundabout. Take the second exit left, passing the convent of San Francisco and a large sculpture on your left hand side. The long tree-lined avenue, (N-240), continues straight on to cross the river Cinca. A few metres further on, exit the N-240 to the left onto the A-130. After 200m take an earthen track to the right that passes under the railway.

2.4km/2.4km Railway Bridge. The Camino climbs up the track and goes straight on through a junction, until it reaches some railway sidings.

1.4km/3.8km Train Line. Cross the unprotected railway crossing and turn left on an earthen track. Turn right onto an asphalt track to cross a minor road. Continue straight on past industrial unit, keep straight on an asphalt street until you meet an dirt track. After the industrial unit continue straight on along a short rough stretch of track, until you meet a better earthen track again. Go straight on to a junction and turn left to enter Selgua village.

3.6km/7.4km Selgua. Enter along C. Monzón and then turn right. At the corner of C. Romero, turn left until Pl. Joaquín Costa. At the far side of this small square turn right, passing the municipal swimming pool. At the end of the street, take an earthen track to the left that descends to meet the A-1223 road.

1km/8.4km A-1223. Cross the road and at the next fork, by a drainage ditch, turn right. Upon meeting a narrow road, (near the A-1223), turn left and after 100m take the first earthen track to the right.

After 600m, take a farm track to the right, following an irrigation channel for a good distance. Cross over an asphalt track and keep straight on, parallel to the channel. At the next junction turn right to reach the A-1223. Cross straight over to enter the village of Ilche.

5.9km/14.3km Ilche. With the church ahead of you, turn left and at the end of the street, veer left. In a few metres take a farm track to the right, following an elevated irrigation channel. Follow this channel along a path until you reach the A-1223.

0.7km/15km A-1223. Cross the road to follow a farm track. Turn right to follow the drainage channel along a well made earthen track until you reach a bridge by a junction.

1.4km/16.4km Junction. Just before the bridge, turn right onto a dirt track and go straight on at the next junction, now gently climbing. Pass by the chapel of Saint Águeda, situated to the left on a low rise. After 300m the pilgrim meets a crossroad of tracks, where a Roman road once existed.

0.9km/17.3km Roman Road. Turn left, then immediately right, along an earthen track. Turn right onto a minor road for a few metres, then cross over it, to follow a track that leads to an irrigation canal. After crossing it,

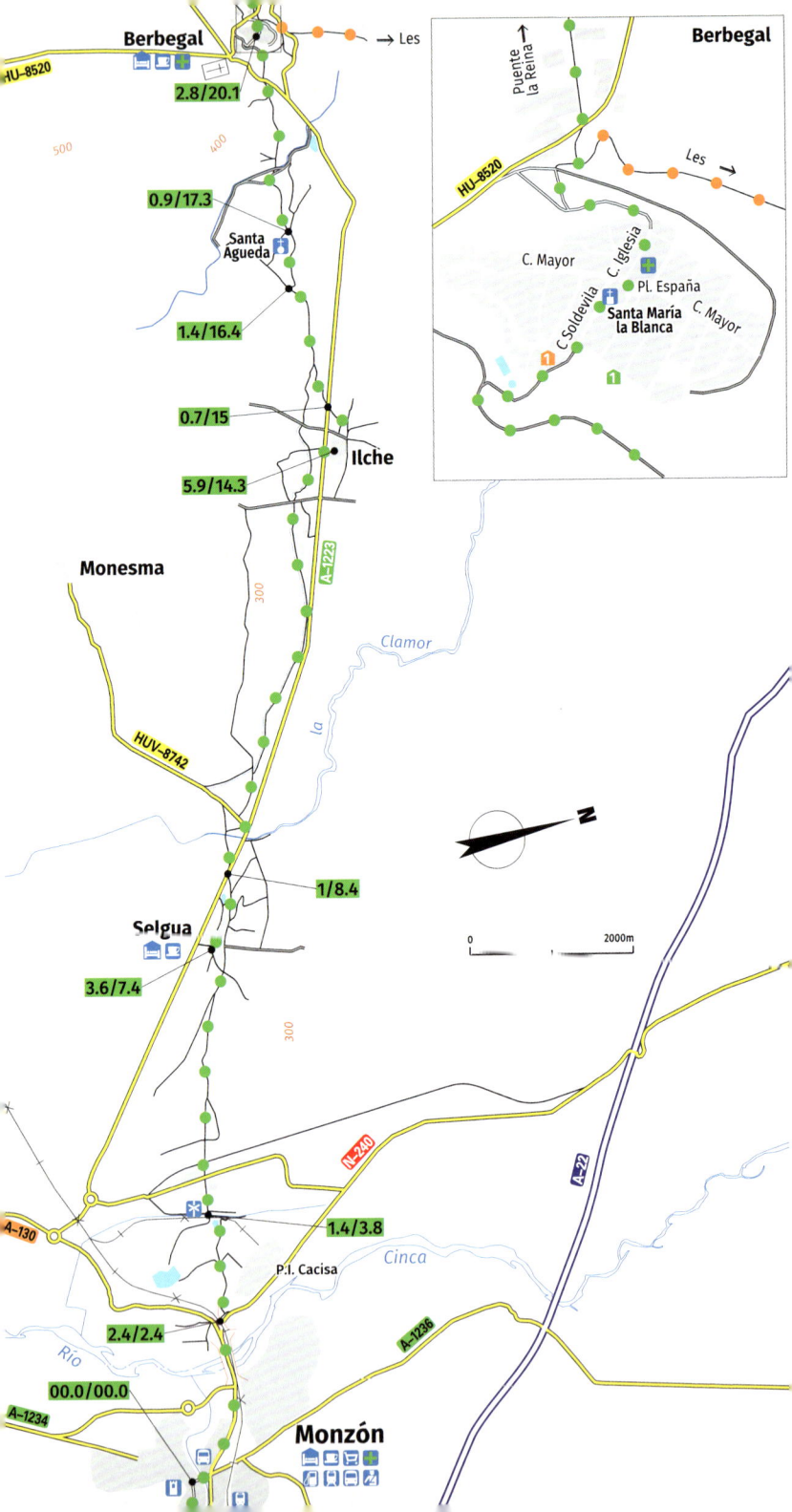

keep straight on along the Roman road until you meet the A-1223. Cross over and follow an asphalt track that climbs upwards to the village. At a fork, turn right and climb to enter the village by C. del Parque. Take C. Soldevilla to arrive at the Pl. España.

©Callum Christie

2.8km/20.1km Berbegal.
Berbegal - pop. 357. An historical village of the Somontano area. Its fortress was guarded in turn by the Knights Templar and the Knights Hospitaller.

Monzón

Selgua
■ **Hostal Casa Forniés**
Tel. 974 417 168

Berbegal
◘ **Casa Rural Bergallo**
Tel. 676 691 958

◘ **Albergue de Peregrinos**
Tel. 974 301 001
        687 297 161

Church of Santa Maria del Romeral, Selgua. Gothic with C18th baroque style remodeling. The tower and archway are worthy of note.
Church of San Juan Bautista, Ilche. Built in the C18th.
Chapel of Santa Águeda, Berbegal. C12th Romanesque. Nearby is the 'Peñon de Las Brujas', an enormous perched boulder.

Church of Santa Maria la Blanca, Berbegal. C12th late Romanesque style. Rebuilt in the Gothic style.
Hospice Arch, Berbegal. The "Medieval Arch" is the only vestige of a hospital set up in 1715 to help the poor as well as weary pilgrims.

6. Berbegal - Pueyo de Fañanás: 28.7km

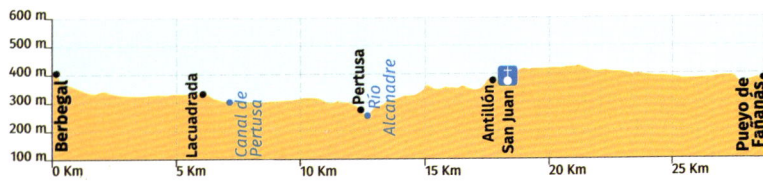

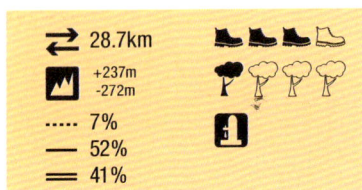

Solitude is the traveler's companion as the Camino enters a region known as the Vale of Huesca (la Hoya de Huesca). It is bordered by the wooded foothills of the Pyrenees to the north and the river Ebro to the south. The plain at its heart is a rich farmland with swathes of cereal and arable crops. This is a long, mostly flat stage to the south of the Sierra de Guara.

Observations: Apart from a few bars in villages, there are very few services available.

0km Berbegal. From the church, take C. de la Iglesia. At its end, turn left and descend a concrete ramp to join an asphalt track. In 50m take a right fork down to an avenue lined with street lamps. Look for an indicated short cut straight ahead by way of a path off the avenue. In a few metres turn left and cross the minor road HU-8250 to continue along an earthen track known as 'El Camino de Laperdiguera'. Continue in a straight line through an expanse of flat fields, at times following little used farm tracks and at others on better defined ways, until the outskirts of Lacuadrada.

6.1km/6.1km Lacuadrada. Enter this very small hamlet, turn right and just past a simple stone cross, turn left downhill on a well used track.

1.1km/7.2km Pertusa Canal. Cross a bridge and turn right along an asphalt track that follows the canal. After the canal disappears underground, keep straight on until a bend where an dirt track appears on the left. A nearby group of trees provide welcome shade for the pilgrim.

3.5km/10.7km Track to Left. Follow the dirt track downhill some 100m to meet the A-1217 road. Turn right to follow the asphalt downhill. After passing a farm to the left, take the next earthen track to your left.

1.2km/11.9km Earthen Track. With the Pertusa church tower in sight, follow this track to its end. Look to take a path down to the right towards the village.

0.6km/12.5km Pertusa. Turn left to enter along the main road to the Pl. Portal. Continue past a children's playpark. Look for a flight of steps down to a bridge across the river Alcanadre. On the far bank take a rough track to the right uphill, in the form of a short cut, to regain the road.

0.4km/12.9km Road to Antillón. Turn right to follow this country road for a long stretch; despite only carrying light traffic, due care should be taken.

3.7km/16.6km Antillón Cemetery. Your first glimpse of Antillón is at a bend in the road. Opposite the turn off to a cemetery, take a track to the right. Descend through a copse of holm oaks and through an area of arable fields before climbing to the village. Enter past some warehouses and turn left past the first few houses. Climb to the road and turn right.

1.1km/17.7km Antillón. From the town hall square continue on the main road, but immediately turn left on C. San Juan to leave the village. Now climb a cemented ramp, passing by the entrance to a chapel on the left. Continue along an earthen track for 300m, and after a farm, take the right fork to keep straight on. Follow the main track along a plateau of arable fields, a sea of cereal crops with almond groves and coppices of holm oaks with extensive views of the Pyrenees.

3.3km/21km Fork. Turn right along a farm track.

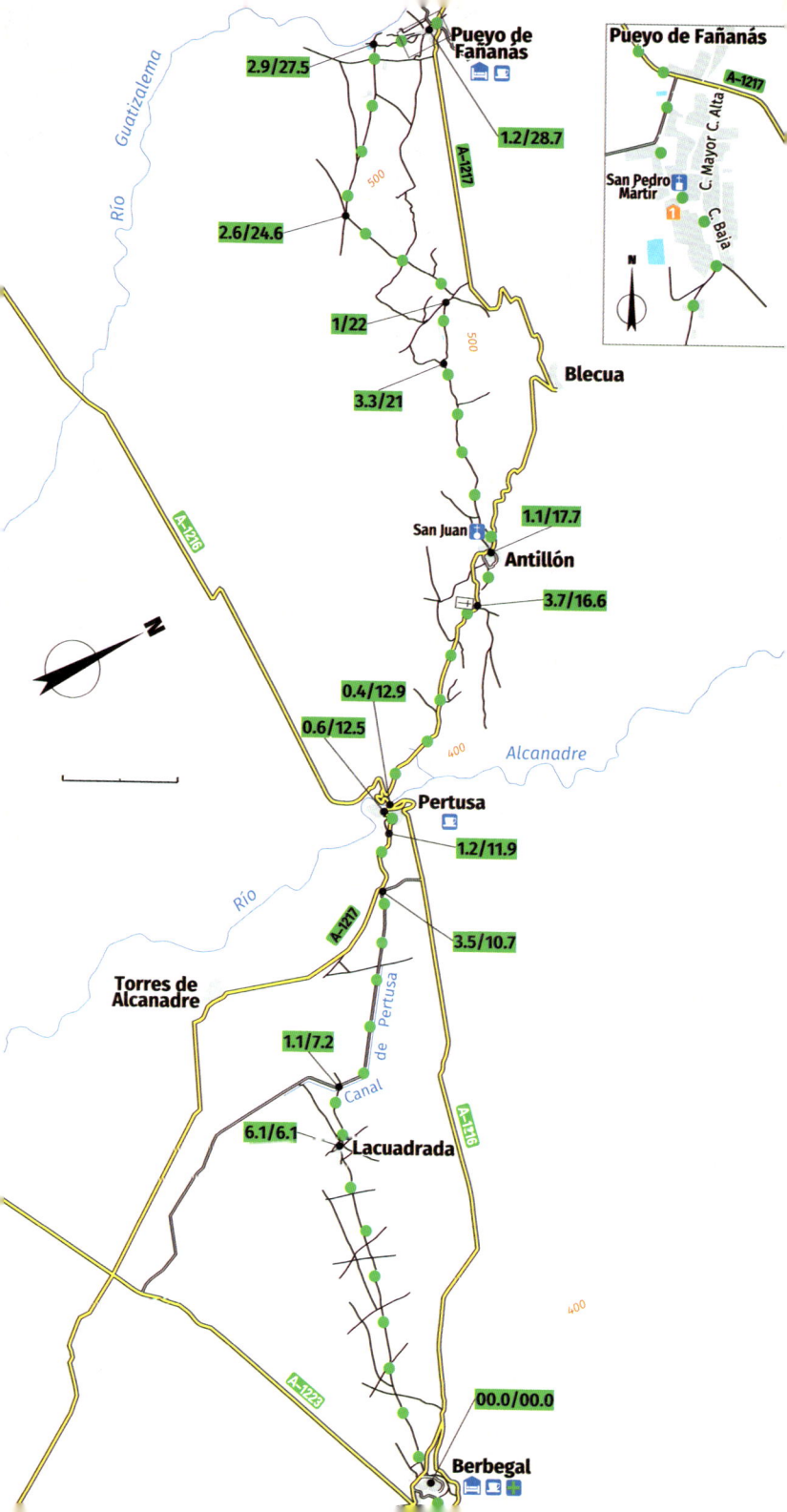

Pertusa (©afCHH. Jon Iceta)

1km/22km Junction of Tracks. Upon meeting a wide track, turn right. In 200m take the first earth track to the left. Carry straight on gently downhill, ignoring a couple of junctions. The Camino occasionally follows more rutted stretches.

2.6km/24.6km Holm Oaks Junction. At a junction by a small coppice of holm oaks, turn right. Keep straight on by the clearest track until a modern farm. The Way now becomes a good track. Carry straight on ignoring all turnings to eventually descend a short steep slope that ends by a small irrigation reservoir.

2.9km/27.5km Reservoir Junction. Turn right and climb to the small village by a rough track.

1.2km/28.7km Pueyo de Fañanás. Arrive at the Pl. Major and the church.

Pueyo de Fañanás - pop. 73. A village administered by the municipality of Alcalá del Obispo.

 Pueyo de Fañanás

Albergue de Peregrinos
Tel. 648 087 099

Church of Santa Maria, Pertusa. C12th Romanesque with a C13th crypt and an attractive bell tower attributed to Juan Herrera built in 1575.

Old Walls, Antillón. Stretches of medieval walls with arches and defense towers.

Church of the Natividad, Antillón. Romanesque in origin with more recent additions.

Church of San Pedro de Verona, Pueyo de Fañanás. Baroque with a C17th bell-tower. The north facing wall is of Moorish origin.

7. PUEYO DE FAÑANÁS - HUESCA: 18KM

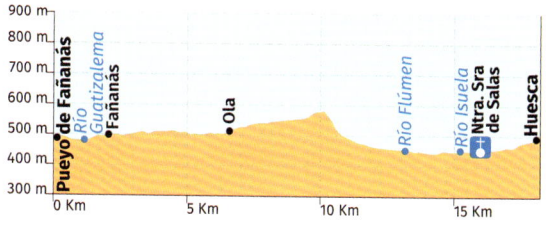

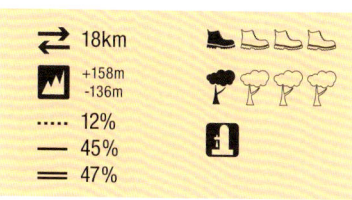

- 18km
- +158m / -136m
- 12%
- 45%
- 47%

The pilgrim's trail to the provincial capital continues through the extensive wheat fields of the 'Hoya de Huesca', with all round views from the high ground of 'Tozal de la Miseria'. The quiet shady path alongside the river Flumen leads to the impressive chapel of Nuestra Señora de Salas on the outskirts of Huesca city.

Observations: Another stage with very few services along the Way.

0km Pueyo de Fañanás. From the bus stop on the outskirts, take the main road to the left and soon cross the river Guatizalema.

1.6km/1.6km Fañanás. Enter the village on C. Bureta to the right. Then turn left onto C. de la Paz which becomes C. del Molino, to leave the village on an earthen track between fields and irrigation channels. After a further 400m at a fork, take the left option to another junction, then turn right for 50m before choosing a farm track to the left. After 1km take an earthen track to the left. Continue straight on for 50m to reach the A-1219 road.

3.4km/5km A-1219. Turn right along this quiet country road until a junction and then turn left toward Ola.

1.5km/6.5km Ola. At the entrance to the village turn right. The Camino climbs a narrow street (past the moorish well and water cisterns) and up to a boundary cross. Proceed uphill on an earthen track to continue straight on between arable fields and clumps of evergreen holm oaks on a steady but gentle incline. Continue in a straight line ignoring turns to a couple of farms. The route becomes a rougher farm track in places and crosses a flatter area until you pass a corral and a small dwelling on your right. In 150m veer to the right and climb a short steep slope. In 500m the fields peter out on the edge of an escarpment by a fire watch tower.

3.6km/10.1km Watch Tower. Take a path ahead, ignoring the other tracks. Descend, in a zig-zag fashion, a hillside of scrub and holm oak. Meet a track and turn left. In just 25m continue on to the left. Keep straight on following the clearest track and soon arrive at a road.

1.8km/11.9km Road to Tierz. Cross over and go straight on at all junctions until you reach a small river.

1.2km/13.1km River Flumen. Cross the river and turn left to follow the shaded banks of this stream along a narrow track. Just before the track recrosses the water, turn right to follow an earthen track away from the river. Keep straight on ignoring all turnings. The track turns to asphalt and goes straight on, soon crossing the Isuela river.

2.5km/15.6km Santuario de Nuestra Senora de Salas. Continue straight on past this chapel until reaching a roundabout.

2.4km/18km Huesca. Enter along Camino de la Cruces, along a bicycle lane until C. Alfonso I. Continue up C. San Lorenzo. From the Coso Bajo take C. Duquesa de Villahermosa to Pl. López Allué. Follow Travesía Cortes, Pl. de San Pedro, Travesía de los Mozárabes, Pl. de los Fueros de Aragón, C. Alfonso de Aragón and C. Palacio to Pl. de la Catedral.

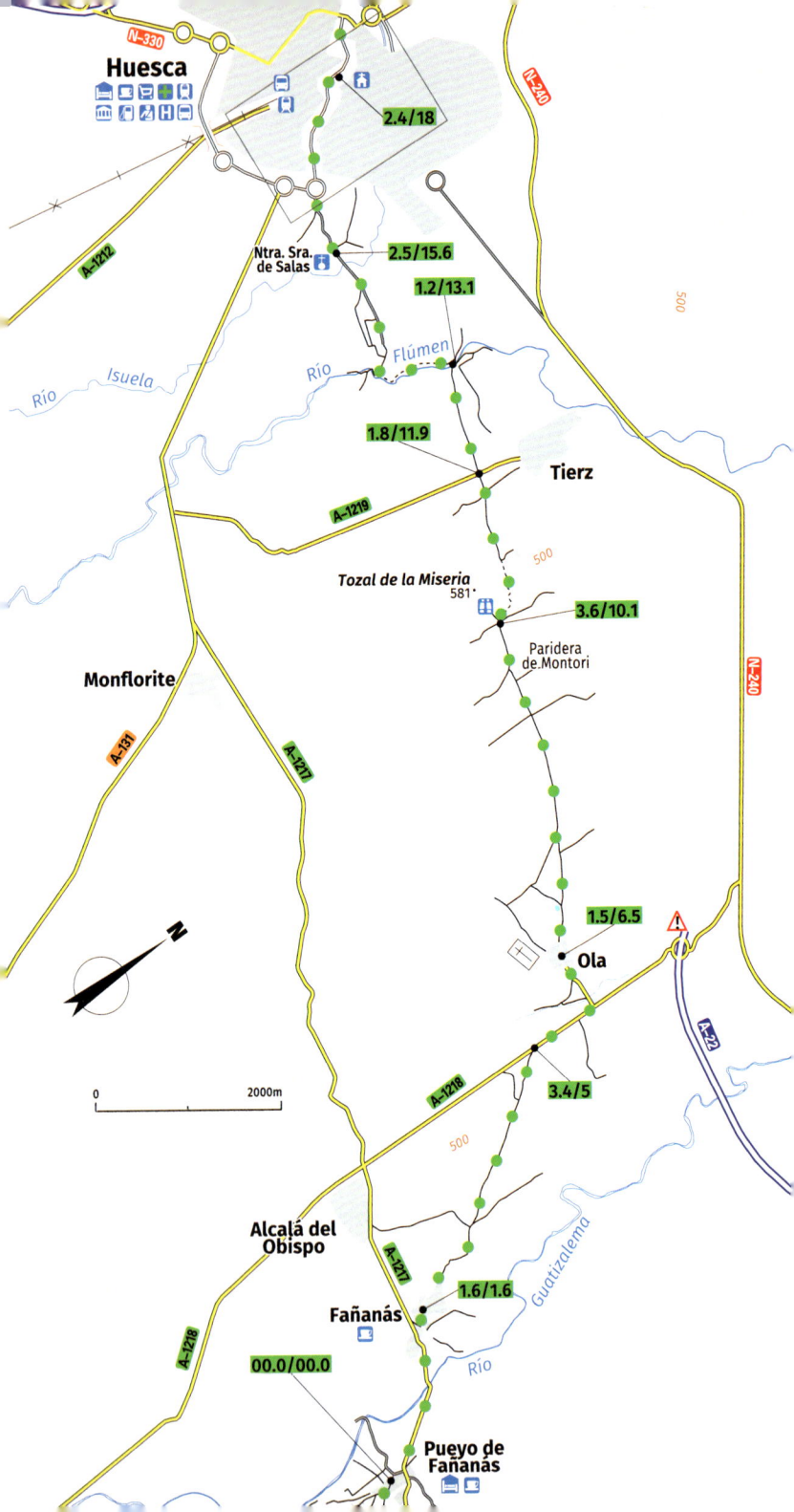

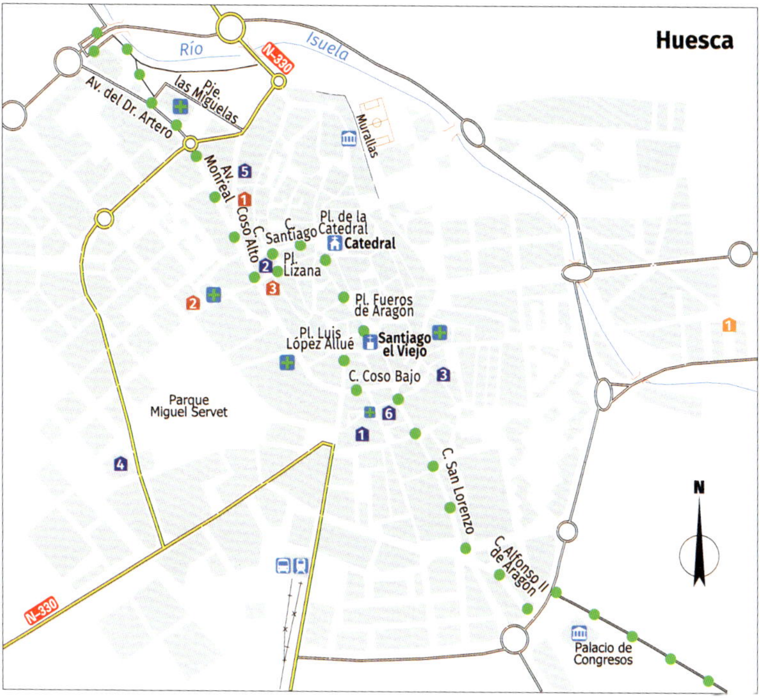

Huesca

Huesca - pop. 52.500. Capital city of the province and of the 'Hoya de Huesca'. Originally an Iberian settlement, it has been inhabited in turn by Romans, Visigoths and Moors, before joining the Kingdom of Aragón.

Huesca
1 Albergue de Peregrinos San Galindo 🛏
Tel. 629 947 956
  659 610 623
1 Pensión Bandrés 🛏
Tel. 630 819 885
2 Hostal Lizana 2 🛏
Tel. 974 220 776
2 Hostal el Centro 🛏
Tel. 974 226 023
4 Hostal Alviz 🛏
Tel. 647 603 834
5 Hostal Joaquín Costa 🛏🛏
Tel. 974 240 857
6 Hostal San Marcos 🛏🛏
Tel. 974 222 931
1 Posada de la Luna 🛏🛏
Tel. 974 240 857
2 Hotel Pedro I de Aragón 🛏🛏🛏
Tel. 974 220 300
3 Hotel Sancho Abarca 🛏🛏🛏
Tel. 974 220 650

Nuestra Señora de Salas (©Callum Christie)

Church of San Juan Bautista, Fañanás. C17th-18th built in a large cross shape with side chapels.
Moorish Well and Cisterns, Ola. C11th al-andaluz in style with a horseshoe arch over the final one of three half-barrel vaults.
Santuario de Nuestra Señora de Salas, Huesca. A very large chapel built in 1200 at the behest of Sancha de Castilla. Once an important pilgrimage destination. It contains an attractive rose window.
Huesca Cathedral. C13th-14th Gothic. Built over the former mosque, of which only one archway in the cloister remains.
City Walls, Huesca. The old town still retains the C9th Moorish walls.
Church of San Pedro el Viejo, Huesca. C12th Romanesque, attached to the monastery of the same name, containing a pantheon of Aragonese monarchs. It has a hexagonal tower.
Town Hall, Huesca. A typical C16th Renaissance style Aragonese nobleman's residence. It houses the famous painting "Campana de Huesca" by José Casado.

8. HUESCA - BOLEA: 21.6KM

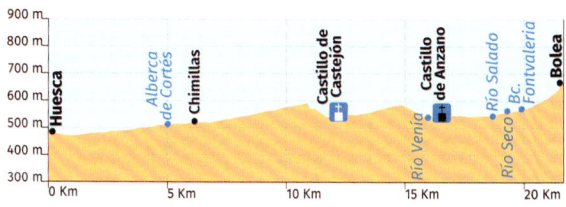

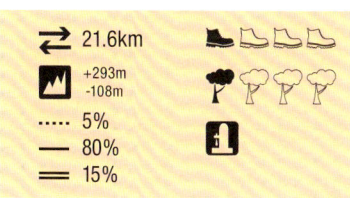

- 21.6km
- +293m / -108m
- 5%
- 80%
- 15%

The Camino continues across the 'breadbasket' of the Vale of Huesca, gradually closing with the foothills of the Pyrenees. The Way remains fairly flat. Arable fields alternate with stands of holm oaks. The landscape is crossed by small streams and dotted with a few large farms known as 'castillos'.

0km Huesca. From Pl. de la Catedral, descend along C. Santiago and onto C. Pedro IV. Continue through Pl Lizana, along Coso Alto, Av. Monreal and onto Av. del Dr. Artero. After 100m take the narrow Pasaje de Las Miguelas to the right. Continue along a rough track until a ring road, by a bridge over the river Isuela. Use a zebra crossing to your left to cross the carriageways and follow a bicycle path back to the bridge. Here, you take a narrow asphalt track to the left and keep straight on ignoring all turnings, then pass under the highway A-23.

2.1km/2.1km A-23. Turn right and continue for a further 400m. At the first fork go straight on to the left along a wide track ignoring all turnings. At the 'Alberca de Cortés', a large reservoir, turn right to follow its banks until a junction, where you veer left by an earthen track, still following the edge of the reservoir. At the next junction, keep straight on, and soon enter Chimillas by an asphalt lane.

3.9km/6km Chimillas. From the town hall and church, go straight on along C. Iglesia to a roundabout. Keep straight ahead on C. Bolea, to leave the village on a dirt track. In a few metres fork to the right. Follow a straight line through arable fields until a triangular junction of tracks. Turn right and in 200m fork to the left. In a further 200m fork right to keep straight on between cultivated fields and holm oaks.

3.6km/9.6km Path. The track becomes fainter upon entering some woodland and becomes a path. At times the path skirts the edge of a field of arable crops. Close attention should be paid to follow yellow arrows.

0.8km/10.4km Small Reservoir. Pass to the right of the reservoir to soon reach a crossing of tracks. Keep straight on, descending, to leave the woods on a well defined track.

1.6km/12km Castillo de Castejón. Drop down past a small lake next to this 'castillo' farm and its chapel. Veer right, and then left and right in quick succession before continuing gently uphill past a row of agricultural barns and warehouses on a wide earthen track. Keep straight on until a fork, where you turn left and descend to cross a stream.

4.2km/16.2km Castillo de Anzano. The Camino veers to the right between this large historic farm (with a ruined chapel) and its outbuildings. After 600m fork left on the main track. Keep straight on ignoring all turnings, through a sea of arable fields, crossing a couple of streams; the river Salado and the river Seco. After 700m cross the Fontvalerla stream.

3.7km/19.9km Fontvaleria Stream. Just before a small building and a reservoir immediately turn right along a farm track. Continue between arable fields. At the outskirts of the village, turn left. Take the first street right and immediately veer left to pick up a lane that ascends to the main village.

1.7km/21.6km Bolea. Enter along C. la Fuente, climbing up to to Pl. Mayor.

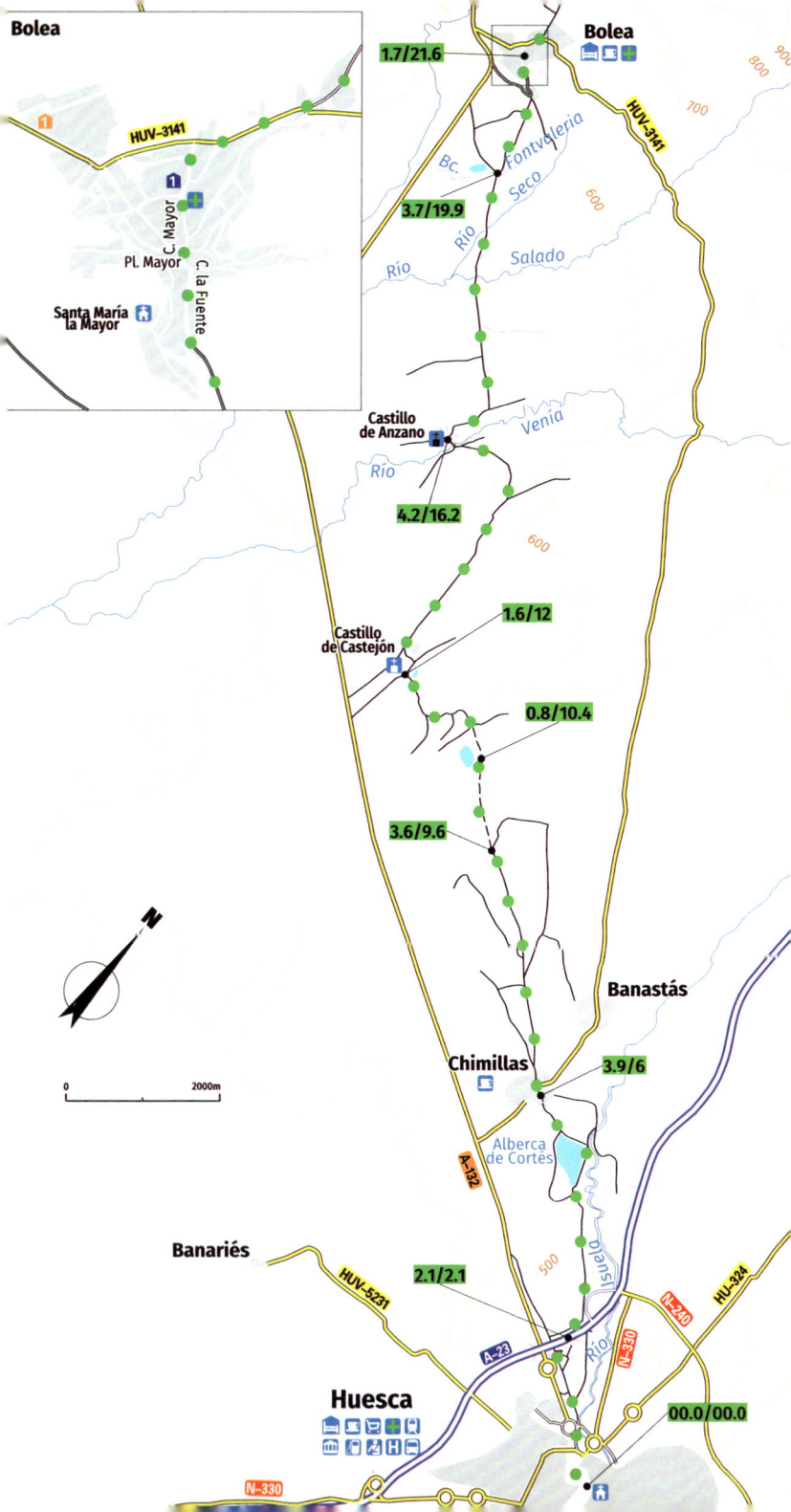

Bolea (©afCHH. Álvaro Calvo)

Bolea - pop. 566. A village of the Hoya de Huesca and capital of a grouping of villages known as La Sotonera.

Bolea
🏠 **Albergue de Peregrinos** ⊝
Tel. 974 272 200

🏠 **Apartamentos Casa Rufino** ⊝⊝
Tel. 687 530 316

Castillo de Castejón. A medieval large farm with a stone built C13th chapel, that would have once served the local populace.
Castillo de Anzano. Sadly the romanesque chapel is in ruins, but there is evidence that a fortified collection of buildings would once have existed whilst the border was in dispute by Christians and Moors.
Collegiate Church of Bolea. Dedicated to Santa Maria la Mayor. A fine C16th example of Aragonese Gothic style as it transitioned to Renaissance. The star shaped vaulted ceilings are outstanding. Contains a chapel dedicated to Saint James.

9. Bolea - La Peña Estación: 29.1km

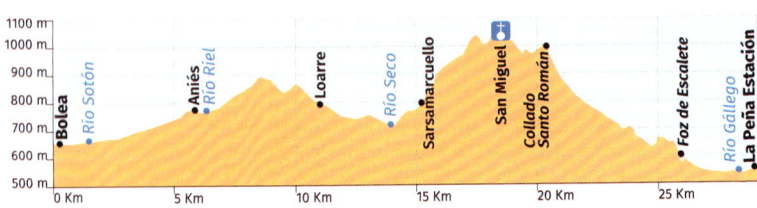

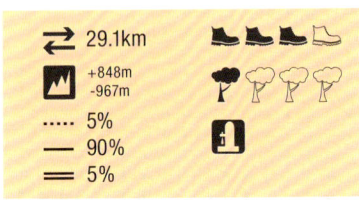

- 29.1km
- +848m / -967m
- 5% / 90% / 5%

Crossing the Sierra de Loarre from the village of Sarsamarcuello up to the chapel of San Miguel requires considerable effort. The walker is rewarded with some spectacular views. The diversity of the landscape, from the plains of the Vale of Huesca, and the mountains and 'Cliffs of Vultures' riven by gulleys, to the pretty narrow valley of the river Gállego by La Peña make for an outstanding experience.

0km Bolea. From the Pl. Mayor descend via C. Mayor to the edge of the village where you turn to the right. Follow this narrow street past a junction to the right to Puibolea and continue to the left, downhill to leave the village on an asphalt track also marked by GR red and white markings. The track soon turns to an earthen way and continues straight ahead until meeting the road to Aniés.

4.6km/4.6km Road to Aniés. A few metres before meeting a road, turn right onto a path that runs parallel to the asphalt. Soon join the road and turn right. In 250m by a tight bend in the road take a path up to the right to emerge on the outskirts of Aniés. Proceed to the church. Fork right along the side of the church to leave the village on a downward slope until you cross a stream, then turning left at a fork. Continue uphill on an earthen track. Ignore a couple of left turns and follow the main track as it undulates over the high ground surrounded by bushy vegetation. As the track starts to descend ignore a track to the right and keep straight on until you meet a road.

Loarre (©afCHH. Jon Iceta)

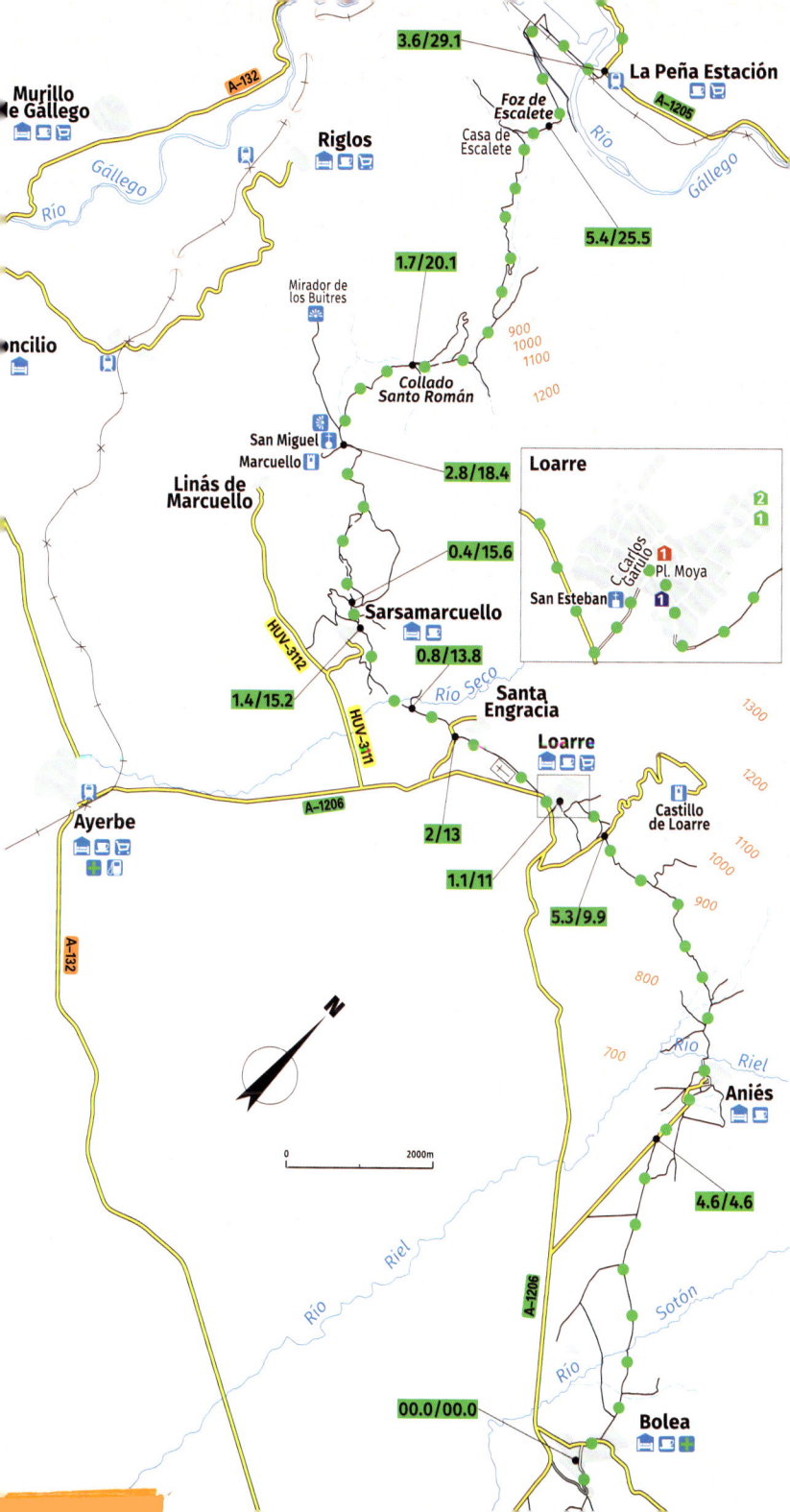

5.3km/9.9km Road to Loarre Castle. Cross over and turn right along the verge for 100m. Take a dirt track to the left that drops sharply to meet an asphalt track. Turn right to enter Loarre.

1.1km/11km Loarre. From the church, descend the main street some 100m and turn right along the road to Ayerbe (A-1206). On the outskirts of Loarre, fork right to pass the cemetery on an earthen track.

2km/13km Road to Santa Engracia. Turn right to join this road. After 150m at a bend in the road, take a dirt track downhill to the left and in 400m continue to the right at a fork.

0.8km/13.8km Path along River Seco. After 250m at a bend in the track, take a path to the left, through holm oaks to cross the bed of the normally dry river. Climb some 300m to join an earthen track and turn right. Continue straight on at the next two junctions, going uphill to enter the upper part of the village of Sarsamarcuello.

1.4km/15.2km Sarsamarcuello. Climb a walled lane to a water deposit, then take a path uphill to reach a track. Cross straight over to continue uphill on the path until you meet another track.

0.4km/15.6km Track. Turn left to keep climbing on this track towards the Marcuello castle. Ignore a track to the right and continue on the main track to a chapel.

2.8km/18.4km San Miguel Chapel. Situated by a turning on the left to the ruined castle. Continue on the main track for 200m until the turning towards the lookout point of 'los Buitres'. Continue to the right, downhill.

1.7km/20.1km Santo Román Pass. A crossing of tracks. Take the second track to the right, a rough eroded stretch that drops to rejoin the better track. Continue downhill for about 1km. At a fork, turn left to climb for a short time before heading once more downhill. At a junction with a small house (Casa de Escalete) to your left, turn right on a steeper downhill section.

5.4km/25.5km Foz de Escalete. A gap in the scenic cliffs that has a bridge with handrail to facilitate the onward progress of the pilgrim. Continue down a wooded slope on the main track, passing through arable fields on the valley floor, then cross a couple of bridges spanning first a railway line and then a wide track. Turn right to join the wide track. Veer left and walk parallel to the rail tracks. Cross the river Gállego, before reaching the main road (A-1205) on the outskirts of Estación de la Peña.

3.6km/29.1km La Peña Estación. Currently there is no accommodation in this hamlet (*see accommodation listing for nearest alternatives*).

La Peña Estación - pop. 38. Small village of the Hoya de Huesca region.

It dates from the early C20th when the railway station was built to facilitate the construction of the nearby Santa Maria reservoir and dam.

Foz de Escaleta (©afCHH. Esteban Anía)

San Miguel (©afCHH. Esteban Anía)

Aniés
- **Casa Bernués**
Tel. 630 616 734

Loarre
- **Casa Pepico**
Tel. 974 382 616
- **El Callejón de Andrés**
Tel. 974 382 735
- **Casa Santos**
Tel. 974 382 605
- **Hospedería de Loarre**
Tel. 974 382 706

Sarsamarcuello
- **Albergue de Peregrinos**
Tel. 974 382 609
   608 536 220

Ayerbe
- **Hotel Villa de Ayerbe**
Tel. 974 380 080

Murillo de Gállego
- **Hostal Los Mallos**
Tel. 974 383 026
- **Casa Jordán**
Tel. 661 338 293
- **Real Posada de Liena**
Tel. 654 767 989
- **La Casona de la Reina**
Tel. 628 096 262
- **Hotel Spa Aguas de los Mallos**
Tel. 974 383 132

Concilio
- **El Corral de Concilio**
Tel. 974 380 898
   659 279 128

Riglos
- **El Refugio**
Tel. 974 383 051
- **Casa Barranquero**
Tel. 678 211 687
- **Casa Escaleretas**
Tel. 687 426 566

Ayerbe
Taxi Ayerbe
Tel. 686 966 024

San Esteban Church, Aniés. Originally Romanesque, rebuilt in the C18th.
Loarre Castle. A magnificent C11th bastion that helped wrest the Vale of Huesca from Moorish forces.
Hospedería, Loarre. A former nobleman's residence of the C16th, built in the Aragonese Renaissance style.
Church of San Esteban, Loarre. C18th, with an attractive belltower.
Marcuello Castle, Sarsamarcuello. C11th fortification now sadly in ruins.
San Miguel chapel, Sarsamarcuello. C12th with a barrel vaulted ceiling.

10. LA PEÑA ESTACIÓN - SANTA CILIA: 31.9KM

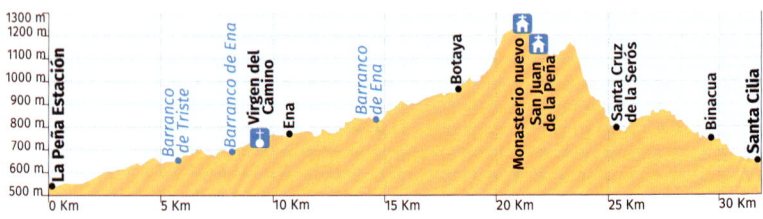

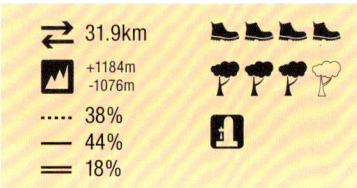

- 31.9km
- +1184m / -1076m
- 38%
- 44%
- 18%

One of the most attractive and solitary stretches of the Camino in Huesca province. Narrow wooded valleys with refreshing mountain streams and picturesque villages lead the walker towards the wide valley of the river Aragón. First, a stop high in the hills at one of the most emblematic spots in the area, the monastery San Juan de la Peña.

Observations: Care should be taken crossing the Barranco de Triste after heavy rains.

0km La Peña Estación. Follow the A-1205 towards Triste.

1.8km/1.8km Path to Ena. Some 100m before a bridge over the Barranco de Triste, take a steep path up to the right to gain the tree line. Continue through pines, gently uphill following the line of valley. The path eventually turns into a track and crosses the stream to continue to a fork. Keep to the right parallel to the stream.

6.6km/8.4km Path. Leave the track, taking a path to the left through the pines, until you join another track and veer left.

0.9km/9.3km Chapel of la Virgen del Camino. After 300m of path, veer left uphill onto a track. Continue straight on uphill and then descend to a junction on the outskirts of Ena. Turn right and up into the village.

1.3km/10.6km Ena. From the pretty church square follow C. Barrio Alto to leave the village. After 200m, at a bend in the road, take a track left towards the cemetery. After 500m take the right fork. Now follow the main dirt track, uphill through woods mainly of pine.

4km/14.6km Track to Botaya. Leaving the dense woods, the track crosses a stream next to a cultivated field. Take a fork to the right following a farm track and in 1km ignore a track to the right. After 400m join another track and keep straight on towards Botaya, through an area of arable fields.

3.6km/18.2km Botaya. Cross the village on the main street to leave by the only access road.

0.9km/19.1km Hairpin Bend. Leave the road, taking a path on the left to climb the steepest section of this stage. As the terrain levels out take a path to the left, through some woods.

1.8km/20.9km New Monastery. Follow a road alongside the monastery. In 150m take a track to the left.

0.3km/21.2km Path to Old Monastery. At the start of this track, to the right, take a path through the woods. After a while you descend on a stony loose surface, ending at some steps that lead to a road. ATTENTION. Beware of traffic on this narrow mountain road. Turn left to arrive at the old monastery of San Juan de la Peña.

0.5km/21.7km Old Monastery. Take a cobbled track opposite the entrance to the monastery that descends steeply on a loose surface. At a junction of path, take the clearer path to the left. After 200m (at another junction), turn left onto a wider path that drops through a gap in a cliff. At a fork by a fire break turn left along a narrow path that leads to a track. Turn right and descend to Santa Cruz de la Serós.

3.2km/24.9km Santa Cruz de la Serós. Enter the Pl. Major with its imposing Santa Maria church. Carry on downhill in a straight line past the humble church of San Capra-

sio, towards Pamplona, along the roadside. On the outskirts of the village take a concrete ramp uphill to the left. After 400m, the track turns into a path through bushes of box and young oaks. Soon start to descend, and at a fork, turn right along an earthen track. On reaching an asphalt track by a water deposit, continue on to the village.

4.2km/29.1km Binacua. Skirt round the village to its church. Leave the village by its only access road and take a path to the left as a shortcut. At the bottom of the hill, veer to the left to cross a stream and immediately turn right, passing some buildings to meet the N-240 main road. ATTENTION due to traffic. Cross the road and take a side avenue towards a roundabout.

2.8km/31.9km Santa Cilia. Keep straight on and turn first right towards the village and its Pl. Mayor.

Santa Cilia - pop. 231. A village of the Jacetania area. Here, our Camino joins the Camino Aragonés that continues on from French border at Somport.

Ena
🏠 **Albergue Municipal de Peregrinos** 🪙
Tel. 636 496 343

Centenero
🟢 **Casa Alamán** 🪙🪙🪙
Tel. 677 620 636

Botaya
🔵 **Albergue Casa del Herrero** 🪙🪙
Tel. 676 488 691

Santa Cruz de la Serós
🔴 **Hostería Santa Cruz** 🪙🪙
Tel. 974 361 975

🔵 **Hotel el Mirador de los Pirineos** 🪙🪙🪙
Tel. 974 355 593

Santa Cilia
🟠 **Albergue de Peregrinos** 🪙
Tel. 974 377 168

 Witch-scarers of Ena. The traditional architecture includes stone built houses with coats of arms, a former municipal jail, the church of San Pedro and a fountain with a trough. The witch tops are designed to prevent any evil spirits alighting or entering households.

Church of San Esteban, Botaya. C17th. Built over a Romanesque church, of which the tympanum still survives.

New Monastery of San Juan de la Peña. C17th. Built after a fire consumed the old monastery.

San Juan de la Peña. The old C10th monastery is built into an overhang of a cliff. The interior contains a pre-romanesque church, a Romanesque cloister, a Gothic chapel and paintings of San Cosme and San Damián. It was a pantheon for the early nobles and monarchs of Aragón.

Church of Santa Maria, Santa Cruz de la Serós. Formed part of a Benedictine abbey that dated from the C11th.

Church of San Caprasio, Santa Cruz de la Serós. Simple but attractive single nave church in the Romanesque Lombardy style. During the C11th and C12th stone masons from Lombardy worked in the Pyrenees and the northern parts of the Iberian peninsular.

Church of Santa Custodias, Binacua. Small and attractive C12th church in Romanesque style.

11. Santa Cilia - Artieda: 27.2km

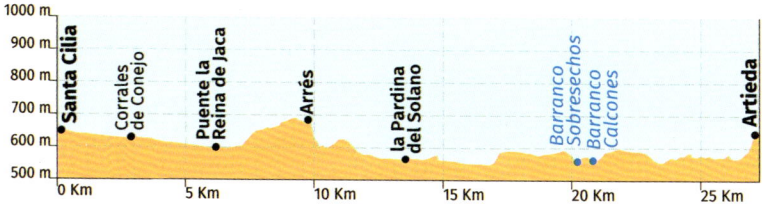

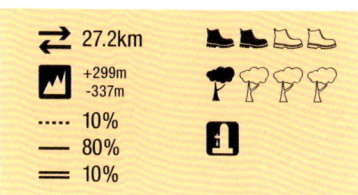

- 27.2km
- +299m / -337m
- 10%
- 80%
- 10%

Once the modern transport routes are left behind, the walker is rewarded with solitude. The tranquility of the farm fields, the gurgling waters of ravines and the welcome stone built villages that stand at the edges of the plains.

Observations: Take care when crossing the N-240. The Sobresechos and Calcones ravines both have footbridges, but care should be taken after heavy rains. There are well marked alternatives should the walker wish to avoid Arrés and Artieda.

0km Santa Cilia. From the Pl. Mayor (and a small playpark), take C. de San Chaime to leave the village. A few metres before the N-240, veer right along a track and keep straight on parallel to the main road.

2.8km/2.8km N-240 Crossing. ATTENTION. Cross the road to continue along a track on the other side. After the first building of Corrales de Conejo take a path to the right that returns to the main road. Veer left to follow the edge of the road.

2.3km/5.1km Recross N-240. ATTENTION. Cross the main road again at a bend in the road to take a pretty path alongside the river Aragón, before regaining the road by a bridge and crossroads.

1km/6.1km Puente la Reina de Jaca. Without crossing the bridge (unless you want to enter this village) continue along the edge of the A-132 road. In a few metres turn right downhill along a country lane to Arrés and a picnic area.

0.9km/7km Path to Arrés. Take a path that climbs the hillside opposite (*the Camino alternative to avoid Arrés continues along the asphalt*). Continue up, through the wooded slopes of Monte Samitier to the village.

2.7km/9.7km Arrés. Leave downhill by the only access road. In 50m take a path to the left that leads to a junction of dirt tracks. Continue straight on via a track that descends to a ravine. At a junction turn right.

2.2km/11.9km Junction. In 600m, back on the flat, turn left to join once again the Camino alternative. Cross the Pardina de Solana stream by a picnic place. Keep straight on by the main track until a bend where you fork to the right. Stay on the main track until you reach a country lane.

4.9km/16.8km Road to Martes. Turn left and immediately take a path up to the right to a fork in the track. Turn right, then continue in a straight line for 800m.

1.2km/18km Junction. Take the first farm track to the right. At an asphalt lane continue straight on to the right. Very soon leave the asphalt and keep straight on along a track until you descend into a ravine.

2.1km/20.1km Barranco Sobresechos. Cross the footbridge and then another, across the nearby ravine of Calcones. After a bend in the track, continue straight on by the main track through all successive junctions.

2.3km/22.4km Asphalt Junction. As you meet the bend of an asphalt lane turn right across an esplanade of bare earth. A farm track quickly turns to a path that descends to follow a stream bed. After 500m join a farm track to continue straight on. Cross an area of arid hillocks, to emerge onto a wider track. Keep straight on, then turn right onto the road up hill to Artieda.

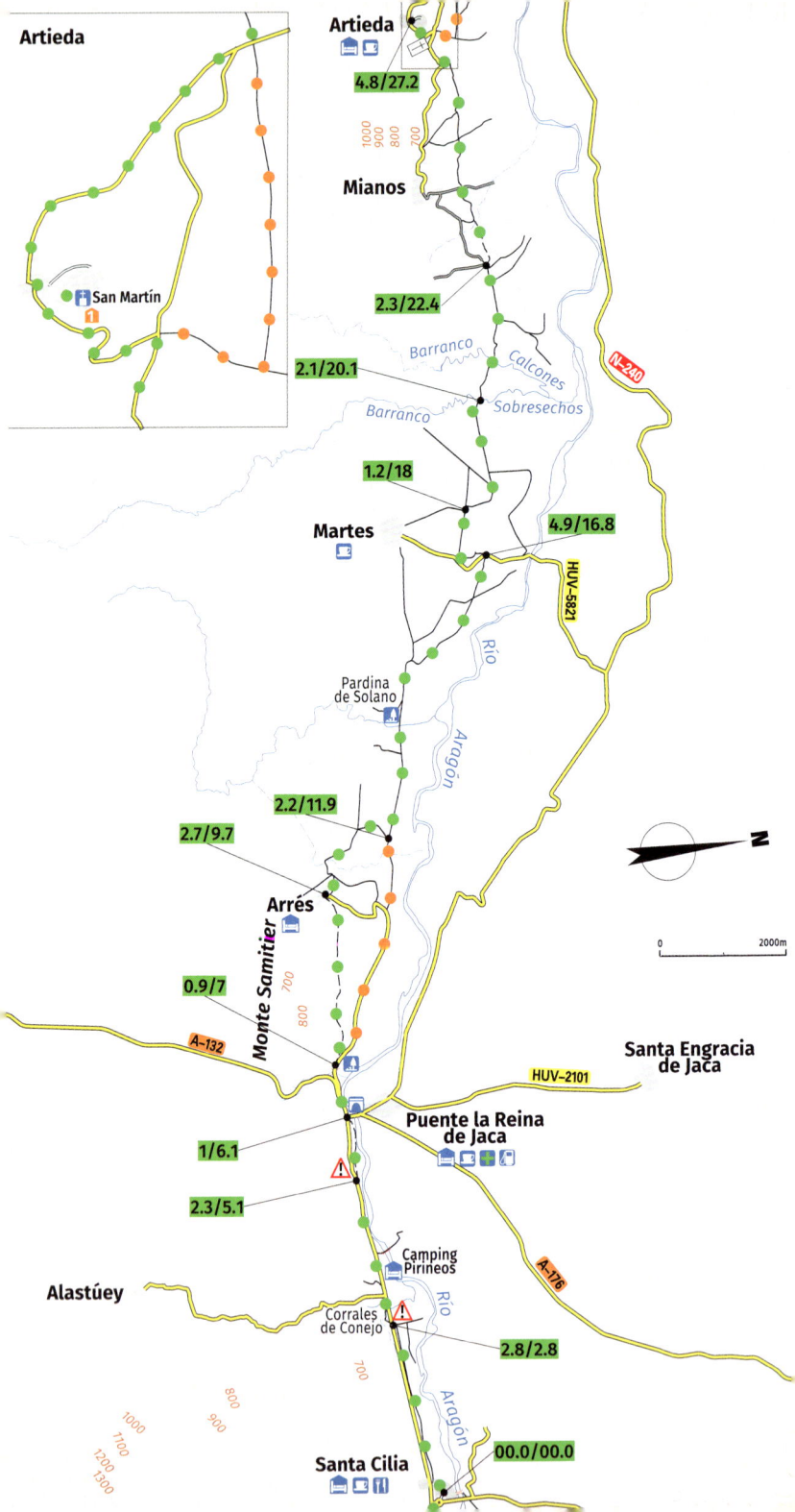

©Callum Christie

4.8km/27.2km Artieda. At the lower entrance to the village, turn left to climb to the centre.

Artieda - pop. 73. A village of the Jacetania area.

Puente la Reina de Jaca
🏠 **Hotel Anaya** ⊖⊖
Tel. 974 377 411
🏠 **Camping Pirineos** ⊖⊖
Tel. 974 377 351

Arrés
🏠 **Albergue de Peregrinos** ⊖
Tel. 974 348 643

Artieda
🏠 **Albergue de Peregrinos** ⊖
Tel. 948 439 316

Puente Nuevo, Puente la Reina de Jaca. Impressive C19th bridge.
Castle, Arrés. C15th Gothic military style.

Church of San Martín de Tours, Artieda. Romanesque single nave church with C16th reformation.

12. ARTIEDA - SANGÜESA: 32.1KM

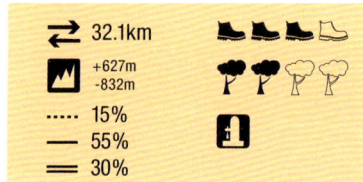

From Artieda atop its hill, the distant majestic western Pyrenees align themselves to the wide valley of the river Aragón. The Camino continues on the southern side of the valley, between the Yeste reservoir and the quiet wooded slopes of the Peña Nalba hills, an area traversed by pilgrims of old.

Observations: At the time of preparing this guide, plans are afoot to further increase the area of lands that will be flooded by the Yeste reservoir. This will most likely affect part of the current route of the Camino between Artieda and Ruesta. The albergue at Artieda will have up to date information.

0km Artieda. From the church, descend on C. Ramón y Cajal and turn right to exit the village. Follow the asphalt lane back down to the valley floor. Merge with another lane and continue 100m to a junction by a small farm.

1.2km/1.2km Junction. Turn left onto a wide earthen track to join the Camino bypass of Artieda.

0.8km/2km A-1601 Road. Turn left to follow the asphalt.

0.7km/2.7km Old Road. Take an older asphalt lane to the right.

3.3km/6km Path. Take a path to the left as a shortcut and then recross the same lane. Follow the path in a straight line ignoring all turnings. Passing close to the ruins of the chapel of San Juan, soon rejoin the road and turn right uphill.

4.1km/10.1km Ruesta. An abandoned village in ruins, apart from the restored pilgrims' hostel. Traverse the centre and leave downhill on an old cobbled path. Follow the path down to a wooden footbridge over the river Regal. Keep straight on by a wider way through an abandoned campsite. Continue ahead on a path to arrive at the chapel of Santiago which is in a sorry state of repair. Soon join a forestry track and follow it uphill to the left.

1.8km/11.9km Chain. At a junction of tracks turn right.

1km/12.9km Junction. After 1km, turn left to start a long climb on a forestry track. Keep to the main track at all junctions during the prolonged climb through the woods.

3.7km/16.6km Country Road. Exit the woods and turn left along a road. In just 50m take the first earthen track to the right, downhill. Keep to the main track.

3.5km/20.1km Fork. With the village of Undués in sight and after a pronounced bend in the track, take a path to the left. This path recrosses the same track and continues to descend to cross a stream bed, before climbing to the village on a cobbled track.

1.4km/21.5km Undués de Lerda. Pass by the church to descend on C. Major. At a small square turn left through a passageway, to leave the village on a dirt track. At times narrowing to a path, the track drops gradually towards a country road.

2.2km/23.7km Road Crossing. Cross over to continue along a track until a junction with some deteriorated asphalt tracks. Keep straight on along a good gravel track ignoring all other turnings or junctions.

5.4km/29.1km Junction by Hill. The Camino turns off to the left as it passes a hill situated to the right. Follow an earthen track around a farm to join an asphalt track. Turn right, staying on the asphalt to cross the "Llano Real", an area with many country

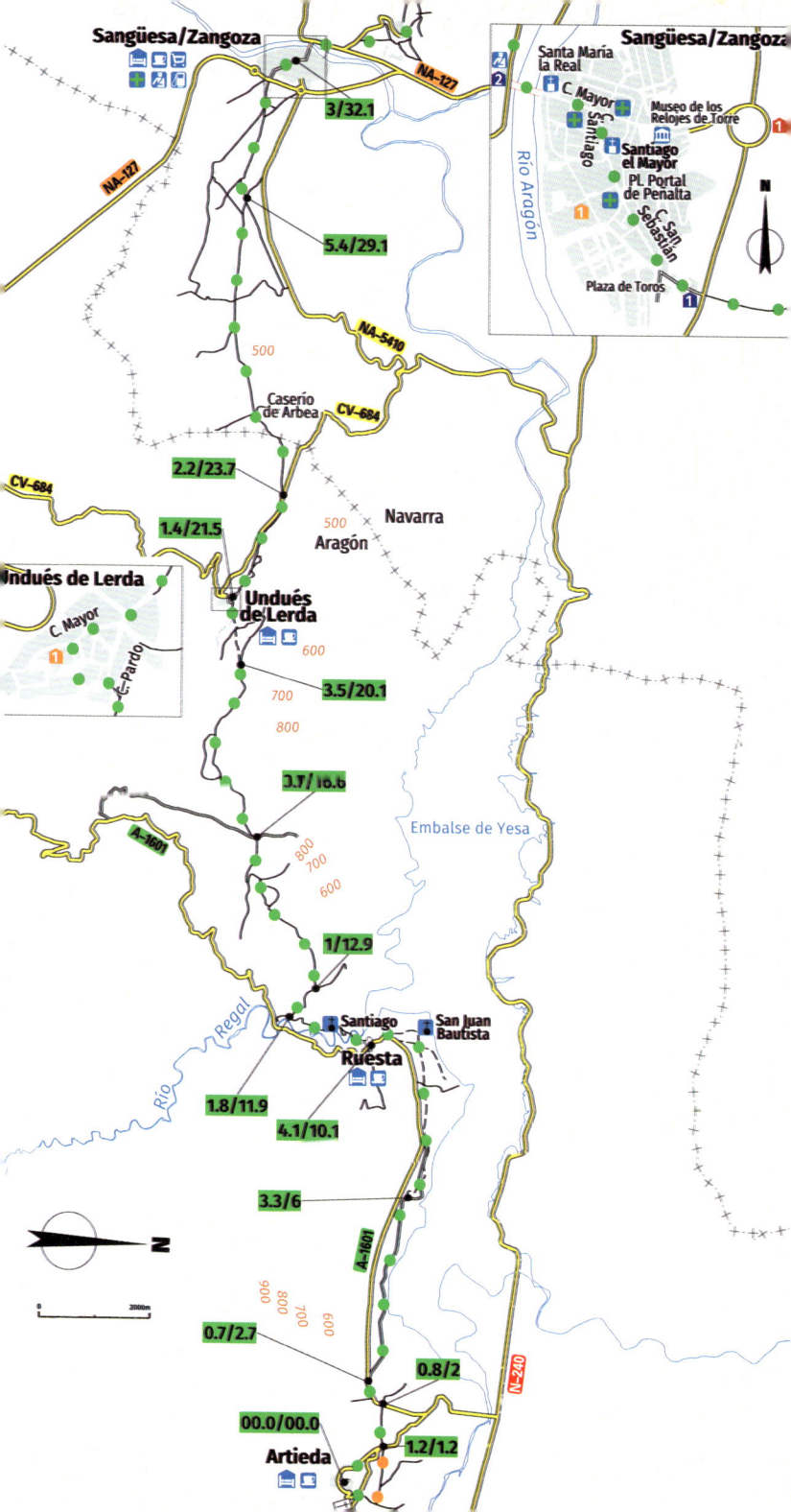

Santiago el Mayor, Sangüesa (©Callum Christie)

houses. Upon reaching a road, turn right. Continue under a ring road bridge to enter the town.
3km/32.1km Sangüesa. At the bullring take C. San Sebastián that ends at Pl. Portal de Peñalta. Take C. Estudio onwards into C. Santiago and the church dedicated to the apostle.
Sangüesa/Zangoza - pop. 5000. A small town of Navarra Media Oriental, that sits on the banks of the river Aragón.

Ruesta
🛏 **Albergue de Peregrinos**
Tel. 948 398 082

Undués de Lerda
🛏 **Albergue de Peregrinos**
Tel. 948 888 105

Sangüesa
🛏 **Albergue de Peregrinos**
Tel. 679 432 348
🛏 **Pensión el Peregrino**
Tel. 608 983 892

🛏 **Hostal JP**
Tel. 948 871 693
🛏 **Hotel Yamaguchi**
Tel. 948 870 127

Ruesta Castle. C11th fortification of which only two towers remain.
Chapel of Santiago, Ruesta. C11th. Single nave chapel with later additions. It would have doubled as a hospice for pilgrims.
Church of San Martín, Undués de Lerda. C16th late Gothic, with a beautifully decorated single nave.
Church of Santiago el Mayor, Sangüesa. Built between C12th-15th to welcome pilgrims.
Church of Santa María la Real, Sangüesa. C12th Romanesque. The doorway is an outstanding example of medieval eclesiastical architecture in Navarre.
Museum of Church Tower Clocks, Sangüesa. A singular collection of clocks from churches and town halls, housed in the Gothic styled convent of San Francisco.

13. SANGÜESA - MONREAL: 26.9KM

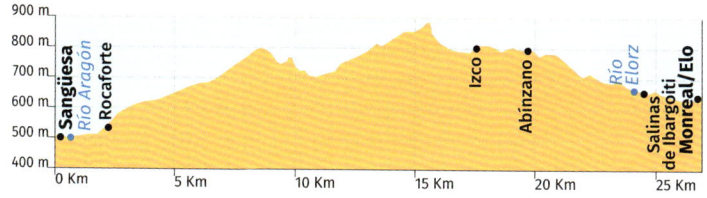

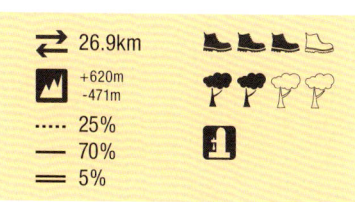

An attractive stage with a range of landscapes; from the open fields of Rocaforte and Izco, to the grazed heights of Alto de Aibar and descent to the shaded banks of the river Elorz.

Observations: The cattle grazing area of Alto de Aibar has a number of gates that should be closed behind the walker.

0km Sangüesa. Leave the town along C. Mayor to cross the metal bridge across the river Aragón and turn right along the NA-127 road towards Liédana.

1km/1km Road to Rocaforte. After 550m turn left. After a short distance take a wide path to the right which soon climbs to the village of Rocaforte.

1.2km/2.2km Rocaforte. Turn left and straight away to the right, uphill on a concrete track to leave the village. The track soon turns to gravel and later passes a picnic area and the San Francisco spring. Continue steeply uphill between fields to reach a ruined corral still with intact arches and a water trough.

2.5km/4.7km Water Trough. Continue along, to the left, on a farm track, that climbs through a pleasant valley. Follow a grassy narrow track to reach a second trough. Turn right along a newly cobbled track that narrows to a path.

3.9km/8.6km NA-534 Road. Pass under the road. The Camino emerges between two roads and continues uphill along a path and into a forest. Soon, the path (sometimes a track) descends to reach the Alto de Aibar, an area grazed by cattle in the form of a long narrow valley. Continue on uphill by an earthen track.

7km/15.6km Cattle Grid. Now on the flat, turn right onto a gravel track and after 50m turn off to the left, following a wide path between pines. Descend to level ground and continue straight on to a village.

2km/17.6km Izco. Pass the church and exit on C. San Martín that becomes a cement track. The surrounding landscape of farm fields is watched over by the distant distinct form of Monte Higa topped by an antenna. Continue straight on at all junctions.

2km/19.6km Abinzano. Enter the village turning downhill on a street to the right before veering to the left along a concrete track that soon becomes an earthen one. At a fork choose the right hand option to keep

Serapias lingua

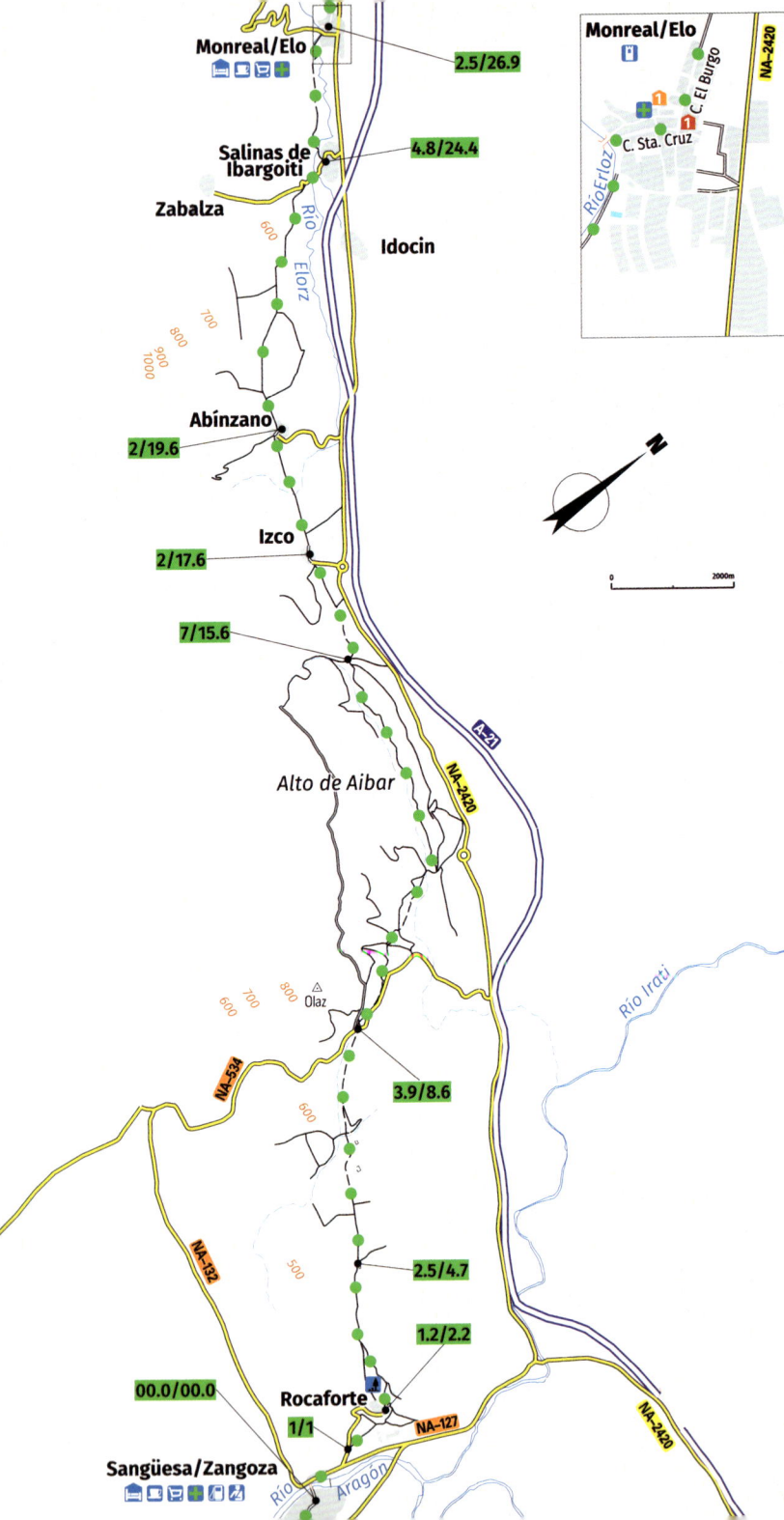

Monreal/Elo (©Javier Campos)

straight on towards Mount Higa following the main track onwards at all the junctions. Upon reaching a country lane turn right. In 100m take a narrow gravel track to the left to cross an old stone bridge. Turn left along a concrete street.
4.8km/24.4km Salinas de Ibargoiti. Before reaching the church, take the first street to the left and leave the village on an earthen track which becomes a path along a shaded stream bank. Return to a dirt track to skirt around a football pitch and cross a footbridge over the river Elorz. Keep straight on to enter the village of Monreal. By a medieval stone bridge, turn right along C. Santa Bárbara.
2.5km/26.9km Monreal.
Monreal/Elo - pop. 470. A village of the Merindad de Sangüesa.

Monreal
🛏 Albergue de Peregrinos 🪙
Tel. 636 492 899

🛏 Etxartenea Monreal 🪙🪙
Tel. 948 362 177 - 669 082 679

🏛 Church of San Pedro, Abinzano. C13th Navarran proto gothic style with a semicircular apse.
Church of San Miguel, Salinas. C14th Gothic with enormous buttresses that support the stonework of the belltower.

River Elorz Medieval Bridge, Monreal. Twin arch bridge with semicircular and pointed arches.
Castle, Monreal. Ruins of C13th fortification.

14. Monreal - Puente La Reina: 31.4km

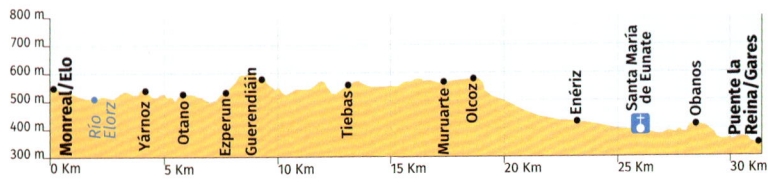

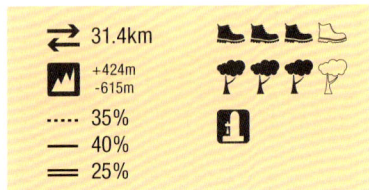

- 31.4km
- +424m / -615m
- 35%
- 40%
- 25%

An outstanding section of the Camino through Navarra due to its quiet pathways through the oak woods of the Alaiz foothills. The views north reveal a rich agricultural tapestry of fields interwoven with irrigation canals. Humble villages line the way, preparing the pilgrim for the simple, yet exquisite style of the chapel of Nuestra Señora de Eunate.

Observations: From Obanos there are two alternative routes to Puente la Reina. You will need to take care if you want to avoid being swept along by the sudden increase in pilgrims that appear along the Camino Francés.

0km Monreal. Follow C. del Burgo leaving the village and join a track towards the river Elorz.

1.2km/1.2km Path. Take a path to the right, following the charming wooded banks of the river. Upon reaching a track turn left. Later the way narrows to a path and leads to the upper part of Yárnoz village.

3km/4.2km Yárnoz. The Camino continues above the church along a flat tarmac track for 500m to the small cemetery. A narrow path leads on from here, following the fringe between woods and farm fields.

1.6km/5.8km Otano. The path crosses a track that leads down to Otano and continues along the flanks of the hillside. The path ends at an asphalt track. It veers left, climbing steeply uphill for 100m. Leave this track for a narrow way to the right, to bypass a gravel quarry.

1.9km/7.7km Ezperun. Meet an earthen track and turn left uphill, away from the village. At a bend in the track, take a path to the right to continue on into oak woods.

1.6km/9.3km Guerendiáin. At the first houses of this village turn left and then leave by the upper part of the village. After the last house fork right on a rough earthen track. After 150m the way turns into a path and enters evergreen oak woods that border farm fields. Ignore a path to the left just before meeting a track. Cross over to continue along the path that winds downhill to rejoin the track. Descend to cross over a road to a quarry and follow the track straight on.

3.8km/13.1km Tiebas. After passing a picnic area to the left, fork right to enter the vil-

Puente la Reina/Gares (©Tur. Navarra)

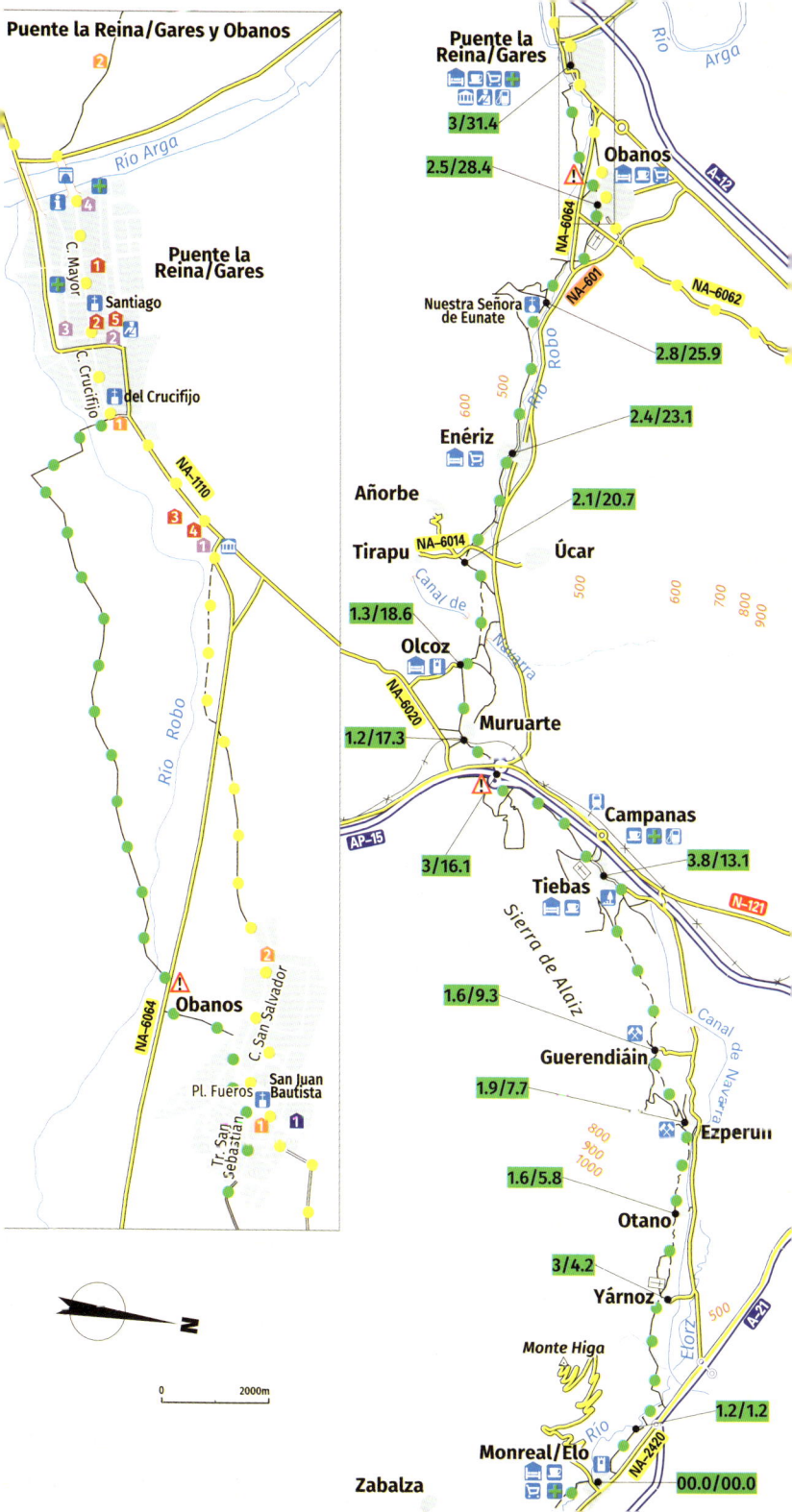

lage along C. Mayor. After the church, fork left at a small cobbled roundabout. Veer left to leave the village and then cross over a road to descend on a wide track past a football pitch. Now follow a farm track past arable fields, parallel to the AP-15.

3km/16.1km AP-15 Roundabout. ATTENTION. The Camino passes through a tunnel under the toll motorway and then under the bridge of the N-121 highway. A few yards further on take a narrow farm track to the left. Reach a railway line and follow it for 150m before turning right to cross under it to emerge by a small wooded village park and playground.

1.2km/17.3km Muruarte. Cross up through the park and turn left to leave the village on a country lane. Soon fork right along a lane to climb towards Olcoz.

1.3km/18.6km Olcoz. At the entrance to the village turn right to skirt the houses and in 150m take the second earth track downhill to the right. After some 350m fork left over the hill through which the Canal de Navarre tunnels its way. Take a path to the left that descends to a junction of tracks. Turn left and continue downhill for 400m.

2.1km/20.7km Path to the Right. As the ground levels out, take this path, following a stream, until it meets the NA-6014 road. Cross straight over to follow an earthen track. Keep straight on as you enter the next village.

2.4km/23.1km Enériz. Follow C. Cofradía to a small square, and veer left along C. San Juan, which flattens out to become the 'Camino de Antillón' as it leaves the village. Before the track begins to climb take a path to the right. Continue along this pleasant route between vineyards until you emerge by the peaceful surrounds to Eunate.

2.8km/25.9km Nuestra Señora de Eunate. Continue straight on along a dirt track for 100m, then take a path to the right. This soon ends at another track where you turn right. Upon meeting a country road (NA-6064) cross straight over to follow an asphalt lane, past the cemetery and uphill into Obanos.

2.5km/28.4km Obanos. The Camino francés also enters Obanos, but our route follows a

Nuestra Señora de Eunate (©Callum Christie)

different onward path. After passing the church, veer left behind the sporting frontón pavilion, then fork left along C. los Infanzones. Continue straight on downhill to leave the village. As the road bends sharply to the left, continue straight on at a crossroads, down some steps and onto a street in a newer part of the village. Keep straight on down to the main road (NA-6064). ATTENTION. Turn right along the edge of this road for 100m and then turn left along an earthen track that leads to the end of this particular Camino!

3km/31.4km Puente la Reina/Gares.
Puente la Reina/Gares - pop. 2800. An important village situated at a strategic point on the river Argas.

Tiebas
- **Albergue de Peregrinos**
  Tel. 600 941 916

Olcoz
- **Hostal El Arriero**
  Tel. 669 214 088

Obanos
- **Albergue de Peregrinos "Usda"**
  Tel. 676 560 927
- **Albergue Atseden**
  Tel. 646 924 912
- **Hostal Mamertos**
  Tel. 649 139 611

Puente la Reina
- **Albergue de Peregrinos "Padres Reparadores"**
  Tel. 948 340 050
- **Albergue "Santiago Apóstol"**
  Tel. 948 340 220
- **Albergue "El Puente"**
  Tel. 661 705 642
- **Albergue "Estrella Guía"**
  Tel. 662 262 431

- **Albergue de Peregrinos Hotel Jakue**
  Tel. 948 341 017
- **Albergue Amalur**
  Tel. 948 341 090
- **Hotel Plaza**
  Tel. 948 340 145
- **Hotel Bidean**
  Tel. 948 341 156
- **Hostal Zubi XXI**
  Tel. 948 340 722
- **Hotel Jakue**
  Tel. 948 341 017
- **Hotel El Cerco**
  948 341 269

Church de la Natividad, Yárnoz. Typical medieval Navarran C13th design with a single nave and a tower with belfry.
Church of the Conception, Ezperun. Of medieval origin, remodelled in the C16th. Contains Baroque altarpieces and a Gothic sculpture of the Virgin.
Church of Santa Eufemia, Tiebas. C13th Gothic with C17th doorway and an elegant atrium with a tower above.
Palatial Tower, Olcoz. C15th strategic tower.
Church of Nuestra Señora de Eunate. C12th octagonal temple with a simple and unique architecture that belies an enigmatic geometry. Surrounded by a beautiful gallery of 33 arches.
Church of San Juan Bautista, Obanos. Neo Gothic, built in 1912 on an earlier church.
Church of Santiago, Puente la Reina. C12th Romanesque with a wooden carving of Santiago of the same period.
Romanesque Bridge, Puente la Reina. Built in the C11th to cross the river Arga. It has a length of 110m, with 7 pointed arches.

TÀRREGA - PINA DE EBRO

Heading westwards, the drier farmlands are soon replaced by a vast patchwork of green fields. Fruit orchards and maize crops are irrigated by a complex network of canals that draw their water from the two main rivers that are crossed along this route. The Way is mostly flat aside from the depressions and escarpments formed by the Segre and Cinca rivers.

Later, the route crosses the dramatic and exposed steppe lands of 'Los Monegros' with its salt pans, where cereal crops survive on scarce rainfall. This harsh arid area can be tough to cross both in high summer due to the lack of shade and in deep winter due to exposure to the elements.

With the securing of Lleida by Christian forces (1149), a new link route between Montserrat and the river Ebro was established. From Lleida the route continued along the ancient Roman road to meet the banks of the Ebro. Pilgrims were drawn by the legend of St. James treading on a thorn as he reached the Roman walls of *Ilerda* by night. Today, on the night before the feast of St. James, boys and girls of the city celebrate "Els Fanalets de Sant Jaume". This festive lantern-filled procession leads to the new cathedral and commemorates the angel who shone a lantern to help the Apostle remove the thorn. A pilgrim hospice was founded in the C15th in Lleida, and the Pia Almoina charity offered pilgrims at least one free meal a day.

©Callum Christie

Lleida - This provincial capital is one of the oldest settlements in Catalonia with recorded finds dating back to the Bronze Age. Iberian tribes defended it against Carthaginian and Roman invasions but eventually *Ilerda* was made a '*municipium*' by the Emperor Augustus. Situated around a flat topped ridge on the Segre river it defended important transport routes to *Tarraco* (Tarragona), one of the three Roman provincial capitals of Hispania.

A university city for over 700 years, Lleida has a maze of narrow pedestrian streets that make up its historic quarter on the right bank of the Segre river. Crowning the ridge is the impressive Moorish castle of la Suda, which later became a royal residence for the Kings of Aragón. Beside it, the striking 'Seu Vella', the old cathedral with an imposing belltower, was converted into a military fortress in the C18th. Today the city is blessed with attractive parks and botanical gardens along with numerous museums.

1. TÀRREGA - EL PALAU D'ANGLESOLA: 23.2KM

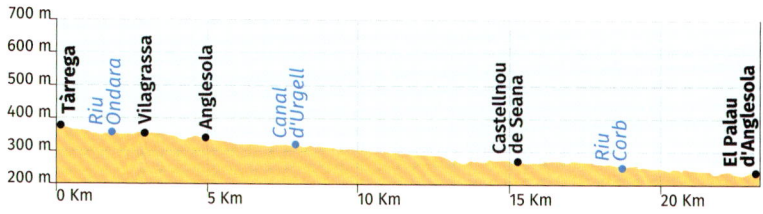

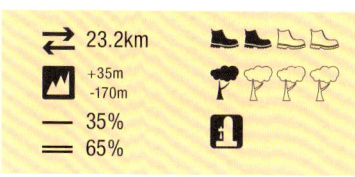

- 23.2km
- +35m / -170m
- 35%
- 65%

The Way crosses the Pla d'Urgell, a plain once dependent on seasonal rain to sustain cereal crops and groves of almonds. It has now been transformed by a system of irrigation canals and small reservoirs making it possible to grow maize and fruit orchards. The villages of the area are small and not too far apart.

0km Tàrrega. From the Pl. Major follow C. d'Urgell to the tree lined Av. de Catalunya and turn left. At a large roundabout the Camino divides; to the right towards Huesca and San Juan de la Peña, or, our Way, straight on towards Lleida. ATTENTION. Follow the margin of the N-II. Cross the river Ondarra. At the entrance to Vilagrassa take the first street right, C.de Tàrrega.

3km/3km Vilagrassa. From Santa Maria church continue along C. d'Anglesola. On leaving the village join the C-53 and turn right. Cross over the A-2, continuing straight on to the outskirts of Anglesola.

2.3km/5.3km Anglesola. Follow C. Major to its end. C. Església takes you to the church of Sant Pau de Narbona. Continue downhill on C. Camí de Barbens and turn left. Leaving the village, take an asphalt lane to your right. After 400m, at a bend, go straight on along an earthen track. Arriving at the Canal d'Urgell, follow it until you join a country road.

2.6km/7.9km Bridge over Canal. Cross over and in 600m (after a big left hand bend in the canal) veer away from the canal, to the right, on a country lane. Keep straight on ignoring all turnings.

3.3km/11.2km LV-3341. Cross straight over this road to continue along a track by the side of a fenced off farm.

1.4km/12.6km LV-3344. At the very end of this track, turn left and follow the road for 300m to its Km 2 marker, before turning right onto an earthen track. In quick succession turn left, then right, still on earthen tracks. Continue straight on to enter Castellnou de Seana. Veer right and proceed to the Pl. Major.

2.6km/15.2km Castellnou de Seana. Follow C. Sant Blai onto C. Major. Leave the village by C. d'Ivars d'Urgell. Cross a road and keep straight on. After a further 250m join another asphalt track to continue ahead (right). In 200m choose the second track on the left just past the entrance to Vilalta farm. Follow this track straight on ignoring all crossroads until you arrive at a country lane by a small bridge that crosses the river Corb.

3.4km/18.6km Road to Vila-sana. Cross this road and continue along the track ahead. Pass by the small Serradal irrigation reservoir and continue straight ahead on along the main track. Cross the L-334 road near an industrial unit and go straight on by another track. Cross the LP-3322 road and continue straight ahead on a track. At the outskirts of Palau d'Anglesola the Camino meets an asphalt minor road and veers right. At the next crossroads turn left over a canal and veer right to enter the village.

4.6km/23.2km El Palau d'Anglesola. Follow C. Nou into C. Sant Josep that in turn emerges at the Pl. Major.

El Palau d'Anglesola - pop. 2100.

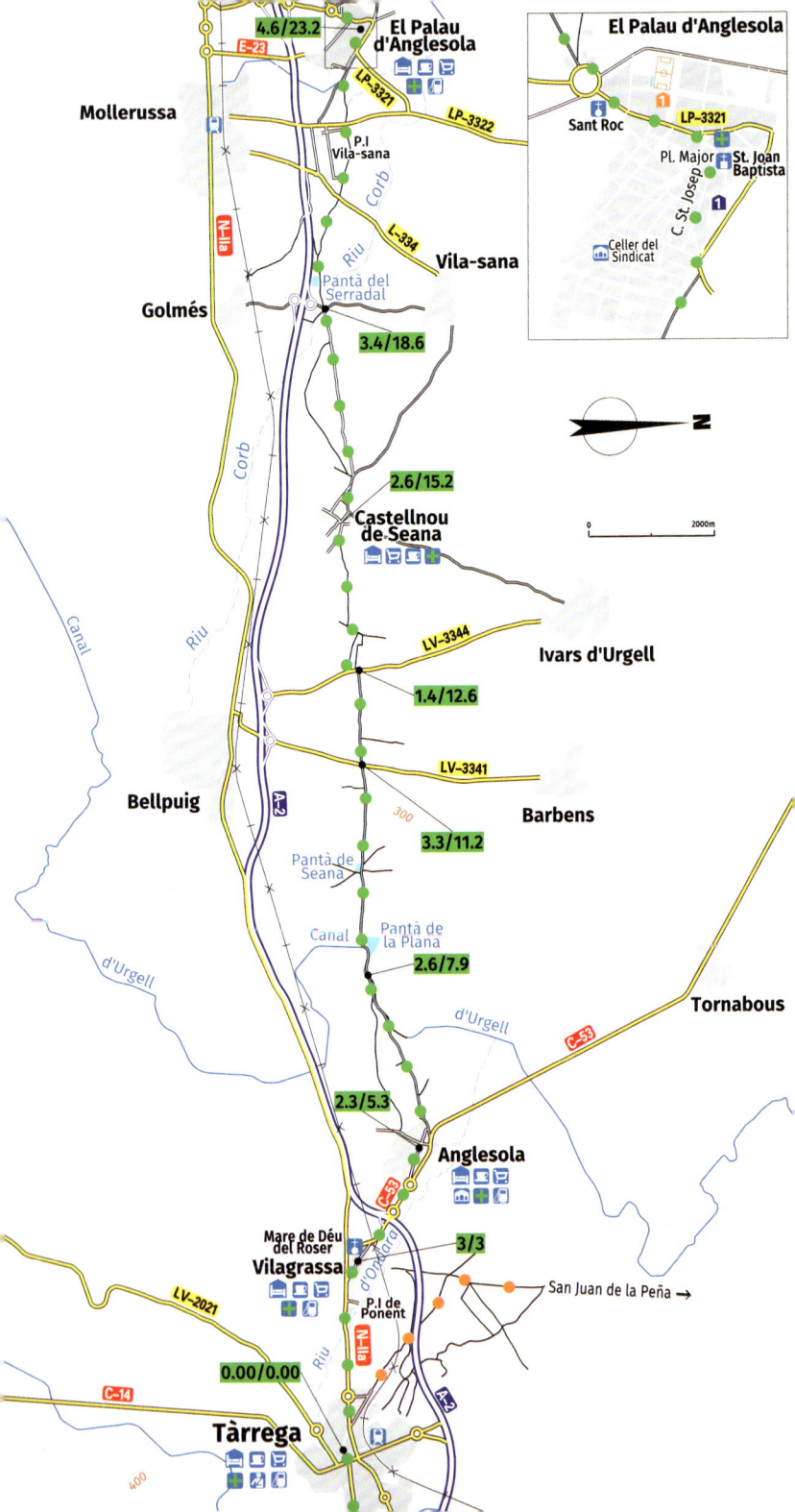

©Julián López-Arenas González

Anglesola
🏠 **Hostal del Carme** 🪙🪙
Tel. 973 311 000
Castellnou de la Seana
🏠 **Cal Puro** 🪙
Tel. 637 81 20 30

El Palau d'Anglesola
🏠 **Acollida de Pelegrins** 🪙
Tel. 629 684 063
🏠 **Pensió Sant Antoni** 🪙
Tel. 973 602 158

 Santa Maria Church, Vilagrassa. Notable for its C13th Romanesque doorway.
Chapel de la Mare de Déu del Roser, Vilagrassa. Hermitage made up of many architectural styles from late Gothic onwards.
Sant Pau de Narbona Church, Anglesola. C16th church, notable for the statues of Saints Peter and Paul taken from an earlier Romanesque church.

Anglesola Hospice. Founded in the C12th to succour pilgrims and the infirm.
Sant Joan Baptista Church, Castellnou de Seana. C16th Baroque with an unusual baptism font.
Celler del Sindicat Agrícola, El Palau d'Anglesola. A typical Cèsar Martinell designed churchlike wine co-operative.

2. El Palau d'Anglesola - Lleida: 24.6km

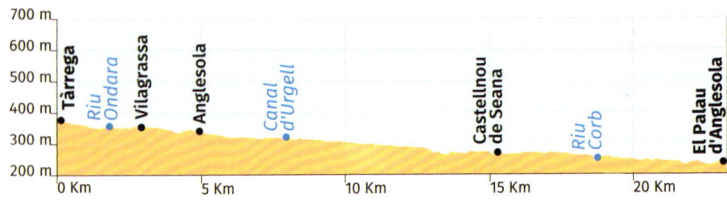

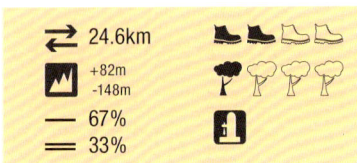

- 24.6km
- +82m / -148m
- 67%
- 33%

A flat stage through the heart of the Pla d'Urgell, with little shade to be had. A fertile area with irrigation channels that water countless fields of maize and fruit orchards. The landscape is broken by the half hidden city of Lleida, which sits on a low ridge within a strategic depression formed by the rio Segre.

0km El Palau d'Anglesola. From the Pl. Major take C. de la Font. At a small park with a stone cross, continue straight on towards a roundabout on the LV-3321, taking the second exit on the right onto a country lane. After 100m keep straight on (left). At the next junction turn right between fruit orchards along an asphalt track.

2.1km/2.1km Auxiliar Canal. Cross by a bridge and turn left onto an earthen track. In 20m take the track to the right and in 300m, at a junction, continue to the left towards a farm building. Keep straight on ignoring side turns whilst continuing parallel to the distant A-2 motorway. At a fork, turn left and then make further left turns until a bridge over the A-2.

4.4km/6.5km Bridge over the A-2. On the other side, turn right along a dirt track. At the gateway of a nearby farm, turn off right, along a track. In 300m turn left parallel to the A-2 on an asphalt track for 500m. At the first fork turn left towards a railway line.

1.5km/8km Level Crossing. ATTENTION. There is no barrier to the rail line. Cross over and in 300m join another track and continue on (right) past some industrial units to a roundabout on the outskirts of Bell-lloc.

1.7km/9.7km Bell-lloc d'Urgell. Continue along the main road then enter the town by a tree lined park and square. Traverse the town to cross the barriered railway track. Turn left, then immediately right. Take C. dels Rosers to the left, leaving the village by a country lane. At a fork, proceed along the left hand hearthen track. Cross a bridge over the A-2 and turn left at the next fork. Keep straight on through the following crossings of tracks, always with the A-2 a short distance to the left.

5.7km/15.4km Fork by Reservoir. Turn right and continue, passing under an electric line. In 600m at a crossroads turn left.

1km/16.4km Les Roquetes Urban Spread. Cross a country road to continue ahead on

La Seu Vella, Lleida (©ACT. M.AS.)

a dirt track skirting the built up area. By the last smallholding cross an asphalt track and continue ahead on a dirt track. Turn right to follow a service track by the A-2. At a road, turn left to cross the A-2.

1.5km/17.9km Bridge over A-2. On the far side, turn left, passing under the bridge and then turn left onto an asphalt track. The way continues straight on soon changing to an earthen surface on the Carrerada de Alcoletge. Join another asphalt track and veer left. Now keep straight on until the first warehouses of a substantial industrial and commercial area.

2.8km/20.7km El Segre Industrial Zone. Continue straight on along a wide road to its end and turn left, still surrounded by commercial units.

1.1km/21.8km Traffic Lights. Turn right along a side road out of the industrial area. ATTENTION. This busy lane with no sidewalk, narrows and then encounters a railway level crossing. Proceed with care and turn left onto a wider country road. Carry on until a canal by the river Segre.

1km/22.8km Canal Bridge. Cross over the canal. The road veers left, leading you to walk along the landscaped embankment of the Segre river under several modern bridges. Upon reaching the stone built Pont Vell (with four arches) cross over to enter the city by the Arc de Pont, an old archway by the statue of Indíbil and Mandoni.

1.0km/24.6km Lloida. Turn left toward the cathedral.

Lleida - pop. 140.000. Capital of the Segrià. Inhabited since ancient times, this city grew around the Seu hill. A strategic river crossing point between the coast and the interior, it was a Roman bastion. During Moorish rule the city was a significant frontier enclave. From the Christian conquest to modern times the city has seen more than its share of warfare. Lleida is surrounded by crops and orchards that are irrigated by water management systems initiated in the Middle Ages.

Hospital de Santa Maria. Lleida (©ACT. Miquel Raurich)

Bell-lloc d'Urgell
Refugi de Peregrins
Tel. 973 560 100
Alcoletge
Alberg del Peregrí
Tel. 973 196 725
　　　625 620 143
Lleida
Alberg Sant Anastasi
Tel. 973 266 099

Pensión Mode
Tel. 973 275 492
Hotel Goya
Tel. 973 266 788
SM Apartaments
Tel. 636 340 039
Hotel Ramon Berenguer IV
Tel. 973 237 345
SM Apartaments Station
Tel. 636 340 039

Hotel Zenit
Tel. 973 229 191
Hotel Acta Rambla
Tel. 973 940 940
Hotel Real
Tel. 973 239 405
Hotel Ciutat de Lleida
Tel. 973 283 910

 La Suda Castle, Lleida. A fortress of moorish origins with a visitor centre.
La Seu Vella, Lleida. The former Cathedral, situated by the castle. Romanesque with elements of Gothic and Renaissance. The doorways, cloister and belltower are breathtaking.
La Paeria, Lleida. A Gothic palace, today housing the town hall.
Chapel of Saint James, Lleida. C14th, simple in design.
La Seu Nova, Lleida. The new Baroque Cathedral was built between 1761 and 1781.

3. LLEIDA - FRAGA: 34.7KM

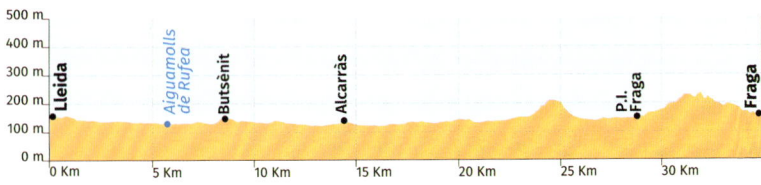

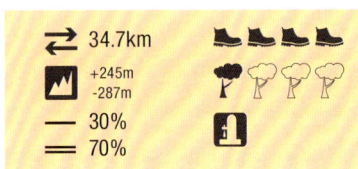

- ⇄ 34.7km
- +245m / -287m
- — 30%
- = 70%

The Way from Lleida to Fraga crosses the boundary between Catalonia and Aragón, as well as the valleys of the rivers Segre and Cinca. Farmed fields, vineyards and irrigated orchards surround the pilgrim's route.

Observations: Great care should be taken when the Camino encounters the busy N-II and the A-2. This stage has a slight change to the signed route to make for the safer progress of the pilgrim.

0km Lleida. From the new Cathedral, join the riverside walkway heading downstream. At the outskirts to the city keep straight on along the asphalted Camí de Rufea. At the first junction, turn left downhill and soon the way follows an earthen track alongside the river Segre.

3.3km/3.3km AVE Viaduct. Soon the Camino passes the wetlands nature reserve of Aiguamolls de Rufea.

3.4km/6.7km River Ford. Ignore a concrete ford over the Segre and continue straight on. After 1km the track turns away from the river and soon meets a local road.

1.7km/8.4km Butsènit. Turn left, past the Mare de Déu de Butsènit chapel. After 200m take an asphalt track to the left. A little further on, the track narrows, turns to dirt and soon descends to cross a stream. Then, just before an irrigation canal, you turn left along a good earthen track. Follow the main track to meet the N-II.

2.5km/10.9km Commercial Units. Turn left, going along to the end of these units and then turn left downhill on the Torrent i Ramell asphalt track. After 800m turn right and follow the track to its end.

2.4km/13.3km Junction. Turn right and after 50m, turn left onto Av. Onze Setembre. At the 3rd crossroad turn right onto Passeig del Riu. Cross the N-II and keep straight on along C. Doctor Castells to Pl. de L'Església.

0.9km/14.2km Alcarràs. Turn left onto C. Major until Pl. Arrabaleta, then turn left onto C. Mossèn Cinto Verdaguer to emerge onto the N-II (Av. Catalunya). Cross over to go straight on along Travessia de Clamor to its end. At a junction of streets choose the second on the left, C. Clamor. Continue straight on out of town on an asphalt track and after 500m, at a junction of tracks, veer right. Continue straight on until the LP-7043 road and turn right onto it for 300m.

2.3km/16.5km Camino Alternative. ATTENTION. Ignore the waymarked Camino that turns left along an earthen track (the red route on the map). *The author considers the waymarked Camino to be too hazardous over the next few kms due to the close proximity of a busy main road and a motorway. There is insufficient protection or separation for the walker from heavy traffic. The mapped alternative only adds 1km and is considered safer and quieter.* Continue straight on along the LP-7043 for 200m until a small roundabout. Cross the N-II with care and continue ahead on the Camí del Polvorí. Follow this asphalt track for 800m.

1.5km/18km A-2 Bridge. Just after crossing the A-2 turn left down an asphalt track that runs parallel to the A-2.

1.3km/19.3km Gas Station Junction. Emerge at a roundabout by the entrance to a gas station, keep straight on along an asphalt track in poor repair, parallel to the service road by the A-2. After 300m turn right, uphill on a dirt track between indus-

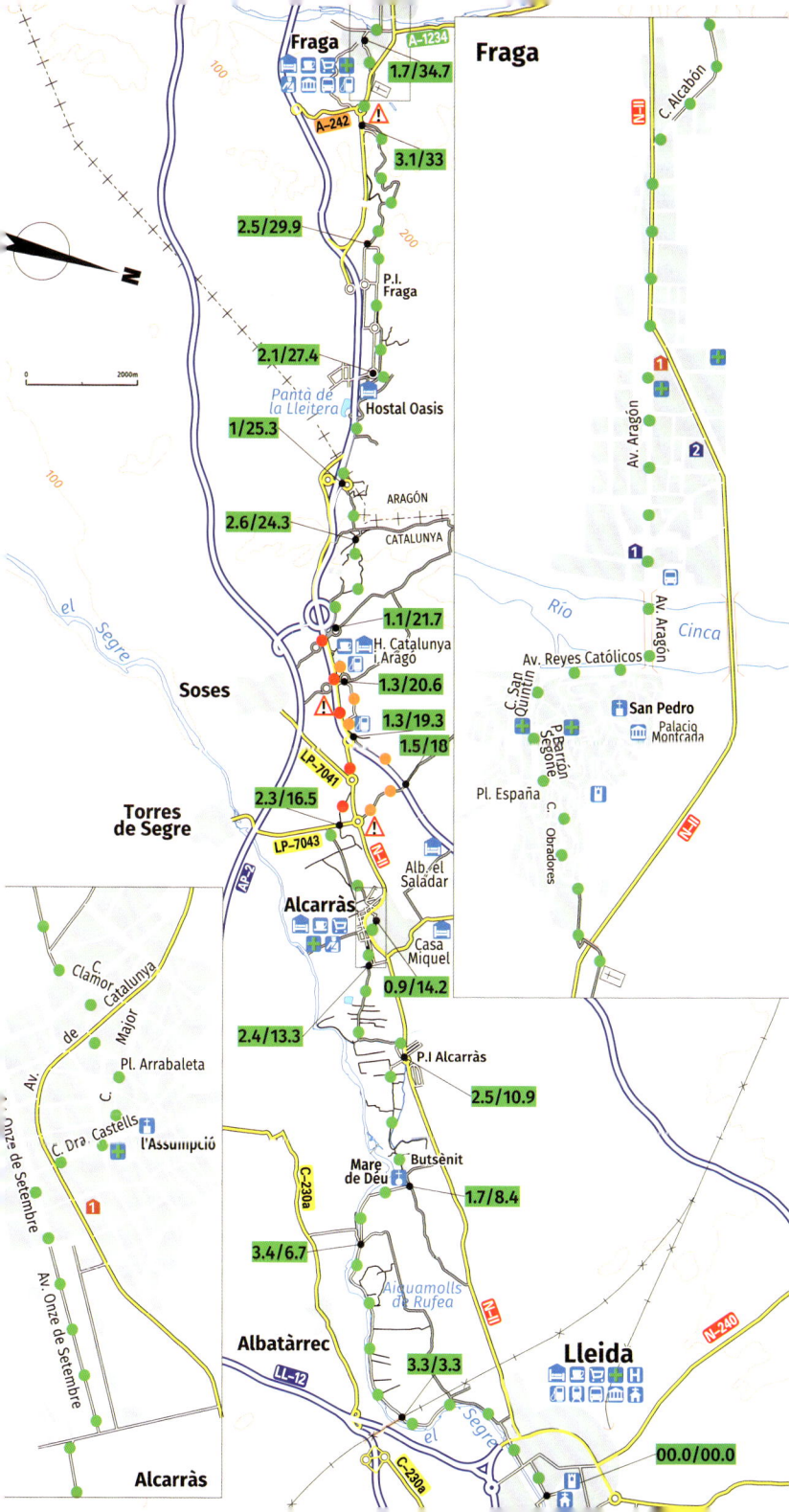

trial yards. Take the first track left, el Camí de Xatarra and follow the main track gently downhill. Join an asphalt track and turn right to a small roundabout.

1.3km/20.6km Roundabout. Continue straight on via the second exit downhill from the roundabout towards the service road by the A-2, where you turn right.

ATTENTION. Beware of traffic. Pass the forecourt of a gas station and then a Hostal/Restaurant. Now, turn right before a night club and join an asphalt track behind this building. Turn left along it, parallel to the service road of the A-2.

1.1km/21.7km Roundabout. At a small roundabout take the second exit along Camí de la Serra Montull, still parallel to the A-2. In 400m avoid entering a large roundabout and

La Seu Vella, Lleida (©ACT. M.A.S.)

veer right, downhill on the Camí de la Serra Montull leaving the A-2 behind. In 600m continue ahead as the asphalt turns into an earthen track. Follow the well made track uphill.

2.6km/24.3km Junction. Join an asphalt track and turn left. In 150m turn right onto the Camí de la Cabanyera, heading downhill to an exit roundabout of the A-2.

1km/25.3km Roundabout. El Camino enters Aragón. Turn right to follow the motorway service road. After 800m continue parallel but now on an asphalt track up to a bridge over the A-2. Without crossing the bridge follow the asphalt and in 200m, just before the service road of the A-2, turn right to continue to the side of a restaurant. In 100m at a fork in the track, keep straight on (left). Just before joining a road, veer right on an earthen track towards a roundabout.

2.1km/27.4km Roundabout. Join the first asphalt track that exits the roundabout. After 50m turn left on to the earthen perimeter track of a new industrial park. After 800m cross into the park at a roundabout and turn right, continuing to the end of the street. Exit the park to the right going uphill on a road to a junction by a narrow canal. Turn right.

2.5km/29.9km Junction. In 900m take the road to the right. At a small roundabout, head downhill through an industrial estate to the N-II.

3.1km/33km N-II ATTENTION. Beware of Traffic. Turn right along the roadside to a roundabout. Keep straight on along a service road parallel to the N-II. After a gas station, follow a flat asphalt track which is parallel to but higher than the N-II. Pass the cemetery surrounded by cypress trees and cross over the N-II by a modern footbridge. Proceed downhill on C. Obradores until you reach the town centre square.

1.7km/34.7km Fraga.

Fraga - pop. 15.000. Capital of the Bajo Cinca. A town whose history can be traced back at least to Visigothic times.

Alcarràs
🟠 **Allotjament de Pelegrins el Saladar** ⊝
Tel. 639 793 004
(policía local)
🔵 **Hostal Catalunya-Aragó** ⊝
Tel. 973 79 71 16

🔵 **Hostal Oasis** ⊝
Tel. 974 470 654
🔴 **Hotel Oyo Can Peixan** ⊝
Tel. 973 791 012
🔴 **Hotel Casa Miquel** ⊝⊝
Tel. 973 791 627

Fraga
🔴 **Hostal Trébol** ⊝
Tel. 974 471 533
🔴 **Pensión Olles** ⊝
Tel. 974 453 834
🔴 **Hotel Casanova** ⊝
Tel. 974 471 990

Mare de Déu de l'Assumpció Church, Alcarràs. Neoclassic in style and built within the ruined castle.

Sant Pere Church, Fraga. Originally Visigothic, it served as a mosque before returning to Christian use. Aragonese Gothic in style.

4. Fraga - Candasnos: 26.5km

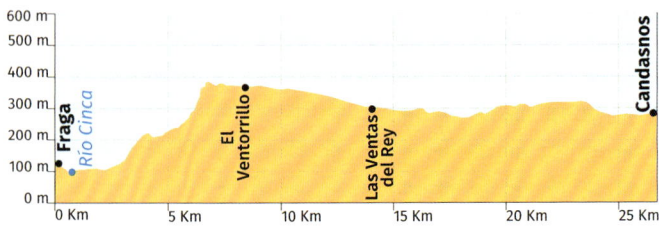

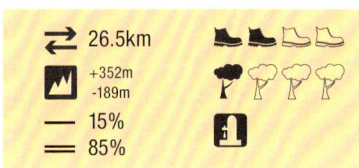

Upon leaving Fraga, the Camino encounters some of the most inhospitable country in this guide. The Monegros, freezing in winter and boiling in summer, is an area of few villages and even fewer wayside inns. Extensive arable lands highly dependent on annual rainfall, are interspersed with the abandoned broken dry stone walls of livestock corrals.
Observations: Carry sufficient drinking water.
0km Fraga. Descend from Pl. España via C. San Quintín. Turn right onto Av. Reyes Católicos and cross the río Cinca to continue ahead on the lengthy Av. de Aragón.
1.9km/1.9km Roundabout. Turn right towards "Los Juzgados" (courthouse). At the next junction keep straight on between commercial units on C. Monasterio de Sigena, an asphalt track that exits the town.
1.1km/3km Crossroads. Continue straight on by an earthen track that soon starts to climb. Turn left at a fork and then immediately right to continue the tough climb. The pilgrim gains views of a very different landscape; a meseta with wide horizons cloaked in fields of cereal.
5km/8km El Ventorrillo. A restaurant at the side of the N-II. The Camino now follows the completely flat Cañada Real de Aragón (Royal Drovers' Road). Continue by a gravel track, parallel to the N-II ignoring all turns to the right.
6km/14km Ventas del Rey. A ruined former wayside inn by a gas station and water reservoir. Continue parallel to the N-II. Eventually zig zag down to a storm tunnel under the N-II.
6.9km/20.9km Tunnel N-II. Cross under the main road and turn right along an earthen track, ignoring all turnings to the left. At a fork just before the A-2, continue straight on (left) towards a bridge.
3.2km/24.1km A-2 Bridge. Cross the A-2 and keep straight on ignoring all turnings.
2.4km/26.5km Candasnos. In a small wooded park to the left, the chapel of Pilar welcomes the traveler.
Candasnos - pop. 320. Village of the Bajo Cinca area.

Burhinus oedicnemus

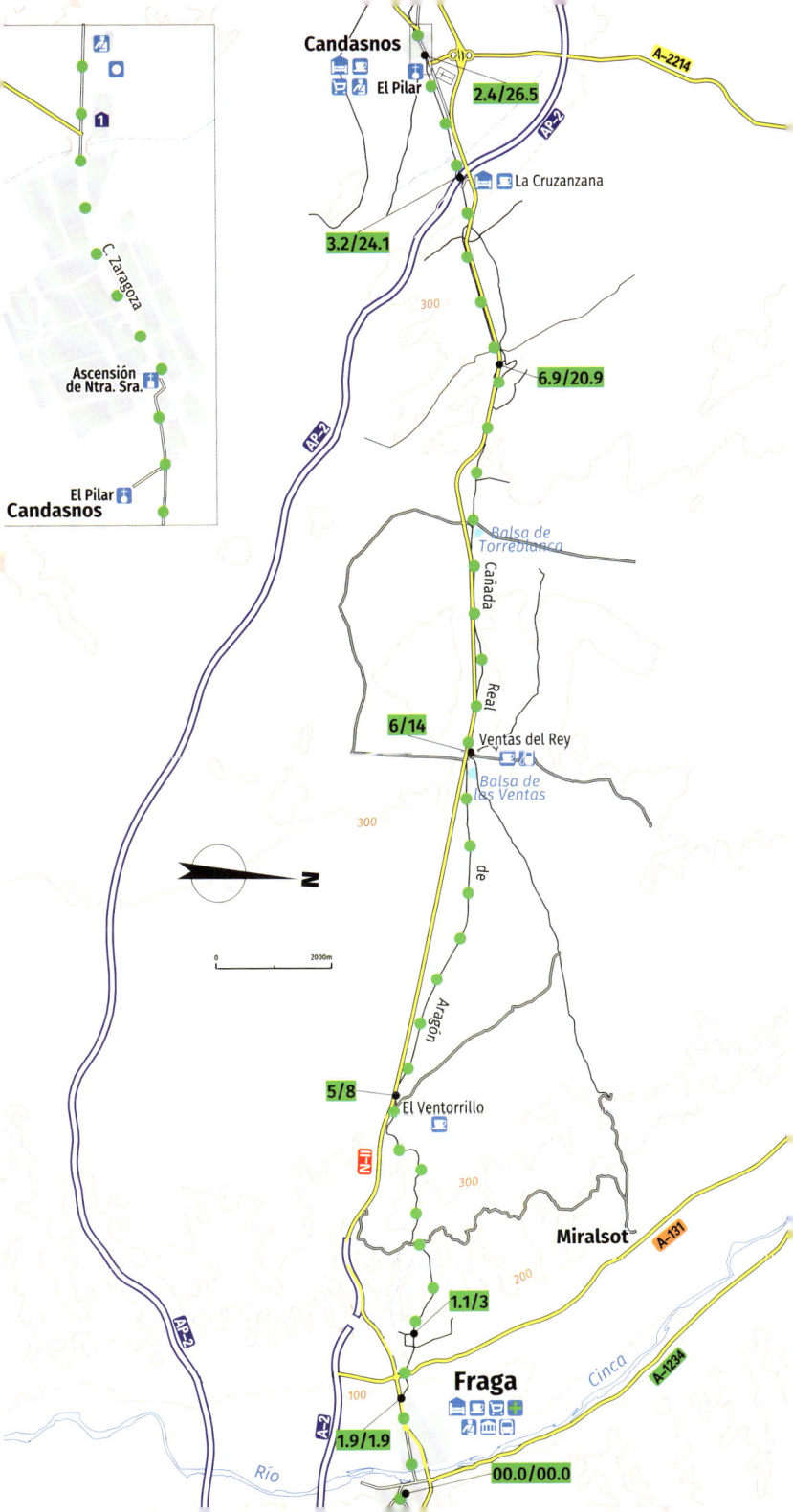

Tossal de la Barbeta, Fraga (©Juan Carlos Borrego Pérez)

Candasnos
- **Pensión El Pilar**
  Tel. 974 463 017
- **Hotel la Cruzanzana**
  Tel. 974 463 044

TAXI
Bujaraloz
Taxis Monegros
Tel. 657 164 472

Fraga
Taxi Juan Alvarez Antich
Tel. 600 485 020
Taxi Verónica Alvaraz Mazariego
Tel. 693 359 450

Chapel of Pilar, Candasnos. Single naved chapel built with hewn rock.
Church of Ascensión de Ntra. Señora, Candasnos. Romanesque with Gothic alterations.

Ice Well, Candasnos. A circular structure, 5.5m in diameter topped with a cupula.

5. CANDASNOS - BUJARALOZ: 20KM

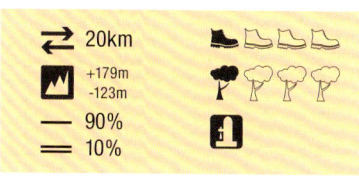

The crossing of Los Monegros steppes continues through its dry and unusual landscape. Hillocks formed of alternate layers of sand and clay reveal ancient petrified water courses, now interspersed by narrow valleys of arable fields where rivers once flowed. The outskirts of Peñalba has modern irrigation canals and channels which nurture a greater variety of crops.

0km Candasnos. Leave the village by its main road, C. Zaragoza and take the first road to the left towards Caspe (A-2410). After just 50m take a gravel track to the right. Continue parallel to the N-II ignoring all turns to either side. At a crossing of tracks, with a corral to the right, go straight on up the slope to a picnic area.

4.8km/4.8km Picnic Area. Continue straight on by a track, which you soon leave to take a rough path to the right. Cross an area of scrub and pines following the N-II closely.

1.5km/6.3km Bridge. The path turns into a track and then crosses a bridge over a water channel "Colector num.2". Turn right to climb a low hill. Upon reaching the N-II take a track left downhill. Follow the main track until you join another and turn right into a flatter area with many farms. Continue straight on at all junctions until you are closely following the Valcuerna gulley, watched over by the chapel of Santa Quitería. Follow this water course without crossing it until you pass under the N-II bridge with its three arches.

3.3km/9.6km Peñalba. At the first junction, turn left to cross the Valcuerna stream by way of a bridge. Enter the village along C. Ramón y Cajal, passing the church of Santa Cruz. Continue on by C. Joaquín Costa and at its end veer right to climb a slope to the Pl. de San Jorge. Continue uphill to leave the village on an earthen track through arable fields. At the first junction turn left to meet a country road. Turn right, uphill on the asphalt. After 150m take an earthen track to the left. Descend on the main track to a junction. Turn right and in 200m you reach another junction just before an intensive livestock farm.

3.5km/13.1km Farm Junction. Turn left and in 200m cross a low bridge, continuing straight on, parallel to the N-II again and ignoring all turnings. Turn right at a fork, still on a gravel track, then in 150m, turn left to continue with the N-II to the left.

Bujaraloz

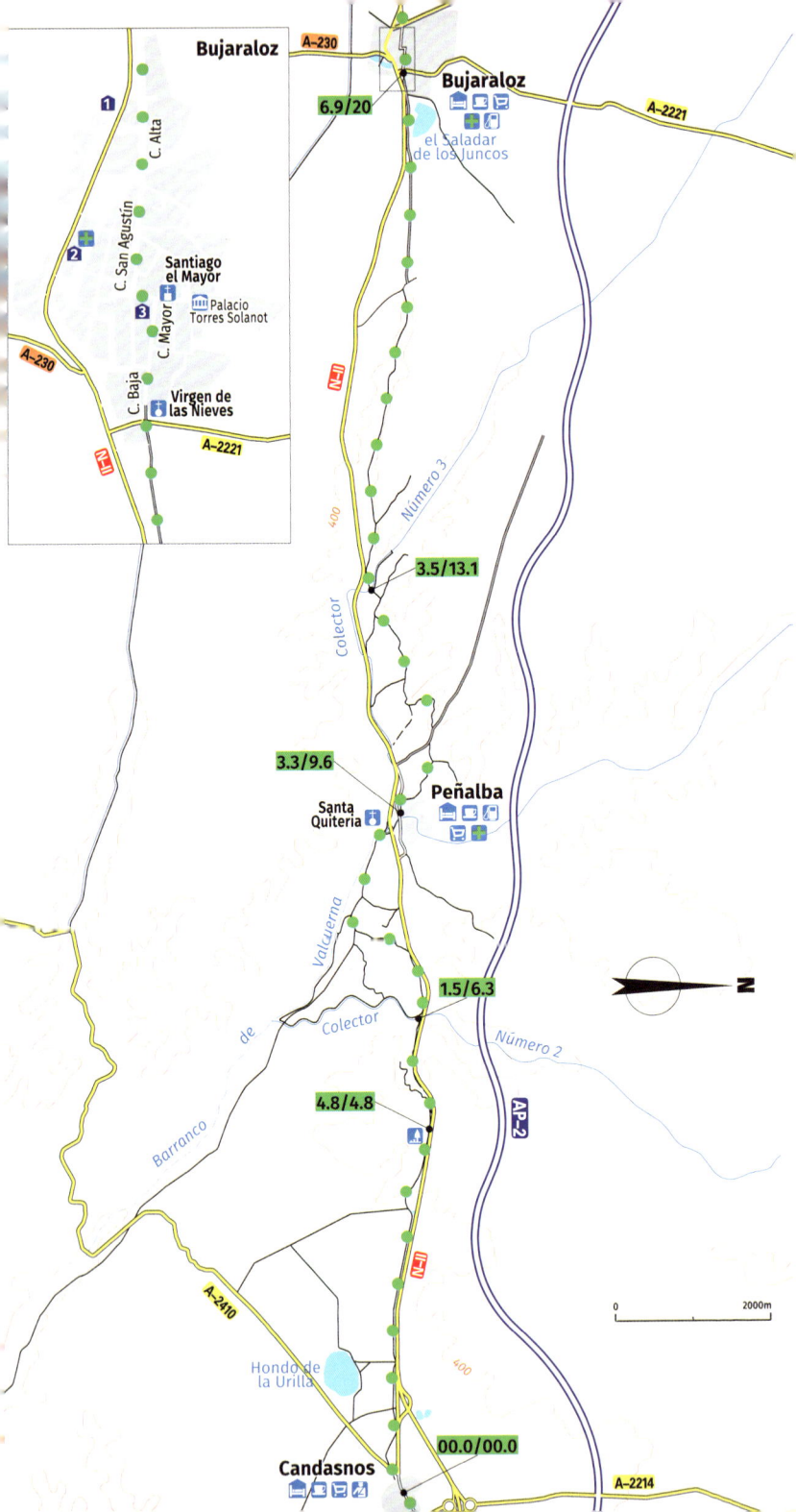

Las Saladas, Bujaraloz (©Darío Martínez Ibáñez)

6.9km/20km Bujaraloz. Enter the village by first passing the 'Saladar de los Juncos' pool and then the chapel of the Virgen de las Nieves. Continue along C. Baja and onto C. Major until you reach the church of Santiago el Mayor.
Bujaraloz - pop. 1000. Village of Los Monegros area.

Peñalba
🟢 **Casa el Balsetón** ⊖⊖
Tel. 649 54 54 50

Bujaraloz
❶ **Hostal el Español** ⊖
Tel. 976 17 31 92

❷ **Hostal los Monegros III** ⊖
Tel. 976 17 35 47
❸ **Hostal las Sabinas** ⊖
Tel. 976 17 34 50

🏛 **Chapel of Santa Quiteria, Peñalba.** A devotion to this saint was introduced by French pilgrims in medieval times.
Church of Santa Cruz, Peñalba. C17th with a Greek orthodox floor plan and a barrel vault.
Church of Santiago el Mayor, Bujaraloz. Originally C13th Gothic style built on the site of a mosque tower. The current look is from the C18th, with further reconstruction after the Civil War.

Torres Solanot Palace, Bujaraloz. C17th Nobleman's residence with a curious doorway onto the square. The interior houses a chapel dedicated to the Virgen de las Nieves.
Las Saladas Lagoons, Bujaraloz. Rain-fed salt pans typical to Los Monegros. Locally produced salt with a slightly bitter flavour has been used for curing since ancient times.

6. BUJARALOZ - PINA DE EBRO: 38,2KM

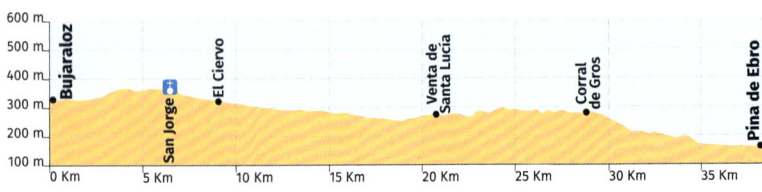

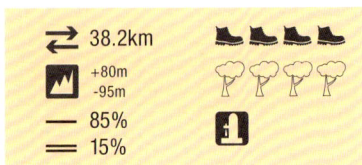

- 38.2km
- +80m / -95m
- 85%
- 15%

The final stretch of the Monegros is almost devoid of shade. It is a steppe landscape interspersed with farm fields. The N-II road, a constant reference through much of this area, follows the ancient lines of communication that once linked the Cinca and Ebro river valleys. The Imperial Roman road and later, the Royal Aragón Drovers' road created a legacy of infrastructure to serve the traveller. Many of the hospices and wayside inns have now disappeared, but some have survived and adapted to modern times.

Observations: Given the length of this stage, many pilgrims will favour dividing it in half, by stopping at Venta Lucia. *See taxi and public bus contact details to help you plan where you overnight.*

0km Bujaraloz. From the church follow C. Santa Ana. Turn right onto C. San Agustin which joins C. Alta and continues straight on out of the village on an asphalt track that soon becomes an earthen track. Continue parallel to the N-II.

4.4km/4.4km Cross the N-II. ATTENTION. Cross the main road with great care. Continue on a track still parallel to the N-II.

2.1km/6.5km Chapel of San Jorge. The chapel is not far off route, to the left. Continue on the same track parallel to the main road, ignoring all left turns.

2.7km/9.2km El Ciervo. The route passes to the rear of this wayside inn and gas station continuing parallel to the main road.

8.3km/17.5km Road to Gelsa. Turn left onto this minor road gently downhill towards Gelsa.

1.5km/19km Track to Venta de Santa Lucia. Take the first farm track to the right between worked fields. Climb gently back towards the N-II past more farmed fields and ridges of scrub.

1.7km/20.7km Venta de Santa Lucía. Pass the front of this roadside inn and turn left to pick up a track at the end of the car park, leaving the main road behind. After 200m fork right to continue on the main track.

1.6km/22.3km Crossroads by a Building. Keep straight where the tracks cross by a small building and a watering trough to your left.

2.4km/24.7km Fork. Choose the left option, straight on and round a gentle bend to the left.

1.1km/25.8km Double Bend Fork. Turn to the right as the track divides very sharply to each side.

1.8km/27.6km Fork. Continue straight on choosing the left option and in 250m pass three identical structures by a watering trough.

1.1km/28.7km Fork at Corral del Gros. At a large enclosure for farm animals to your right, continue straight on by the right hand option. After 400m choose the left fork and follow the main track downhill until you reach the N-II main road.

2.9km/31.6km N-II. Just before the main road, veer left along a track that follows a line of small electricity pylons.

2km/33.6km Pina de Ebro Industrial Park. The Camino veers left onto the asphalt that continues around the outskirts of these industrial units. Take an earthen track to the left, leaving the units behind. Continue until you reach the A-1107 road. Turn left along a parallel track towards Pina del Ebro. Continue along the left hand side of the road taking care when the size of the verge becomes reduced.

3.3km/36.9km Crossroads. At the outskirts of Pina de Ebro veer left at a fork in the road.

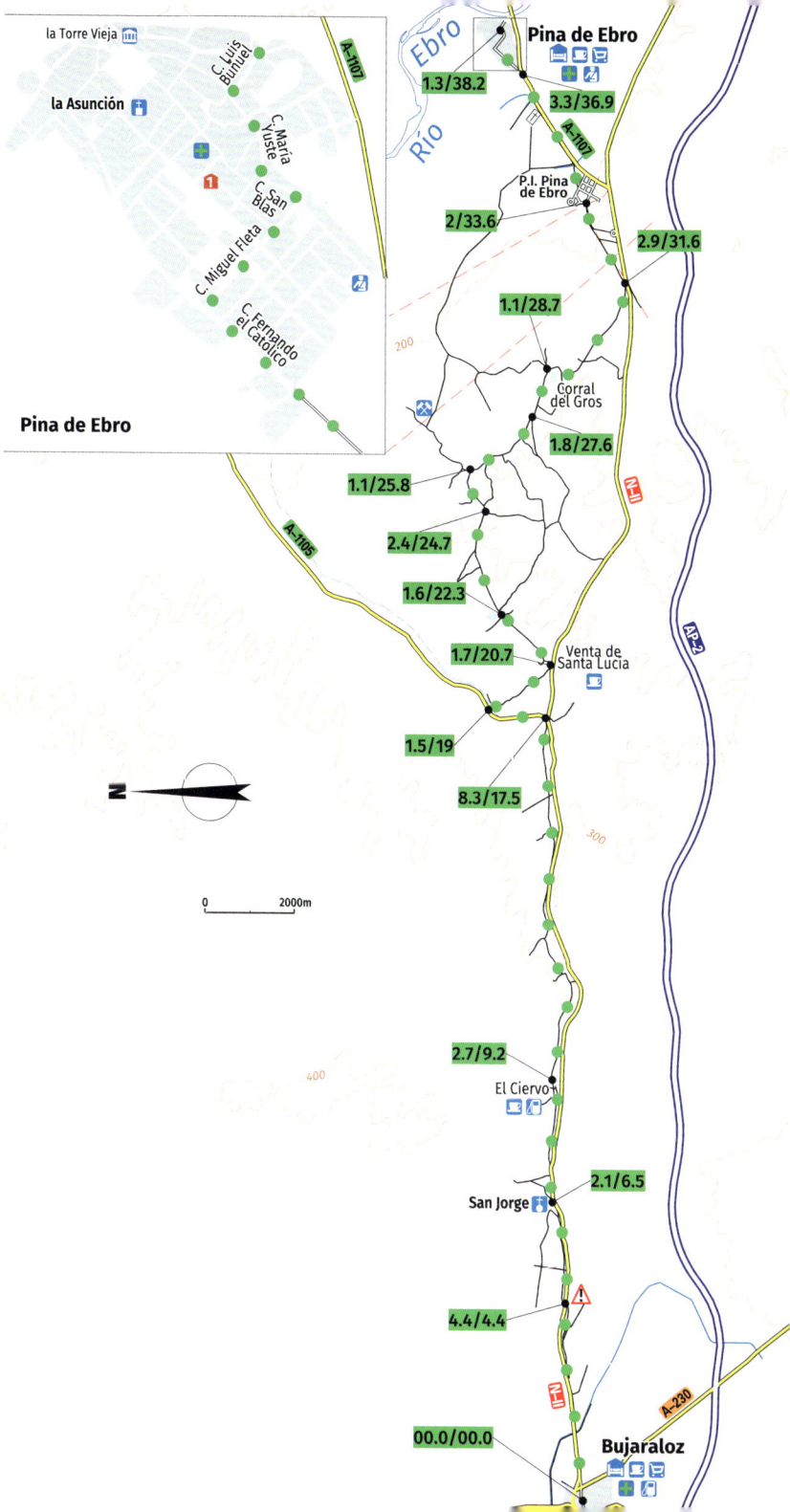

Hieraaetus pennatus

El Ebro (©Darío Martínez Ibáñez)

1.3km/38.2km Pina de Ebro. Continue straight on to enter the village along C. Fernando el Católico. Turn right into C. Miguel Fleta and continue to its end reaching a small park on the right. Now turn left along C. San Blas and at the end of this street turn right along the narrow C. María Ruste taking you through the center of the village to the Pl. de España.

Pina de Ebro - pop. 2400. A village of the Ribera Baja del Ebro area.

■ **Camino towards Logroño - p. 174**

Pina de Ebro
🔴 **Los Valles**
Tel. 976 165 553

Agreda Bus
www.agredabus.es
Tel. 976 300 080

Bujaraloz
Taxis Monegros
Tel. 657 164 472
Taxi de Osera de Ebro
Tel. 679 49 29 04

 Venta de Santa Lucía. A centuries-old watering hole and wayside inn.
Church of la Asunción, Pina de Ebro. C14th Mudéjar style church enlarged in the second half of the C18th.

La Torre Vieja, Pina de Ebro. A Baroque tower; the only remaining feature of the church of Santa Maria la Mayor.

TORTOSA - LOGROÑO

From the humid Mediterranean coastal plain, surrounded by citrus orchards and rice paddies, this section passes over the compact Serra de Pandols and the vineyards of 'Terra Alta' before entering the vast Ebro valley. The mesmerising riverside journey provides scant shade as it winds its way to Logroño before joining the Camino Frances. The route traverses areas of irrigated agricultural production and complex canal systems, all supplied by the headwaters that gather on the southern slopes of the Pyrenees. Today, as in ancient times, Spain's longest river brings life to the cities and farms throughout the interior and the Eastern seaboard.

This historic pilgrim trail to Santiago first became popular in the C12th. 'The Camino del Ebro', was generally chosen by pilgrims from territories in the Mediterranean that belonged to the Crown of Aragón (Sicily, Sardinia, Naples, Athens) or from its overseas trading centres. Disembarking at medieval ports on the river delta (Port Fangós, el Grau or els Alfacs), pilgrims would arrive at the Cathedral city of Tortosa by small boat. They could then proceed either by boat (as the Ebro was navigable to Zaragoza in medieval times), or on foot along its banks. During some periods this Camino suffered from banditry leading the bishopric of Tortosa and its city authorities to subsidise Pilgrims on their way to Santiago and maintain the roads ahead.

This site of Our Lady of the Pillar Basilica in Zaragoza has its origins in antiquity and according to Catholic tradition marks the first Marian apparition. It states that the Virgin Mary appeared atop a pillar to James the Apostle on this spot in 40 CE during his challenging journey through the Iberian peninsula. She encouraged his endeavours and instructed him and his followers to build a church in her honour. In 1456 Pope Callixtus III granted indulgences for visitors to the shrine where today the diminutive image of the Virgin stands atop a column of jasper. The site has attracted pilgrims in its own right for centuries and continues to be a popular pilgrimage destination.

Zaragoza - The capital city of Aragón lies in the centre of a vast arid depression, where the fertile alluvial plains of the Huerva, Gállego and Ebro rivers meet. The site of the important Iberian town of *Salduba* later became the Roman colony of *Caesaraugusta*, founded by the Empe-

Monasterio de Rueda (©Darío Martínez Ibáñez)

El Ebro (©Darío Martínez Ibáñez)

ror Augustus. Many archaeological remains from this important military and commercial centre can still be seen today. The city flourished as an international and cosmopolitan centre of trade under Moorish rule from around 714. *Saraqusta* rose to splendour from 1018 as the capital of a large and powerful Taifa, whose dominion extended all the way to Tortosa and the Ebro delta. The spectacular Aljafería was built as the royal palace and also housed the important polymath Avempace.

King Alfonso I of Aragón took the city in 1118 making it his new capital. Subsequent Aragonese kings were crowned in the Cathedral 'La Seo', formerly the site of the main mosque. This, along with the churches of La Magdalena, San Gil, San Pablo and San Miguel, form a nucleus of Aragonese Mudejar architecture, often with their towers built around former minarets. The magnificent C16th 'Lonja' was built as the trading exchange in Renaissance 'Plateresque' style. Along with the building of aristocratic palaces and founding of the university it reflected the city's growing importance and wealth at that time.

The immense C17th Basilica del Pilar with its cupolas and towers dominates the horizon from miles around. Today the Basilica and its surrounds are the focus of a national holiday and celebration of the feast of Our Lady of the Pillar, patron saint of Spain, on October 12. Today Zaragoza is a modern vibrant place that accounts for over half of Aragón's population and is Spain's fifth largest city. Industrialisation in the C20th has maintained the city's importance as an economic hub.

Mudejar architecture - Deriving from a fusion of Romanesque, Gothic and Arabic elements, the structural and decorative motifs in brick and stucco were inherited from Al Andalus craftsmen and became popular with the Christian conquerors. The style was employed here from the C12th-C17th by Mudejar artisans, Muslims who remained in Christian territories without initially abandoning their religion. The unique Mudejar architecture of Aragón is recognised by Unesco and can be found along the Way from Zaragoza to the churches of the towns and villages further west.

1. TORTOSA - ESTACIÓ DE BENIFALLET: 22.7KM

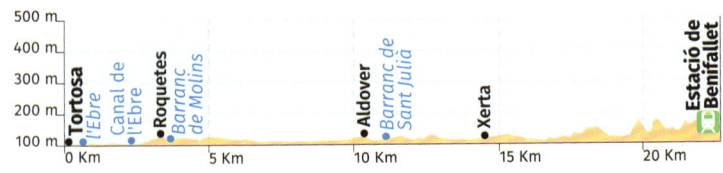

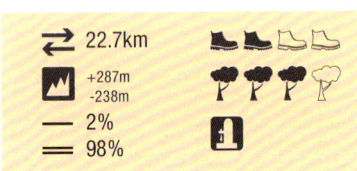

- 22.7km
- +287m / -238m
- 2%
- 98%

The Val de Zafán railway line has been turned into a 'Via Verde' bicycle track that follows the right bank of the river Ebro. Citrus orchards, vegetable plots, farm houses and old defensive towers as well as some small towns line this pleasant and mostly flat route. The long distance walking route along the Ebro, the GR 99, is also followed, but it ducks in and out from here to Logroño, sometimes to be followed, other times to be avoided.

Observations: Some of the route is shared by vehicles. A torch will be useful in the longer tunnels.

0km Tortosa Cathedral. The Camino heads downstream along the river to cross by the iron Pont Roig or 'Red Bridge'.

0.7km/0.7km Pont Roig. Upon reaching the far side of the Ebro the asphalt Via Verde track begins. It crosses through an industrial park and passes small vegetable farm plots. When you meet the TV-3421 road, keep straight on along a street to enter Roquetes.

3km/3.7km Junction. At the far end of the village, turn left for a few metres before turning right, downhill to cross a bridge over the Barranc dels Molins.

0.8km/4.5km Picnic Area. The cycle track is interrupted here as you descend and cross a country lane. Further on, pass under the C-12 main road. To the left the Torre d'en Corder tower stands out. The way continues between a canal and the C-12.

5.8km/10.3km Aldover Old Station. Situated at the entrance to a village which is crossed by the Via Verde. 500m later leave the old railway line and turn left along a track towards the C-12.

0.9km/11.2km C-12 Underpass. ATTENTION. To avoid crossing this busy road you leave the Via Verde and follow a track to the left, down and under the C-12. Then turn right to reach the far side of the road. The Camino follows the verge for a few metres before returning to the former line of the railway.

2.1km/13.3km Detour. The Via Verde is blocked by a privately owned farm. Leave the former railway line by a track to the left which then passes under the line and the C-12. Turn left onto a country lane towards Xerta. At the entrance to the village fork right to continue parallel to the Canal del Ebro. In 350m take a street to the left to the Pl. Major and the church of l'Assumpció.

1.1km/14.4km Xerta. Turn right along C. Santa Anna then left by C. Santa Quitèria. Continue straight on by C. Calvari and then Av. de l'Estació. At the former Xerta railway station turn right to rejoin the Via Verde.

Tortosa (©PT Diputació de Tarragona)

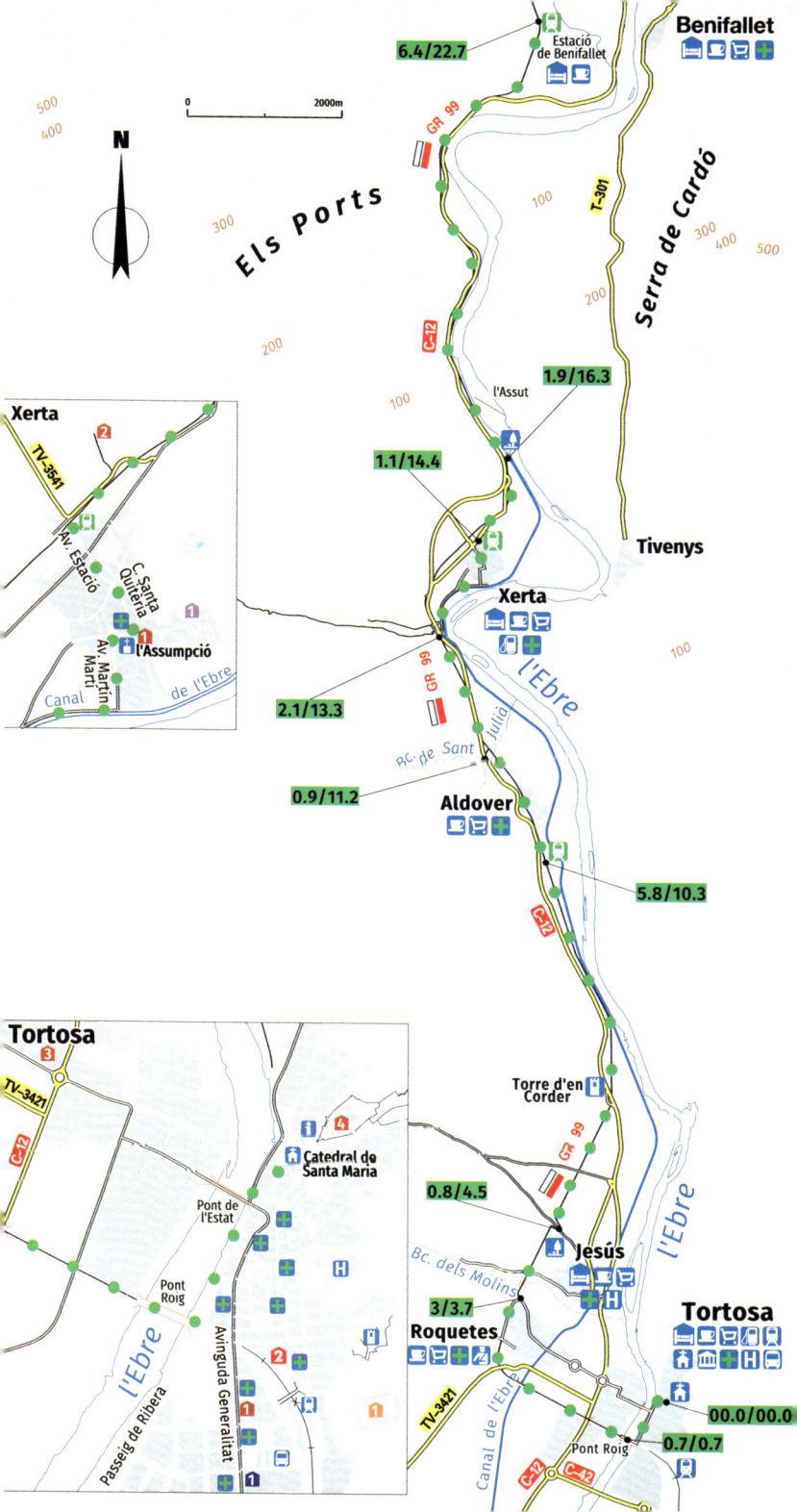

Tortosa (©PT Diputació de Tarragona)

Tortosa
- **Alberg del Seminari** ◌
  Tel. 977 44 02 00
- **Hostal Virgínia** ◌◌
  Tel. 977 444 186
- **Hotel Tortosa Parc** ◌◌
  Tel. 977 446 112
- **Hotel Berenguer IV** ◌◌
  Tel. 977 449 580
- **Hotel Corona
  de Tortosa** ◌◌
  Tel. 977 580 433
- **El Parador
  de Tortosa** ◌◌◌
  Tel. 977 444 450

Jesús
- **Alberg de Joventut
  Enric d'Osso i Casa
  d'Espiritualitat** ◌
  Tel. 977 500 786

Xerta
- **Alberg Assut** ◌
  Tel. 678 67 67 67
- **Hotel Casa
  Ceremines** ◌◌◌
  Tel. 977 473 664
       609 155 077
- **Hotel
  Villa Retiro** ◌◌◌
  Tel. 977 473 003

Benifallet
- **Estació
  de Benifallet** ◌◌
  Tel. 977 094 185
- **Hotel Pep** ◌
  Tel. 977 462 200
- **Casa Puntes** ◌◌◌
  Tel. 610 367 024

1.9km/16.3km Ebro Navigation Channel. At a picnic area follow the river with the man-made water channels closeby (see historic note).

6.4km/22.7km Benifallet Station. The Via Verde continues by way of several long tunnels and many viaducts. It turns away from the river Ebro, entering a wooded landscape and the end of the stage.

Tortosa - pob. 33.000. Capital of the Baix Ebre. Historians believe that this was the site of Hibera (ancient capital of the Ilervacones, an Iberian tribe), later renamed *Dertosa* by the Romans. The area was conquered by the Moors in 714. Their legacy includes the impressive 'Suda' castle that sits above Tortosa. The Christian arrival in 1148 oversaw a flowering of the local economy that reached its zenith during the Renaissance, with many of the existing palaces and monuments dating from this period.

Benifallet - pop. 700. A village of the Baix Ebre. Situated on the far banks of the Ebro, the river was crossed by a ferry before the modern Llaguters bridge was built.

Xerta (©Juan Carlos Borrego Pérez)

🏛 **Tortosa Cathedral.** Dedicated to Santa María, this Gothic style temple was begun in 1347 on the site of a Romanesque church, which in turn was situated on the former mosque. According to recent archaeological digs this was once the site of the Roman forum. The current Baroque façade was completed in 1757.

La Suda, Tortosa. A castle of Roman origin located on a promontory that overlooks the city. Used by both Moors and Christians, the current fortification dates from the reign of the caliph Abderramán III.

L'Escorxador. Originally the city slaughterhouse, this late C19th Modernist building now houses a museum displaying the history of Tortosa and the Ebro area.

Torre d'en Corder, Tortosa. A square C12th watchtower, 20m in height.

Xerta Church. C14th. Built with a limnimeter on the façade that has recorded each flood of the nearby Ebro since 1617.

The Assut and River Ebro Canal Locks. A diagonal weir built by the Moors (and extended laterally from C12-14th under Christian rule) to divert water from the Ebro to create hydraulic power and supply mills and irrigation channels. C19th canal and locks facilitate the movement of boats upstream.

2. ESTACIÓ DE BENIFALLET - BATEA: 31KM

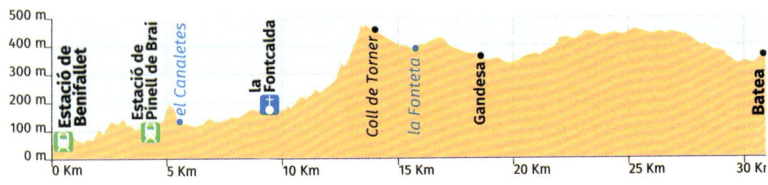

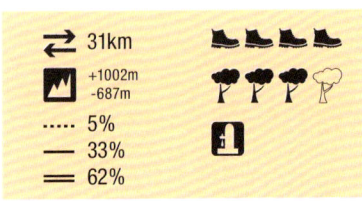

- 31km
- +1002m / -687m
- ····· 5%
- ——— 33%
- ═══ 62%

The river Ebro is left behind for a few stages as the Camino cuts across the Sierra de Pàndols towards the 'Terra Alta' area, a plateau well known for its wine production. This stage contains the longest climb of the Camino del Ebro, but the pilgrim is rewarded by the attractive landscape of extremes; from the solitude of the wild mountain slopes, to the peacefulness of the meticulously attended vineyards.

Observations: Carry a torch for the longer tunnels of the Via Verde.

0km Benifallet Station. Follow the Via Verde through tunnels and over viaducts that follow the course of the rio Canaletes.

4.5km/4.5km Pinell de Brai Station. A former railway stop, sadly now in ruins.

3.4km/7.9km Blocked Tunnel. Follow a parallel earthen track to the right to avoid this obstacle before returning to the former railway line.

1.3Km/9.2km Wooden Bridge. The Camino leaves the Via Verde behind. Follow the red and white markings of the GR 171 on an earth track downhill to cross the rio Canaletes by a footbridge.

0.2km/9.4km La Fontcalda. Turn left along a riverside path with a handrail, from which the waterfalls of the river can be admired.

0.7km/10.1km Vall del Frare. After passing a house, take a dirt track to the right, leaving the river behind, to start a long climb up a narrow valley through olive and almond groves. After 1km of steep inclines, continue on the well made track, ignoring the GR 171 that heads off to the right following a path. Further on, to the right hand side, are the Joan Batista Manyà viewpoint and a curious geological formation in the shape of a monk that gives its name to this valley.

3.7km/13.8km Coll d'en Torner. The highest point of the day; as the way joins an asphalt track and turns left.

1.8km/15.6km La Fonteta. Just before reaching this spring and the C-43 road, turn left uphill on a path. It quickly joins a wider track where you turn right, climbing along a pine crested ridge, parallel to the C-43.

1.1km/16.7km Junction. Upon reaching an earthen track, turn left past a vineyard. In 250m, ignore a track to the left by a water deposit and keep straight on, following the main track towards warehouses on the outskirts of Gandesa.

1.7km/18.4km Gandesa. At the C-43 main road, veer left until you reach the Town Hall square. Turn left along C. Miravet to the church of L'Assumpció. Turn right along C. Major on through Pl. del Comerç, reaching Pl. de la Farola, where you veer left along Av. Aragó on the N-240 road.

0.3km/18.7km Bridge. After 300m leave the main road to go downhill and swing right to go under the main road bridge. In a few metres at a junction, turn left along the asphalted Camí Vell de Batea. Continue straight on by this country lane ignoring all turnings as you climb gently through vineyards.

4.3km/23km Junction of Caminos. Ignore a signed alternative to the right. Continue straight on the asphalt lane, over a plateau of vineyards with some small areas of woodland. At every junction keep straight on along the asphalt. The lane descends to reach the C-221 road where you turn right, following the verge.

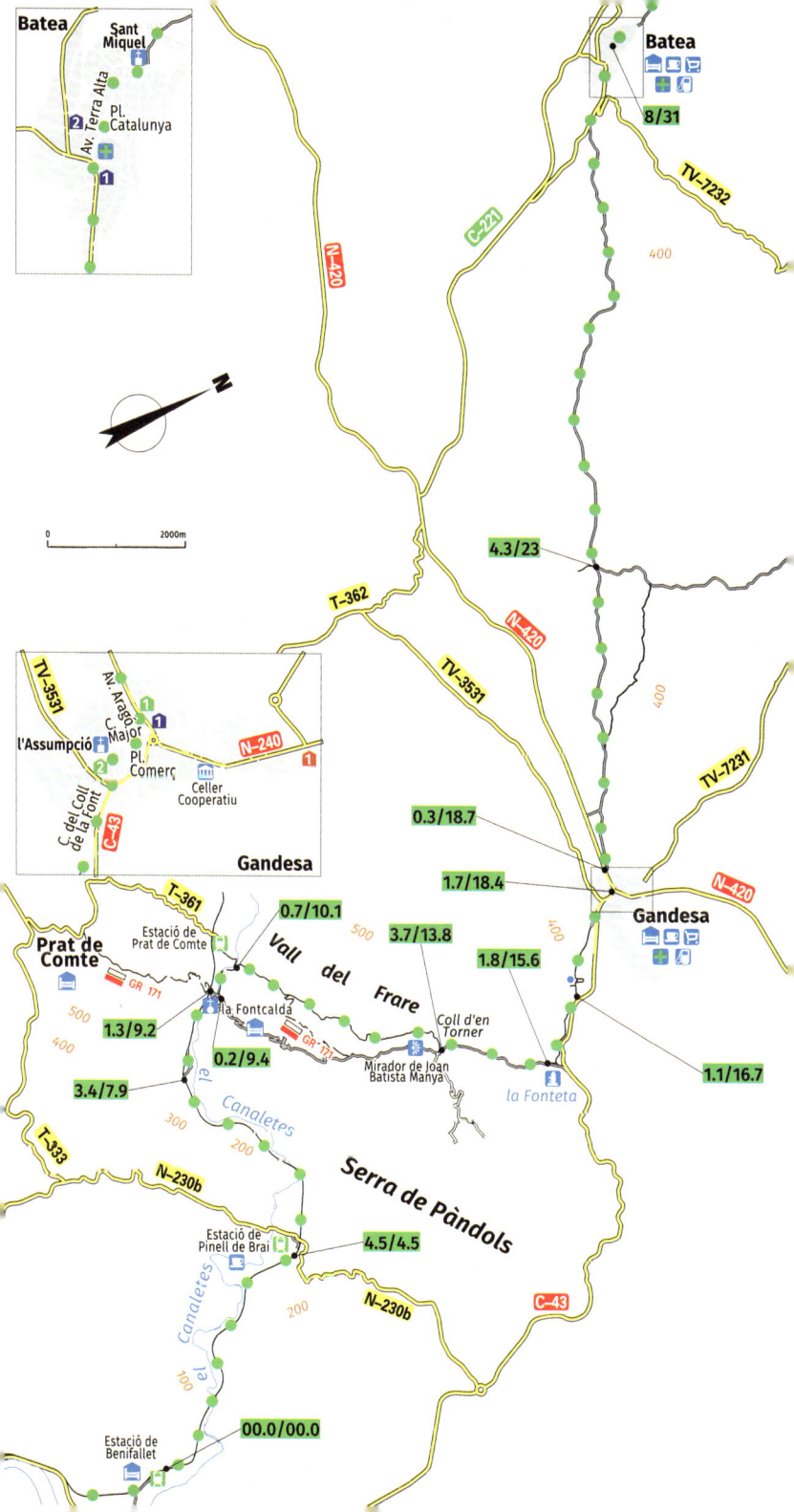

La Fontcalda (©PT Diputació de Tarragona)

8km/31km Batea. Continue straight on to Pl. Catalunya, then along C. Major to the church.
Gandesa - pop. 3000. Capital of the Terra Alta. A village with historical noblemen's houses. There is also a Study Centre dedicated to the Battle of the Ebro.
Batea - pop. 2000. A village with a long history of winemaking. It has an attractive array of traditional architecture.

Prat de Comte
Ca l'Àngels
Tel. 977 42 83 09
Gandesa
Ca Tibària
Tel. 977 42 00 89

Casa dels Abeuradors
Tel. 649 905 252
Fonda Serres
Tel. 977 42 05 12
Hotel Piqué
Tel. 977 42 00 68

Batea
Hostal de l'Anton
Tel. 977 43 00 10
Rural
Celler Piñol
Tel. 977 43 05 05

La Fontcalda, Prat de Comte. The Fontcalda Sanctuary has a chapel that attracts a devoted following in the Terra Alta area. It owes its name to the nearby hot water springs.
Celler Cooperatiu, Gandesa. A catalan Modernism style winemaking cooperative. It is considered one of the 'Cathedrals of Wine' and in 2007 was voted one of the Seven Wonders of Catalonia.
Church of l'Assumpció, Gandesa. Built during the transition between Romanesque and Gothic styles. It has a noteworthy doorway and a 40m tall belltower.
Church of Sant Miquel, Batea. Very large construction of the C18th.
Batea's Historic Centre. Colonnades and arches abound in the old centre of this pretty stone built village. The calle Major, town hall and the surrounding streets conceal attractive nooks, doorways and chapels.

3. Batea - Fabara: 17.7km

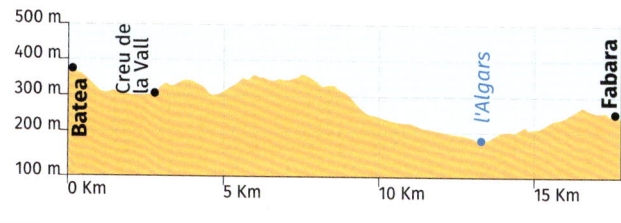

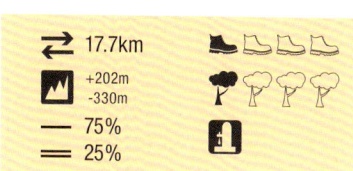

The transition from the Terra Alta in Catalonia to the Mataraña district of Aragón is a delightful stretch of mostly earthen tracks through olive and almond groves, and well tended vineyards. The river Algars winds its way through this peaceful landscape.

Observations: At the date of publishing there was no accommodation in Fabara.

0km Batea. From Sant Miquel church turn right to descend on C. del Torelló. Turn left along C.del Molí to leave the village on a country lane.

1.4km/1.4Km Roundabout. Turn right towards Nonaspe.

1.3km/2.7km Creu de la Vall. Turn left by this covered cross that marks the beginning of the Vall Bona track. Climb up the main track ignoring side turns into vineyards.

2km/4.7km Three Way Junction. Take the right hand track and after 400m turn left past an olive grove. In 50m fork right to start a climb uphill through pine woods. After 900m the way levels out to continue straight on.

2.1km/6.8km Fork by a Wood. Veer right to stay on the high ground. After 500m fork right again to continue by the main track between woods and olive groves.

1.6km/8.4km Junction by Camino Board. Turn right by a sunbleached route info panel that marks your entry into Aragón. After 400m, turn sharply left on an earthen track, descending through a wooded valley that soon opens out. Follow the main track downhill between olive groves on the right and woods on the left ignoring all minor turnings until you reach the river Algars.

4.8km/13.2km Río Algars Bridge. Cross the river and follow the main track (ignoring all turnings), gently uphill through a landscape of olive and almond groves and small farms. Continue straight on when the route becomes asphalt. On the outskirts of Fabara, turn right at a triangular little park. At the end of this street turn left and in 50m fork right along C. Aragón. Take the third street on the right, C. Frare, and follow it to the Pl. de España and the town hall.

4.5km/17.7km Fabara.

Fabara de Mataraña - pop. 1100. A village of the Bajo Aragón - Caspe area.

Batea (©Ajuntament de Batea)

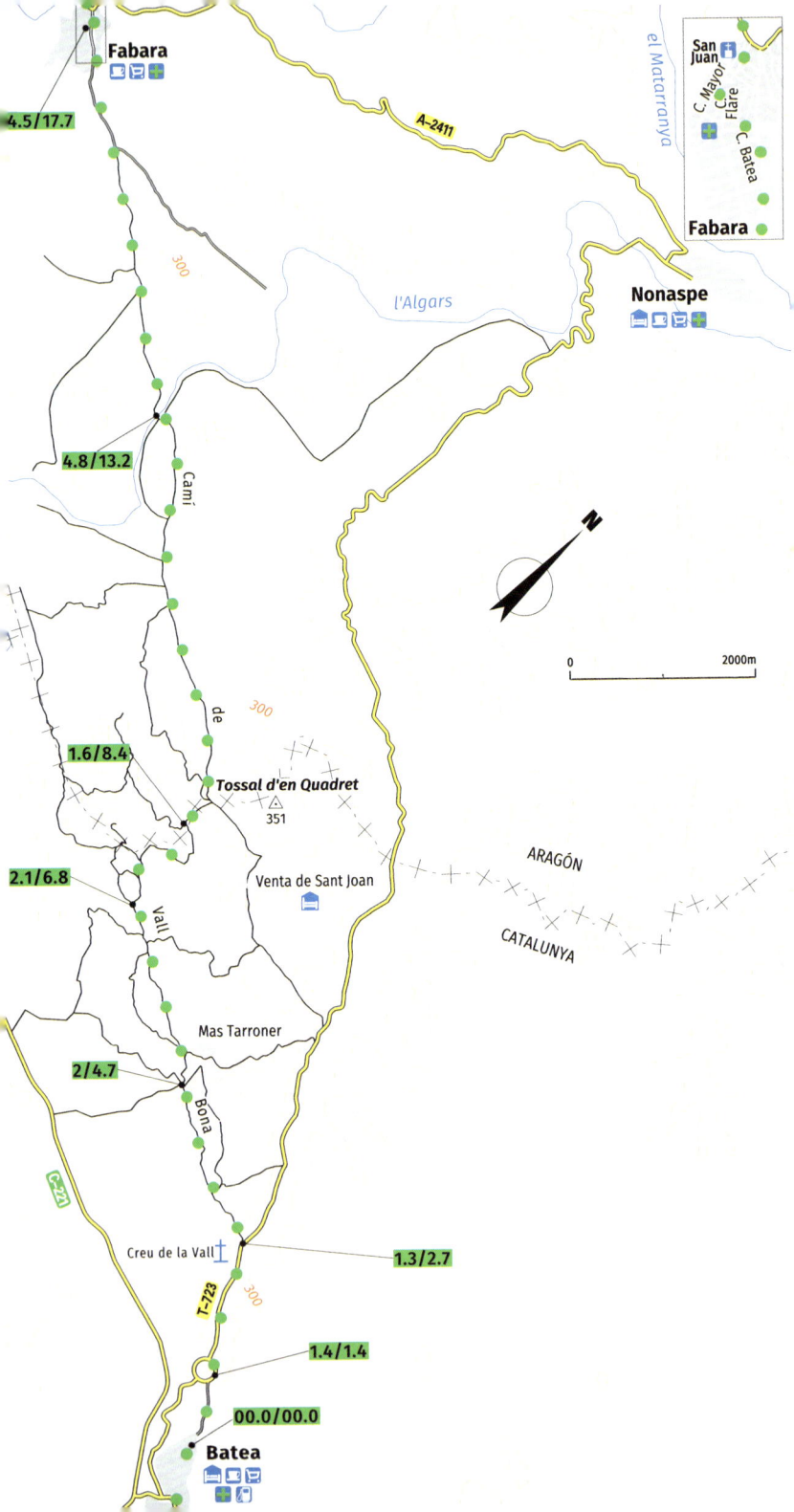

Creu de la Vall (©Ajuntament de Batea)

Batea
🛏 **Venta de Sant Joan** 💰💰
Tel. 649 644 724

Nonaspe
🛏 **Albergue Municipal Nonaspe** 💰
Tel. 976 63 60 01

🛏 **La Presó de Nonasp** 💰
Tel. 665 979 672
Batea
Taxis Lluís Busom Llop
Tel. 690 751 778

Church of Sant Joan Baptista, Fabara. C15th Gothic. Topped by battlements that give the impression of a fortified church.

Roman Mausoleum, Fabara. One of the finest preserved C2nd tombs of its kind in Spain.

4. Fabara - Caspe: 21.6km

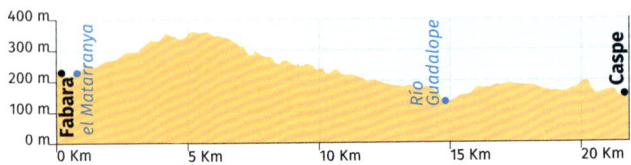

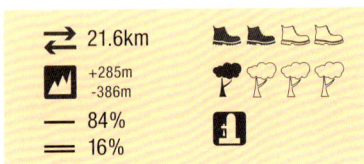

A stage that crosses the Caspe Sierra between the rivers Matarranya and Guadalope. Clumps of pines and scrub vegetation populate a dry and harsh landscape that is dotted with olive and almond groves. The descent through the Fabara valley travels through terraces of arable fields and fruit orchards.

0km Fabara. From the Pl. España, continue to the left of the town hall toward the church of Sant Joan Baptista. Pass to the right of the church and descend steps and a ramp to the right. Turn left along the second street opening, C. Mesón. At the end of this street turn left and keep straight on to leave the village and cross the bridge over the river Matarranya.

0.9/0.9km Track to Left. 250m after the bridge, at the first bend in the road, climb a track on the left. Soon after passing a quarry the Camino reaches a road.

0.7km/1.6km A-1411. ATTENTION. Cross the road and continue straight on by an earthen track. Follow the main track uphill between olive and almond groves, interspersed with wild scrub and rocky ground. Ignore all side turns as the way ascends along the crest of a ridge. The track levels out and soon starts to gently descend.

4.8km/6.4km Junction of Tracks. Turn left to drop steeply into the Fabara valley through its terraced fields. Continue downhill following the main track.

7.5km/13.9km A-221. A few metres before the track reaches the main road, turn right along a track that runs parallel to the road. Then follow a path steeply uphill before reaching an old road.

0.7km/14.6km Old Road. Turn right to follow the aging asphalt and cross the river Guadalope by the old bridge. ATTENTION. Upon reaching the A-221 main road, cross straight over to continue along an earthen track. After 300m, near a pine wood, veer right following the main dirt track and ignoring all minor farm tracks. The track approaches the main road and veers left to follow it closely before meeting a side road.

2.5km/17.1km CHE-901. Turn left along the asphalt and after 50m turn right along an earthen track between olive groves. After 500m fork left and continue to a farm. Veer left between farm buildings, then a few metres on at a junction of tracks, keep straight on along a gravel track. Follow the main track passing farms and greenhouses before reaching the A-221 main road.

2.4km/19.5km Cemetery. ATTENTION. Cross the A-221 and turn left. After 100m, take a lane uphill to the right between industrial units and a cemetery. At the end of the industrial area, at a crossroads, continue straight on towards the Torre de Salamanca. The Camino drops gently downhill following the 'Stations of the Cross' (pillars topped by a cross). After 400m veer right on a short dirt track that leads to a square where the first station of the cross is situated. Fork right along C. Cruces and follow it to its end. Turn right and then take the second street to the right, C. San Francisco. In 50m at Pl. Matea, turn right onto C. Hilarza. Keep straight on, passing the chapel of San Roque, then downhill to the Pl. Montserrat, with its chapel and viewing point. Turn left to continue downhill to the Pl. del Compromiso and the Collegiate church.

2.1km/21.6km Colegiata de Caspe.

Caspe - pop. 9500. Capital of Bajo Aragón-Caspe. A town with many historic monuments and setting of the Caspe Compromiso of 1412.

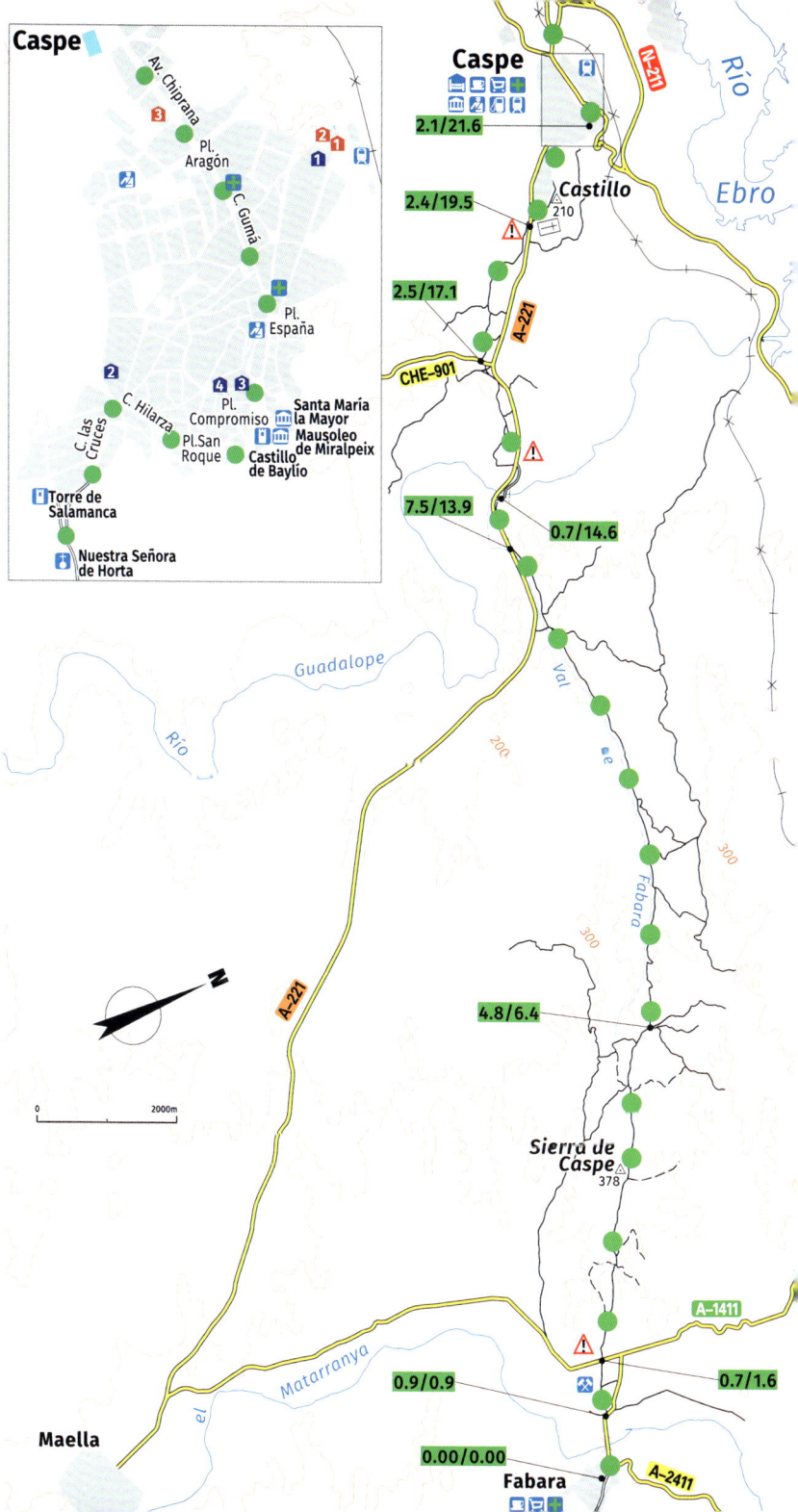

Caspe (©Juan Carlos Borrego Pérez)

Caspe

❶ Pensión Los Jardines
Tel. 976 632 248
❷ Hostal el Surtidor
Tel. 976 639 453
❸ Pensión La Cabaña
Tel. 976 630 678
❹ Pensión Camino Jacobeo del Ebro
Tel. 689 485 122
❶ Hotel Magallón
Tel. 976 630 222
❷ Hotel Mar de Aragón
Tel. 976 639 052
❸ Visit Hotel
Tel. 976 630 055
Taxis
Pertronella Buksar Soponyainé
Tel. 608 622 436

Chapel of Santa María de Horta. Caspe. Romanesque C12-13th. The chapel was originally situated 3kms away, but after suffering damage from floods on the banks of the Mequinenza reservoir, it was dismantled and rebuilt in Caspe.
Baylío Castle, Caspe. Military residence of the Administrator of the Order of St. John of Jerusalem. In 1412 the Caspe Compromise was signed here, electing as successor to the crown of Aragón, Fernando de Trastámara after king Martín I of Aragón had died with no heir.

Collegiate Church of Santa María la Mayor, Caspe. Gothic style. Built over the site of a mosque, it became a collegiate in 1394. The tower is C19th.
The Salamanca Tower, Caspe. Late C19th fort built during the Carlist Wars.
Miralpeix Mausoleum, Caspe. A Roman funereal monument dating back to C2nd-C3rd. Originally sited on the banks of the Ebro, it was moved block by block to Caspe when the river was dammed to create the Mequinenza reservoir.

5. CASPE - ESCATRÓN: 30.5KM

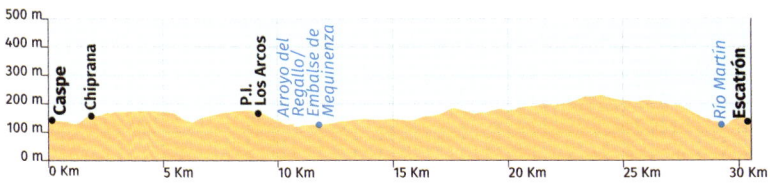

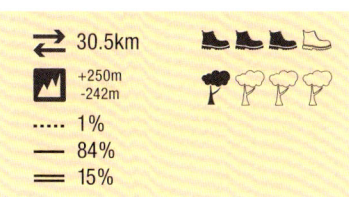

Despite the proximity of the mighty Ebro and its Mequinenza reservoir, this is a very arid stretch of the Camino with little shade.

Observations: Be sure to carry sufficient water. There are no villages or 'cafes' during this stage.

0km Collegiate of Santa María la Mayor. Take a straight line along C. Mayor, then C. Santa Lucía, passing the church of Santa Lucía and onto C. Gumá. At a roundabout, keep straight on along the left hand side of Av. de Chiprana.

1.1km/1.1km Alcañiz Junction. Turn left along the roadside and 250m later, after a roundabout, take an asphalt lane to the right that coincides with GR99 markings. Climb up past a small industrial park and continue straight on.

1.5km/2.6km Tunnel under the N-221. A few metres after the tunnel turn right, following an irrigation channel as you continue uphill.

1.4km/4km Train Tunnel. As the nearby train line exits a tunnel, fork right, gently downhill. Turn left upon meeting an asphalt lane, and after 300m leave the lane and take an earthen track to the right. By an electric pylon, fork to the left and descend on a path which turns into a farm track. After 200m, near a small house fork left and follow the track down to meet a road.

2.8km/6.8km A-221 Crossing. ATTENTION. Cross straight over and take a dirt track to the left, parallel to the A-221. Keep straight on until a minor road. Turn right along it, to a roundabout.

2.2km/9km Roundabout. Turn left following signs to the 'estación F.C.'. 50m before passing under the main road, leave the asphalt to take an earthen track to the right. Descend towards the Ebro river. ATTENTION. At the end of the track, join the A-221 and continue along the right hand verge, reaching a road bridge over the Arroyo de Regallo, a tributary of the Ebro.

2.9km/11.9km Track to Left. ATTENTION: 250m after the bridge, cross the road to take an earthen track to the left. Pass a field of solar panels to meet a junction with an asphalt track. Keep straight on along an earthen track passing through the Saladas de Chiprana, an area of small lagoons. Follow the main track at all junctions (at one of them the GR99 turns off to the right) until you reach a bend near a small hill.

5.1km/17km Junction. Turn right onto a less well used dirt track. Descend to cross over another track and continue gently uphill.

2.3km/19.3km Double Junction. Keep straight on at this crossing of tracks to follow a farm track between small arable fields. After 500m, at a junction under two overhead electricity lines, continue straight on along a pebbled track. Follow this main track ignoring minor turnings to either side until you reach a main road.

3.7km/23km A-221. Turn left to follow a parallel trail on the left hand side of the road until you join a stretch of old road to your left.

4.8km/27.8km A-221 Crossing. ATTENTION. Cross the main road to follow the old road downhill. Pass by the entrance to the cemetery, soon crossing the river Martín and climb towards the village. At the first junction, keep straight on, to the right, to enter the village up Av. Goya.

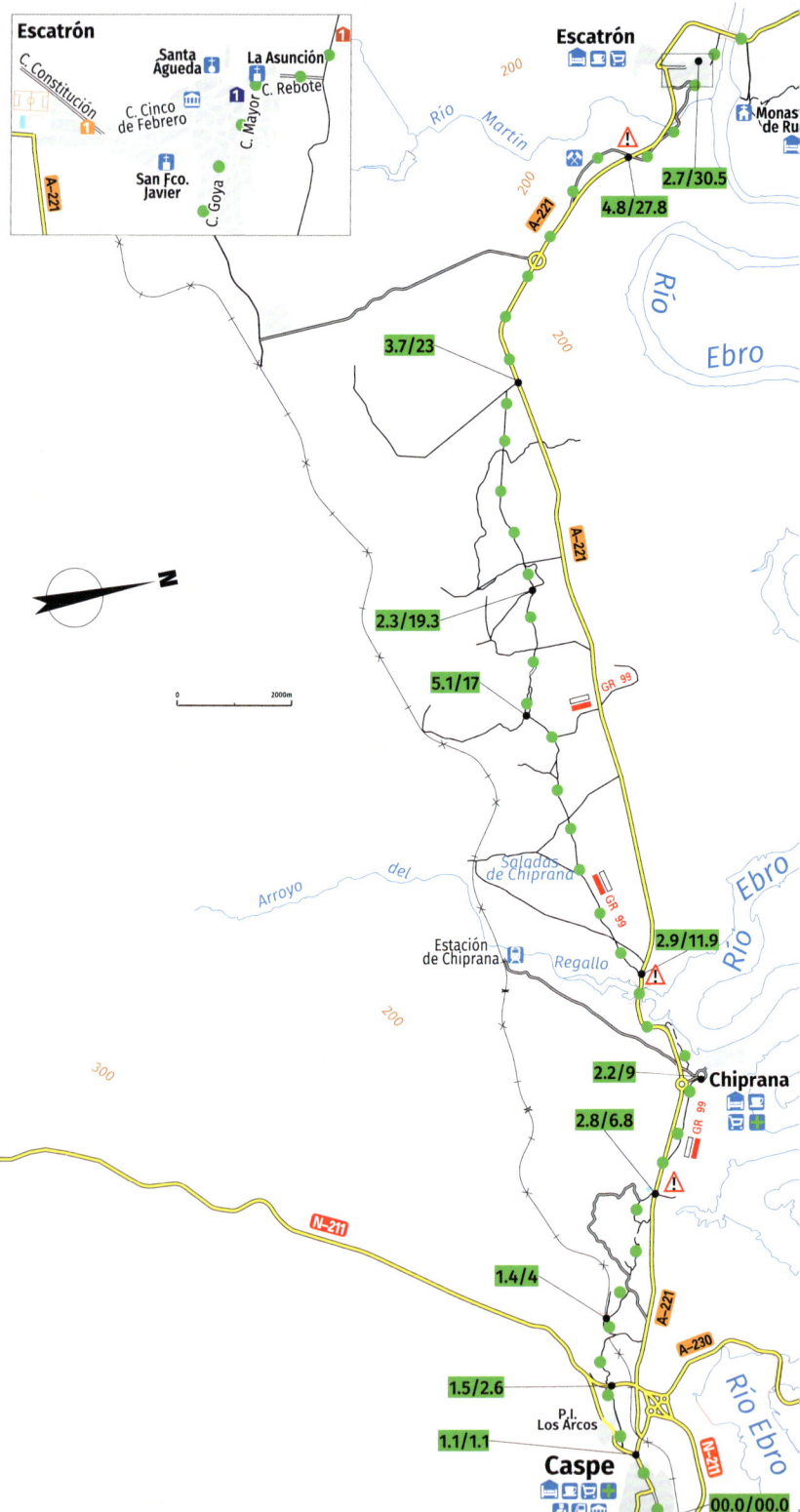

2.7km/30.5km Escatrón. Continue along C. Mayor to its end to find the church of la Asunción.

Escatrón - pop. 1100. A village of the Ribera Baja del Ebro area.

Escatrón (©Bautista Antorán Zabay)

Chiprana
- **Las Saladas**
  Tel. 660 891 346
- **Casa Rural La Curva**
  Tel. 630 463 188

Escatrón
- **Albergue Municipal**
  Tel. 976 17 00 06
- **Pensión Mayor**
  Tel. 976 170 194

- **Hotel El Embarcadero**
  Tel. 976 170 300
- **Hospedería del Monasterio de Rueda**
  Tel. 976 877 930

Church of la Asunción, Escatrón. This Baroque construction has Renaissance style chapels and some Gothic additions. The altarpiece of 1607 was made by maestro Esteban and is the outstanding element of the church.

Chapel of Santa Águeda, Escatrón. C18th large building whose doorway was a gathering point for pilgrims.

6. ESCATRÓN - QUINTO: 35KM

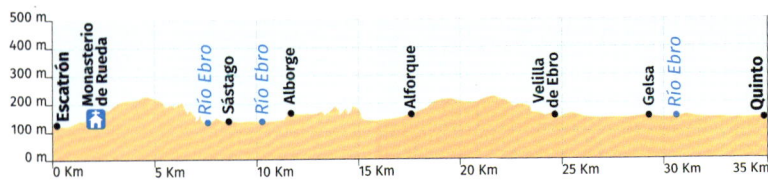

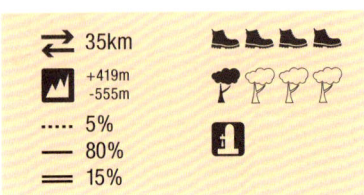

This long stage is broken up by the meanderings and crossings of the Ebro. The irrigated lands of the riverside villages contrast with the arid, arable and scrubland found further away from the fluvial waters.

Observations: Allow a couple of hours if you take the guided tour of the Rueda Monastery.

0km Church of la Asunción. Follow C. Rebote from the rear of the church, to descend towards the river Ebro. Veer left following the banks of the river to the nearby road bridge. Cross the bridge and take the first asphalt lane on the right towards the monastery.

2.1km/2.1km Rueda Monastery. At the entrance of the car park fork left uphill to another carpark. By the entrance to a ruined corral to the left, take a path uphill that passes by the ruins of the Rueda chapel to your right. The path joins an earthen track and the Camino turns left, continuing uphill. After 50m, leave the track to rejoin a path on the right that climbs to join another track. Veer left, climbing through a dry rugged landscape dotted with pine woods. Ignore all minor turnings to continue the ascent to a corral.

2.5km/4.6km Track by Corral. 100m before reaching a modern corral turn to the left, This track begins to descend and reaches the A-2105 road.

1.9km/6.5km Viewpoint of the Ebro Meanderings. Situated at the cross roads of the A-221 and A2105. Cross the A2105 to the right hand edge of the viewpoint. Follow a path down the steep slope to join a track and turn left towards a bridge over the Ebro. After crossing the bridge and a short straight stretch of road the Camino enters Sástago.

1.3km/7.8km Sástago. Keep straight on along Av. de Aragón. At the end of this street turn left along an earthen track parallel to the river until you reach the CV-411 road.

2.3km/10.1km Bridge. Turn right to cross the Ebro and then immediately turn left along an asphalt lane which soon becomes an earthen track. Take the second track on the left to enter Alborge.

1.4km/11.5km Alborge Church. Skirt around the church to its square and take C. Mayor to the left. Follow this narrow street in a straight line to leave the village. At a crossroads turn left towards Alforque on the VP-017A minor road. After 200m ignore a track to the right with a Camino variant to Velilla. Continue along the country lane towards Alforque for a good while until you reach the banks of the Ebro.

3.5km/15km Path to the Left. Just as the asphalt peels away from the river, and before the first farm field, take a path to the left that follows the river bank. It soon turns into a farm track. Take the first track to the right, leaving the river behind and continue towards a roundabout on the outskirts of a village.

2.5km/17.5km Alforque Roundabout. Continue straight ahead on a minor road towards Gelsa.

2.8km/20.3km Track to the Left. Look out for yellow arrows on the road surface indicating this turn off. Continue gently uphill on a farm track across an area of arable fields. After 500m ignore a track to the right, and at the next crossing of tracks, keep straight on. After 400m take the next track to the right, downhill through an area of rough scrubland.

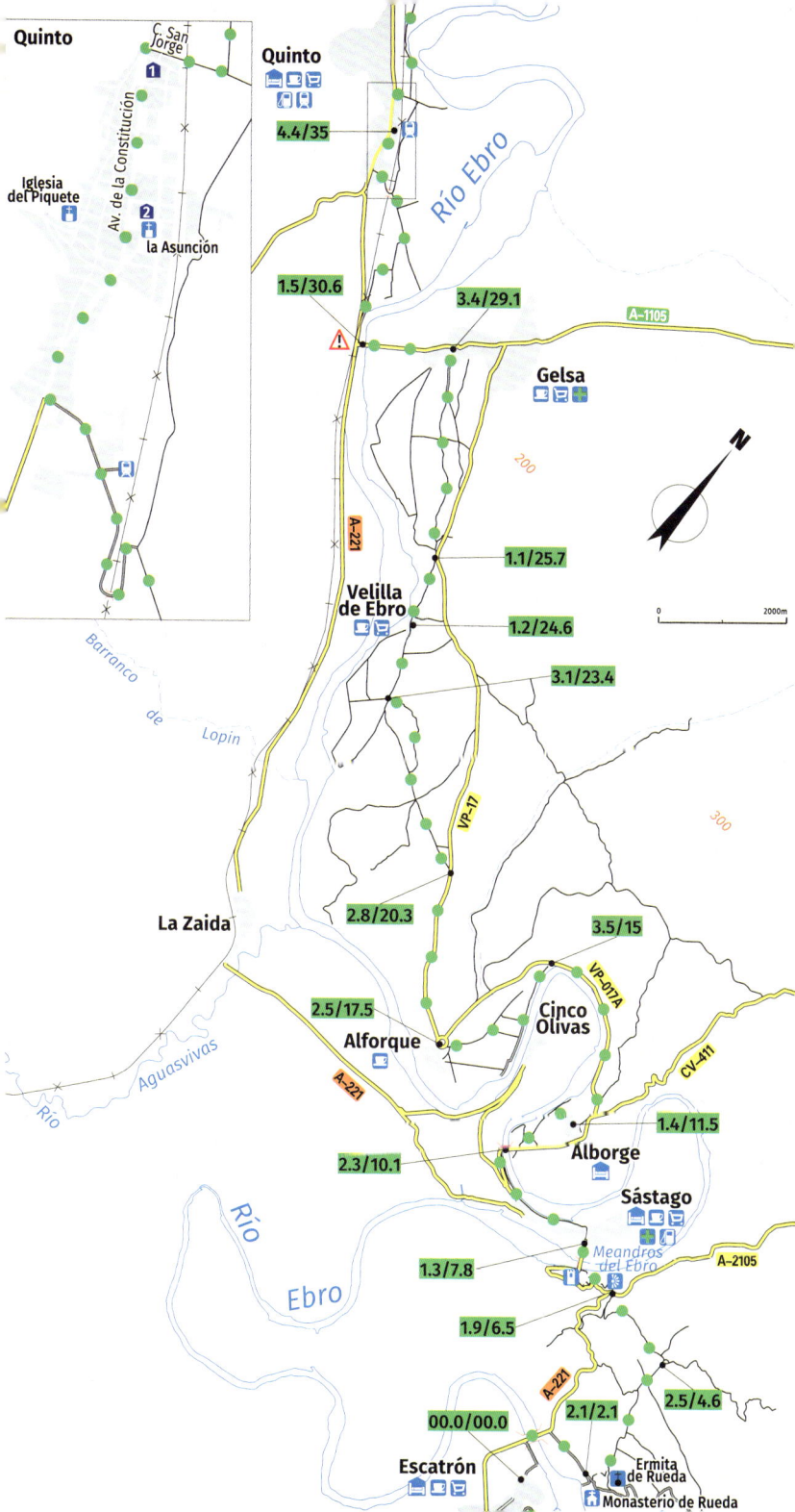

Real Monasterio de Rueda (©Bautista Antorán Zabay)

3.1km/23.4km Junction. At the first junction, by irrigated fields, turn right.

1.2km/24.6km Velilla. From the Pl. de la Iglesia, continue straight along a narrow street. At its end, turn left downhill towards a small park. Turn right to leave the village on an asphalt lane.

1.1km/25.7km Track to the Left. The track splits just before reaching a road. Here take a farm track to the left. After 150m continue straight on and then at the next junction, turn left. Follow an irrigation channel between farm fields. Pass a farm on the right, then go straight ahead through a junction, on towards Gelsa Village.

3.4km/29.1km Gelsa. From the church of San Pedro, turn left gently downhill on C. Cortes de Aragón and the Carretera del Puente, to leave the village. At a roundabout continue straight on past a gas station. ATTENTION. Continue along the narrow verge of the A-1105 road. Cross the bridge over the Ebro using the right hand narrow verge.

1.5km/30.6km Junction. ATTENTION. Turn right to follow the roadside for a few metres then take great care to cross the road and follow an earthen track between the road and the railway line. Cross under the road to continue between the river Ebro and the railway. Leaving firstly, the river and then the railway behind, the farm track veers to the right. At the next junction between fields, turn left and soon after a house turn left again. At the next crossing of tracks turn left to cross a bridge over the railway line. Pass by the railway station and continue straight on to reach the N-232 main road on the edge of the town of Quinto. Turn right to reach the town centre.

4.4km/35km Quinto.

Quinto - pop. 2000. A village of la Ribera Baja del Ebro.

Sástago
Hostal Monasterio de Rueda ⊜⊜
Tel. 976 178 287

Hospedería del Monasterio de Rueda ⊜⊜⊜
Tel. 976 877 930

Alborge
Casa de los Diezmos ⊜
Tel. 628 233 777

Quinto
❶ Hostal Rioja ⊜
Tel. 976 177 218
❷ Pensión Plaza ⊜
Tel. 976 177 248

Royal Monastery of Nuestra Señora de Rueda, Sástago. A former Cistercian monastery, restored during the C20th thanks to the persistence of the local community and now converted into a hotel. It has a Gothic cloister, a slim mudéjar tower and a huge (16m diameter) working water wheel (rueda), hence its name. It is recommended you make a reservation should you wish to take a guided tour. 974 35 51 19 visitasrueda@aragon.es

Hydroelectric Station, Sástago. C20th Modernistl style with decorated brickwork.
Celsa Roman Museum, Velilla de Ebro. Features the nearby archaeological dig of a roman settlement.
The former Church of la Asunción, Quinto. C15th. Built with its defence in mind. It has a mudéjar tower. It now houses the Museum of Mummies.

7. Quinto - Fuentes de Ebro: 16.6km

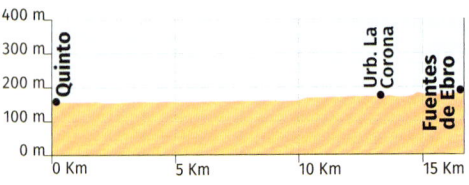

- ⇄ 16.6km
- +39m / -0m
- — 80%
- = 20%

A short and flat stage through fertile irrigated fields. Now and again the slow lazy waters of the Ebro meander into view. The Camino from Tàrrega joins us half way through the route.

0km Quinto Town Hall. Leave the village on the Av. Constitución towards Zaragoza. On the outskirts, opposite the Los Baños de Quinto park, turn right towards the Embarcadero de Quinto and cross a bridge over the railway. At the next junction turn left along an asphalt lane that also carries the GR 99 walking route. At the end of the straight stretch turn left. Without crossing the train line continue straight on, to a fork.

1.7km/1.7km Fork to Left. The GR 99 splits off as the Camino continues to the left, closely following the railway line. At the next fork, continue to the left. After 600m there is a crossing of tracks. Keep straight on towards the railway and follow it on dirt tracks for a significant distance without crossing it.

7.4km/9.1km A-1107 Bridge. The Camino from Tarrega and Pino de Ebro joins here (see below). Pass a ruined building and continue under a road bridge to a junction. Turn left uphill to cross a small bridge over a canal and reach the railway line again without crossing it. Continue along a straight stretch parallel to the rails. Pass under a road bridge and continue on next to the railway. At the end of the straight, ignore a turning to an area of modern housing and instead, cross a bridge over the railway line. Now continue with the high speed AVE rail track to your right, then after 200m veer right to pass under this line.

4.2km/13.3km Tunnel under AVE. Leave the train line behind and continue straight along an earthen track passing a gravel pit to your left. Ignore turns to the left and soon continue along an asphalt lane towards the outskirts of Fuentes de Ebro. Enter on C. Río Ebro, then straight, along C. Baño. Turn left into Av. Lorenzo Pardo and continue on C. Ramón y Cajal. Turn right onto C. Mayor to reach the Pl. de la Iglesia.

3.3km/16.6km Fuentes de Ebro Church.

Directions from Pina de Ebro

0km Pina de Ebro. From the Pl. España take a pedestrian passageway to the rear of the old bell tower. By the banks of the Ebro river turn right until the A-1107 road. Turn left to cross a long bridge over the Ebro. ATTENTION.

Nycticorax nycticorax

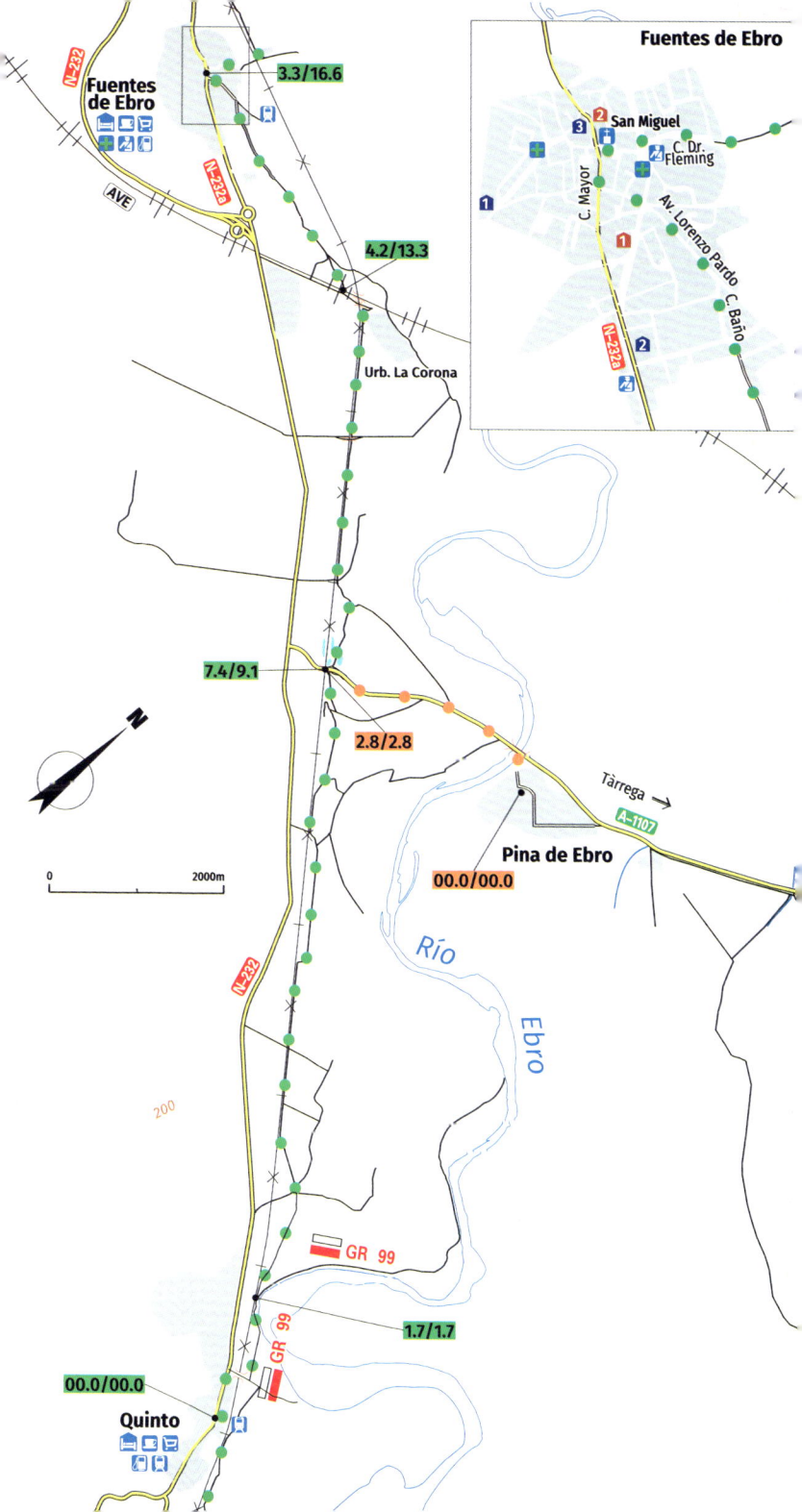

El Ebro (©Darío Martínez Ibáñez)

Follow the verge of the road for a long stretch. Some 200m before the road crosses a railway line, take an earthen track to the left. By a ruined building, turn right along another track and under the road bridge, to follow the railway line.

2.8km/2.8km You have now joined the Ebro Camino to Logroño.
Fuentes de Ebro - pop. 4500. A village of the Comarca Central in the province of Zaragoza.

Fuentes de Ebro
❶ Hotel Texas ⬤
Tel. 976 160 419

❷ Hotel Texas II ⬤
Tel. 976 161 070
　　686 960 753
❶ Hostal El Patio ⬤
Tel. 640 206 149

❷ Hostal Elena ⬤
Tel. 976 160 267
❸ Hostal San Miguel ⬤⬤
Tel. 976 169 071

Church of San Miguel Arcángel, Fuentes de Ebro. C16th. Renaissance with a single nave. The belltower is mid C20th, replacing the original that was destroyed during the Spanish Civil War.

8. FUENTES DE EBRO - ZARAGOZA: 30.8KM

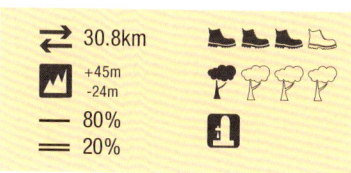

A long but flat stage sees the pilgrim reach Zaragoza, the largest city of the Ebro Camino with a rich array of historic architecture. The route crosses irrigated fields, riverside woodlands and nature reserves rich with birds and wildlife.

0km Fuentes de Ebro Church. Continue along C. Dr. Zamenhof. At a square with the Guardia Civil barracks, follow C. Dr. Fleming to the left. At the end of this street continue straight on, leaving the village to cross the railway line. Immediately turn left along a gravel track parallel to the railway. After 700m, keep straight on to reach a junction where you turn right. Continue straight on by the main track ignoring all turnings.

5.9km/5.9km El Espartal Industrial Park. Cross an irrigation canal and continue straight on along a street with a park on the left. At the end of the industrial units continue along an earth track parallel to another canal. After 500m pass under a motorway and continue to follow the main track. Cross an asphalt lane and continue straight on along an earthen track to pass to the rear side of an urbanisation and the nearby chapel of Nuestra Señora de Zaragoza la Vieja. Upon reaching an asphalt lane turn right and in 250m turn right again towards El Burgo.

7.2km/13.1km El Burgo de Ebro. Enter along C. Ramón y Cajal. At a bus stop, fork right along C. Pl. de Toros that runs into C. Mayor. At the end of this street turn right, then immediately left to continue straight on along a tree-lined street with new houses (C. de las Torrecicas). At its end continue on a flat lane and after a walled tennis court, keep straight on using the middle of three dirt tracks. After 500m, continue straight on, soon walking along the banks of the river Ebro. At the next junction turn right onto an earthen track parallel to the N-232 main road as it broadens into a motorway. The track continues along a viaduct to cross a gulley.

5.1km/18.2km Los Galachos. A nature reserve on the banks of the Ebro with a viewing platform. Continue along the main track passing under a minor road.

3.2km/21.4km Cartuja Baja. A suburb of

La Seo (©Tur. Zaragoza. Agustín Martínez)

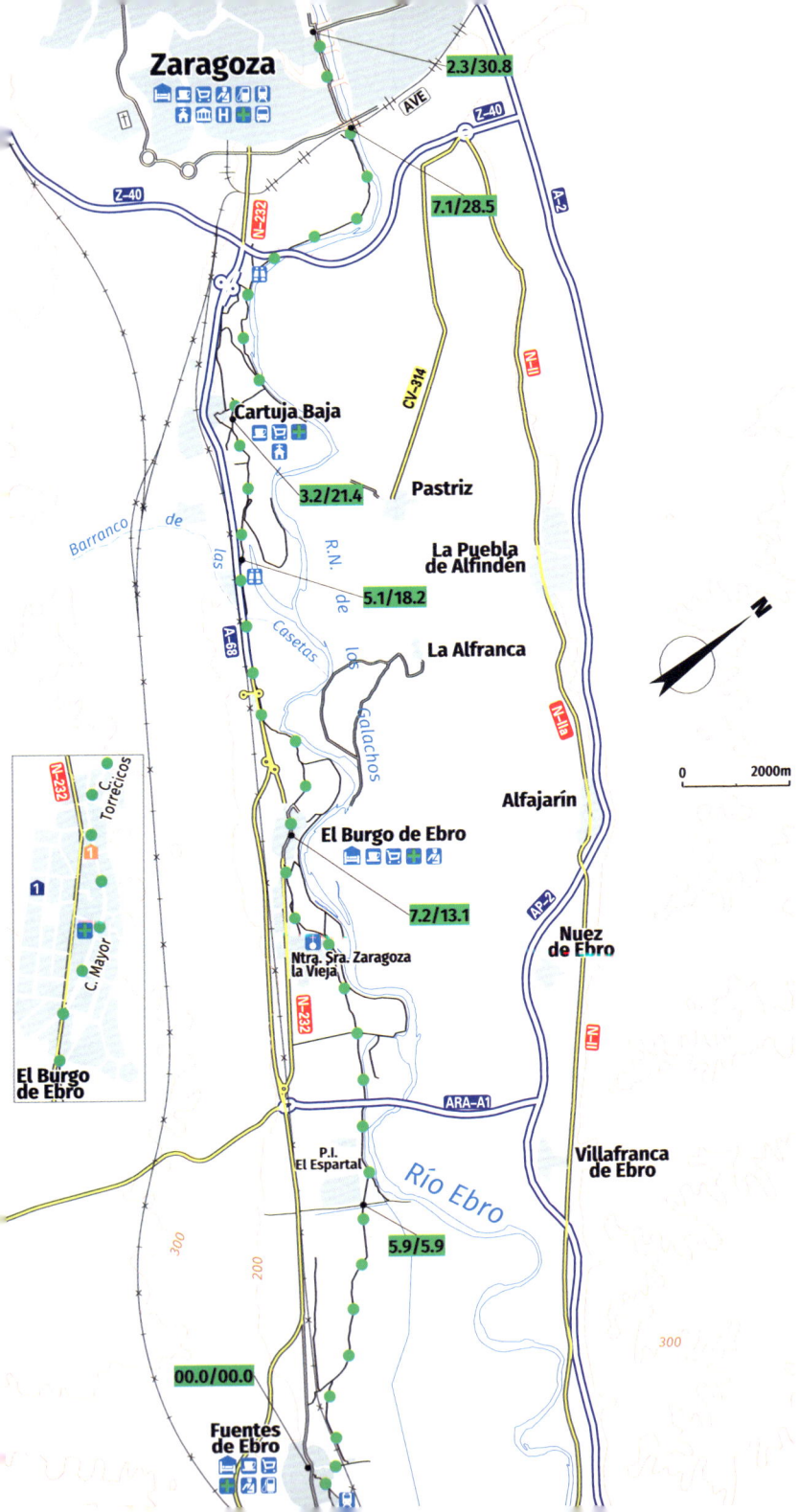

Zaragoza that was once the site of a monastery. On entering, there are two Camino alternatives. Choose the Camino del Ebro to the right which leads to the river and veers left to follow a green corridor all the way to the city along a wide earth track. Pass the Alfranca nature viewing platform. Keep straight on parallel to the river and under the Z-40 ring road. Continue along the river track between farm fields and river woodland.

7.1km/28.5km AVE Bridge. Enter Zaragoza under the railway bridge. Follow a delightful riverside walkway past a variety of different bridges until you reach the C15th Puente de Piedra with its graceful seven arches built of stone. Turn left to enter the historic city centre.

2.3km/30.8km El Pilar Basilica.

Zaragoza - pop. 660.000. Capital of the Autonomous Community of Aragón. A historic city founded by the Romans in 19BC and known then as *Caesaraugusta*.

El Pilar. Zaragoza (©Tur. Zaragoza. Ester Casas)

La Aljafería (©Tur. Zaragoza. Agustín Martínez)

El Burgo de Ebro
1. **Albergue Municipal**
Tel. 976 105 005
1. **Hostal Danae**
Tel. 625 715 878

Zaragoza
1. **Albergue Behostels**
Tel. 976 282 043
1. **Hostal Plaza**
Tel. 876 707 052
2. **Hostal Central**
Tel. 976 395 978
3. **Hostal El Bridge**
Tel. 627 307 932
1. **Hotel San Jorge**
Tel. 976 397 462
2. **Hotel Tibur**
Tel. 976 202 020
3. **Hotel Hispania**
Tel. 976 284 928
4. **Hotel Inca**
Tel. 976 390 091
5. **Hotel NH Ciudad de Zaragoza**
Tel. 976 442 100
6. **Hotel Sauce**
Tel. 976 205 050
7. **Hotel Río Arga**
Tel. 976 399 065
8. **Hotel Catalonia El Pilar**
Tel. 976 205 858
9. **Hotel Pilar Plaza**
Tel. 976 394 250
10. **Hotel Oriente**
Tel. 976 203 282
11. **Hotel Alfonso**
Tel. 876 541 118
12. **Hotel Don Jaime 54**
Tel. 976 399 065

Los Galachos Nature Reserve. Situated on both banks, 'galachos' are oxbow lakes formed by natural changes to the course of the river Ebro. Especially rich in birdlife.

Basilica of Our Lady of the Pillar. Home to 'la Pilarica', patron of Aragón. According to tradition this marks the spot where the Virgin Mary appeared to Saint James the Greater to encourage him on his apostolic work in Hispania.

The Cathedral of la Seo. Also known as the San Salvador Cathedral, built over the former site of the Roman forum and mosque.

Roman City Walls. Two stretches of wall remain, built between C1st - C3rd AD.

La Aljafería. A C11th Royal Palace fortified from the Taifa period of Zaragoza. A unique example of its type from that era.

Mudéjar Churches. The importance of Mudéjar art is portrayed in the C14th churches of San Pablo, San Miguel de los Navarros and Santa Magdalena.

9. ZARAGOZA - ALAGÓN: 29KM

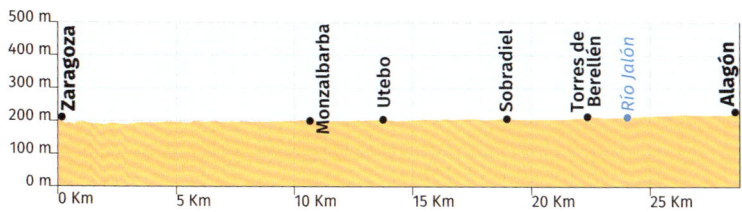

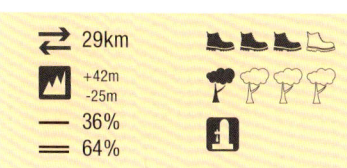

- 29km
- +42m / -25m
- 36%
- 64%

The Camino enters the upper reaches of the Ebro valley. Villages with ornate mudéjar church towers are interspersed with irrigated fields. The left bank of the river valley is enclosed by the Alfocea hills, a wild and bare escarpment, crowned by the white-washed chapel of Castellar.

0km El Pilar. From the Pl. del Pilar, return to the riverside walk to continue upstream along the Paseo Echegaray y Caballero without crossing the river at any point. Upon reaching the Pl. Europa with its obelisk, cross the road and turn right to descend a ramp sidewalk towards the river. Veer left to follow the river bank upstream.

2.9km/2.9km Expo 2008. Continue alongside the river, past the modern arch of the Tercer Milenio bridge following a footpath past a large parking area.

1.9km/4.8km Camino de Monzalbarba. Take a signed country lane to the left, away from the river towards the motorway ring road flyovers. After crossing under these main roads, turn left at a fork and continue through an area of arable fields. Ignore all junctions to follow the main asfalt lane in a straight line.

5.7km/10.5km Monzalbarba. Cross the village in a straight line along Paseo la Sagrada. On the far outskirts turn right on the asfalt lane of 'camino de La Mejana' for 50m, then turn first left onto an earth track. Traverse an area of arable fields before crossing a bridge over the A-68 to continue straight on.

3km/13.5km Utebo. Enter this pretty village along C. Antonio Machado. Turn left along the facade of the church and its magnificent tower. Continue along a narrow street and take the second opening on the right, C. Huerta Alta. On the outskirts, cross

Utebo (©Juan Carlos Borrego Pérez)

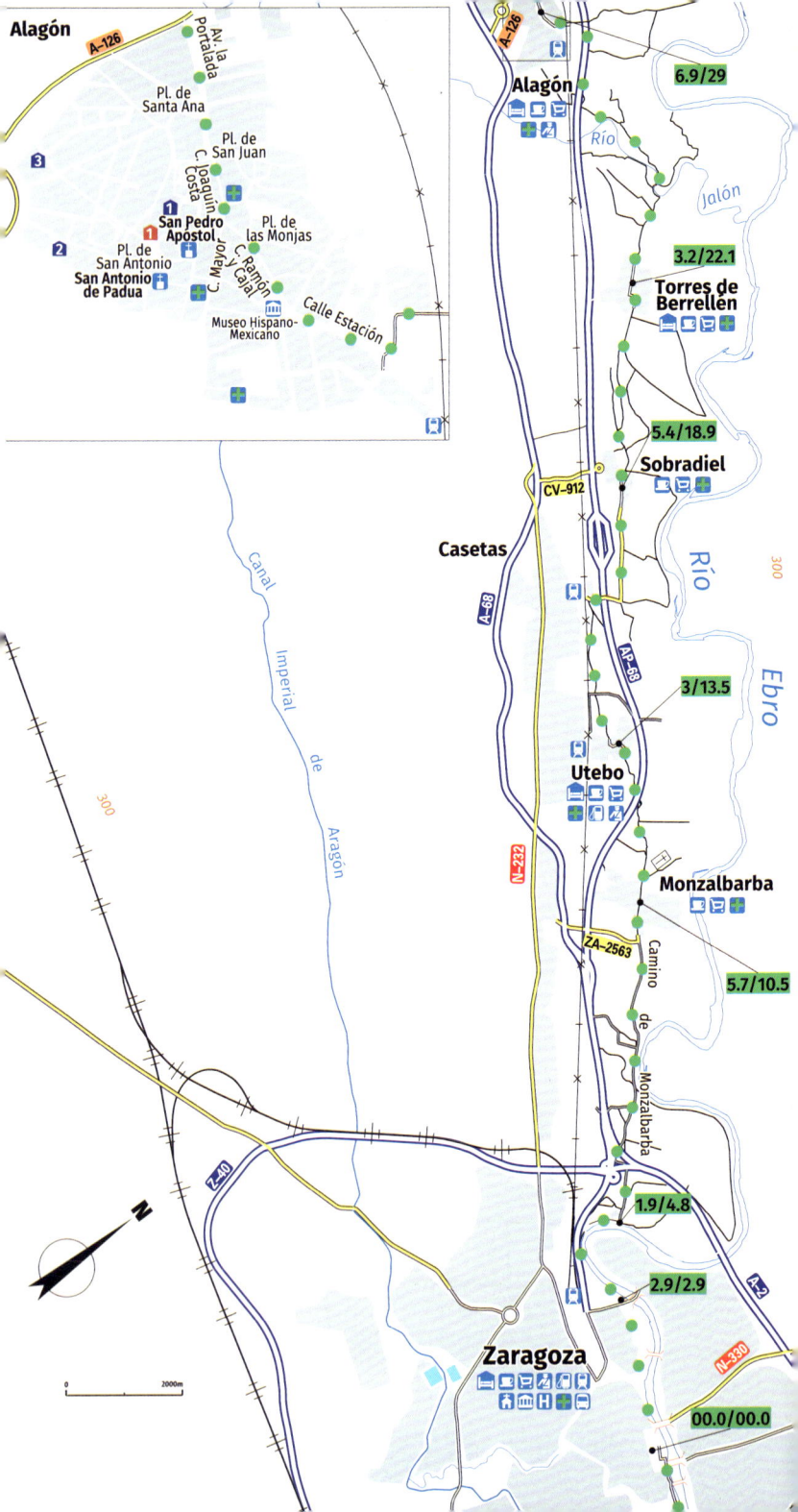

a road and keep straight ahead on an earthen track. Upon reaching some modern warehouses, the lane veers to the right, reaching a roundabout. Continue straight on to cross over the motorway and follow a country lane ignoring all turnings.

5.4km/18.9km Sobradiel. Enter the village in a straight line along C. del Pino. At its end, turn right onto C. Conde and after 50m turn left onto C. Camino de Santiago. At the end of this street, now on the outskirts, turn right for a few metres, to cross an irrigation channel and turn left onto an earthen track. Follow this main track until a fork, where you continue straight on by the left track.

3.2km/22.1km Torres de Berrellén. Enter along C. Miguel de Cervantes until a junction where there are two Camino directions. The option to the right passes by the church of San Andres (front entrance takes some finding). Both options join up at Pl. Puente Alto, from where the Camino continues along C. Garfilán. At the end of this street continue straight on along a country lane to leave the village. By the river Jalón, leave the lane to keep straight on over the water by an old causeway. At the other side turn left for 100m and then turn right to rejoin the asphalt lane. The lane passes a bridge over the AP-68 without crossing it, instead continuing straight on, parallel to the motorway. At the next bridge, turn left to cross over the motorway and then the railway.

6.9km/29km Alagón. Enter along C. Estación and after a roundabout fork right along C. Ramón y Cajal towards the historic centre and the hilltop churches.

Alagón - pop. 7000. A small town of the Ribera Alta del Ebro. Originally inhabited by the Vascones and later an important Roman town. The Moors in turn, were displaced by Alfonso I.

Utebo
- **Hostal Silvano**
Tel. 976 611 340

Torres de Berrellén
- **Albergue Municipal**
Tel. 976 65 3101

Alagón
- **1 Hostal Baraka**
Tel. 976 616 011
- **2 Pensión Mari Carmen**
Tel. 670 762 554
- **3 Pensión Jarea**
Tel. 629 489 776
- **1 Hotel Los Ángeles**
Tel. 976 611 340

Mudéjar Tower, Monzalbarba. C16th brick built. Its three floors each have a distinctive pattern.

Mudéjar Tower, Utebo. One of the most important examples of Aragonese mudéjar architecture.

Church of Santiago, Sobradiel. Late C17th Barroque style. Made of brick.

Church of Sn. Andres, Torres de Berrellén. C16th mudéjar style with a neo mudéjar tower.

Church of San Antonio of Padua, Alagón. Baroque style. The Museum of Contemporary Hispano-Mexican Art is housed next door.

Chapel of the Virgin of the Castle, Alagón. C16th. Dedicated to the appearance of the Virgin during the taking of Alagón by Alfonso I the Battler.

Church of San Pedro Apóstol, Alagón. C13th-14th. The octagonal tower is C11th and thought to preserve aspects of the mosque's minaret; considered one of the most attractive mudejar towers.

10. Alagón - Mallén: 30.9km

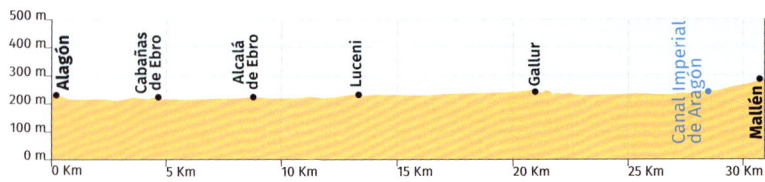

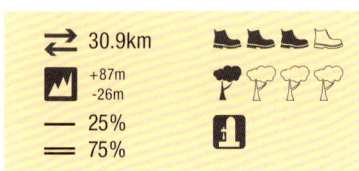

- 30.9km
- +87m / -26m
- 25%
- 75%

The fertile flat river valley landscape, with its patchwork of small fields watered by a complex system of irrigation channels, is dotted with small villages. The distant diminishing outline of the Moncayo massif to the left of the Camino breaks the otherwise level horizon.

Observations: Before reaching Mallén, an alternative Camino route is available that follows the Imperial Aragón Canal. It is shown on the map but has no accompanying directional text.

0km Alagón. From the highest point of the town, the Pl. del Castillo, follow C. las Escalericas del Castillo to the rear of the Chapel of Virgen del Castillo. Descend a flight of steps to continue along C. Cofradías to its end and turn left to follow Av. Portalada in a straight line to the outskirts. At a corner by a school, cross a road and take an asphalt lane straight ahead. In 300m leave the lane and fork right on an earthen track which soon passes under the train line and the motorway.

1.4km/1.4km VP-24 Road. ATTENTION. Turn left to follow the verge of this country road. At a junction, close to the Ebro, fork right.

3.1km/4.5km Cabañas de Ebro. Enter the village on a straight line by C. Joaquin Costa to the Pl. Fueros de Aragón. Veer left along C. Goya and then right on C. Major. Exit along Camino de Alcalá following the river Ebro. After 1km fork left towards Ínsula Barataria. Follow the main lane to its end, where you turn right at a junction.

4km/8.5km Alcalá de Ebro. Enter along C. Cervantes and at Pl. España turn towards the church. Continue on to C. Camino Real and turn left past the Sancho Panza monument to follow the river Ebro out of the village. Join a lane and keep straight on ignoring all turnings.

4.6km/13.1km Luceni. Cross this village in a straight line along Av. San Juan de la Peña, then C. Daoiz y Velarde. At Pl. España continue straight along C. Ramón y Cajal to leave the village. At a roundabout take the first exit left towards Gallur. ATTENTION. Follow the roadside a good way until a roundabout and go straight on.

7.9km/21km Gallur. Enter along C. Camino Real, passing the Centro Parroquial and then along C. Constitución to the Pl. España and then C. Tudela. Leave the village along an asphalt track at a level above the river plain. After 900m the track descends to the plain as it meets the Imperial Aragón Canal. Follow parallel to the canal, but not by its service track. Just after reaching a small factory cross the Valverde bridge over the canal and turn right.

7.7km/28.7km Fork in Camino. 200m after the bridge there is a split in the Camino. To the right is an option that follows the Imperial Canal (*see maps 10&11*) to Ribaforada. To continue to Mallén fork left, crossing under the railway line and on through an industrial zone, always straight onwards. ATTENTION. Caution should be taken crossing the N-232 main road to enter the village.

2.2km/30.9km Mallén. Continue uphill to the Av. de Zaragoza. Turn right towards the church.

Mallén. pop. 3000. A village of the Campo de Borja.

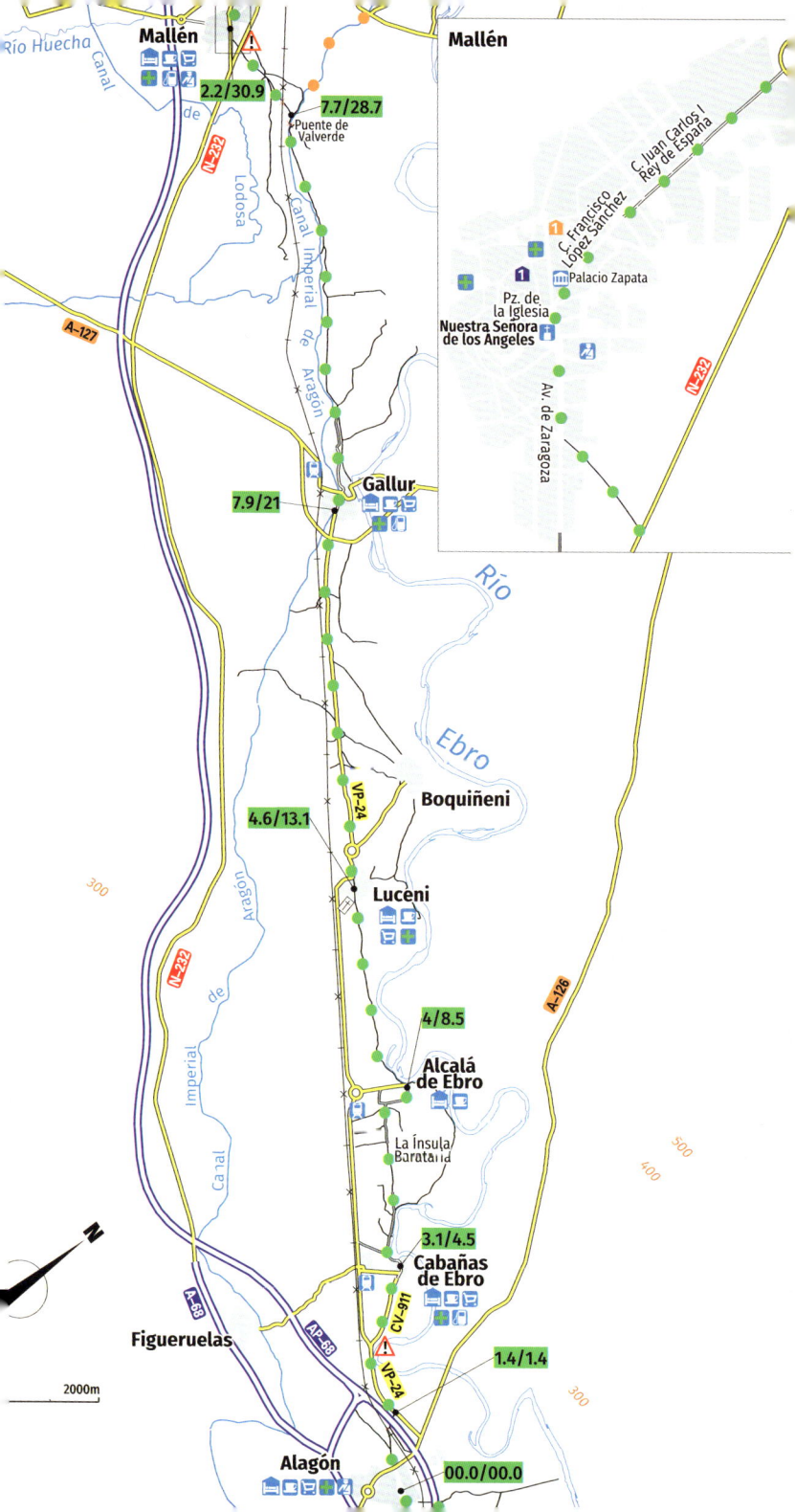

©Juan Carlos Borrego Pérez

Cabañas de Ebro
- Hostal Cubero
Tel. 976 611 720

Alcalá de Ebro
- La Palmera de la Insula
Tel. 685 097 249

Luceni
- Casa Alejandro
Tel. 679 441 838

Gallur
- Hotel El Colono
Tel. 976 864 275
- Albergue Municipal
Tel. 976 611 479

Mallén
- Albergue Municipal
Tel. 618 998 839
- Pensión Pinocho
Tel. 976 850 225

Church of San Idelfonso, Cabañas de Ebro. Baroque style of the C17th.

Mansion of the Dukes of Villahermosa, Alcalá de Ebro. A hunting lodge, conjoined with the remains of a Moorish castle.

Don Quijote and the Ebro, Alcalá de Ebro. Miguel Cervantes in his famous novel, locates Ínsula Barataria, for his servant Sancho Panza to govern, in this region of the Ebro river.

Church of the Purification, Luceni. C13th Gothic with a single nave. Outstanding for its altarpiece depicting a young Jesus in the Temple.

Church of San Pedro, Gallur. Built between 1750 and 1773 over a baroque church, the first floor of its tower once formed part of the castle.

Church of Nuestra Señora de Los Ángeles, Mallén. Built in different styles, from the Romanesque to the C18th.

The Zapata Palace, Mallén. C18th Neoclassic with a baroque style façade and a magnificent interior patio staircase.

11. Mallén - Tudela: 29.9km

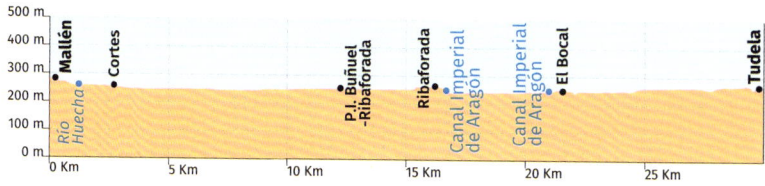

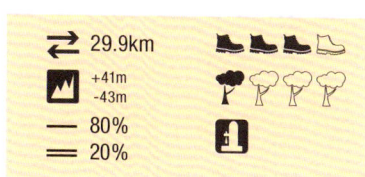

A flat stage that reveals firstly, the hydraulic secrets behind the lush agriculture that surrounds the Ebro and then the majestic hidden architectural gems of the old centre of Tudela.

0km Mallén. From the Pl. de la Iglesia follow C. Francisco López Sánchez in a straight line to the outskirts. Proceed under the N-232 flyover and continue straight on towards Cortes along a cycle lane. Enter the village along C. Azucarera and C. San Miguel.

2.8km/2.8km Castillo de Cortes. Continue past the church along C. Alta and then turn right onto C. Tudela to leave the village. On the outskirts at a roundabout take an earthen track to the left. On meeting the train track, turn right (away from it), then in 800m, turn left towards the train line again and follow it. The track then veers right, away from the railway and climbs to meet a road.

8.9km/11.7km NA-5210 Road. Turn right and after 100m cross the road to enter the Buñuel-Ribaforada industrial estate. Take the second street on the left and then the first to the right. At the end of this street by the sliding gate of a factory, turn left along a narrow earthen track between fences. Upon meeting the railway, turn right on a rough dirt track parallel to the lines. After 700m join a broader track and continue straight on.

4.9km/16.6km Ribaforada. Enter in a straight line along C. Sancho VII. At its end, swing right onto Av. Nuestra Señora del Carmen and continue straight on until the outskirts of the village. Cross over the Imperial Aragón Canal and turn left to follow an earth track parallel to the canal's service track.

4.2km/20.8km Junction. The Camino turns left to cross a small bridge and then turns right alongside the canal. At the Puente de Formigales bridge, turn right without crossing it, to follow a track past a barrier. Continue on until you reach a dam where the waters of the river Ebro enter the canal. Cross over the dam and follow a track to the left, parallel to the canal. After 500m turn right to cross a small bridge and right again to briefly follow a country lane. After 100m take the first track to the left and follow it ignoring all turnings.

5km/25.8km NA-134 Bridge. The track loops under a road bridge, skirting the railway line. Continue through an area of farms and market gardens.

Cortes de Navarra
(©Juan Carlos Borrego Pérez)

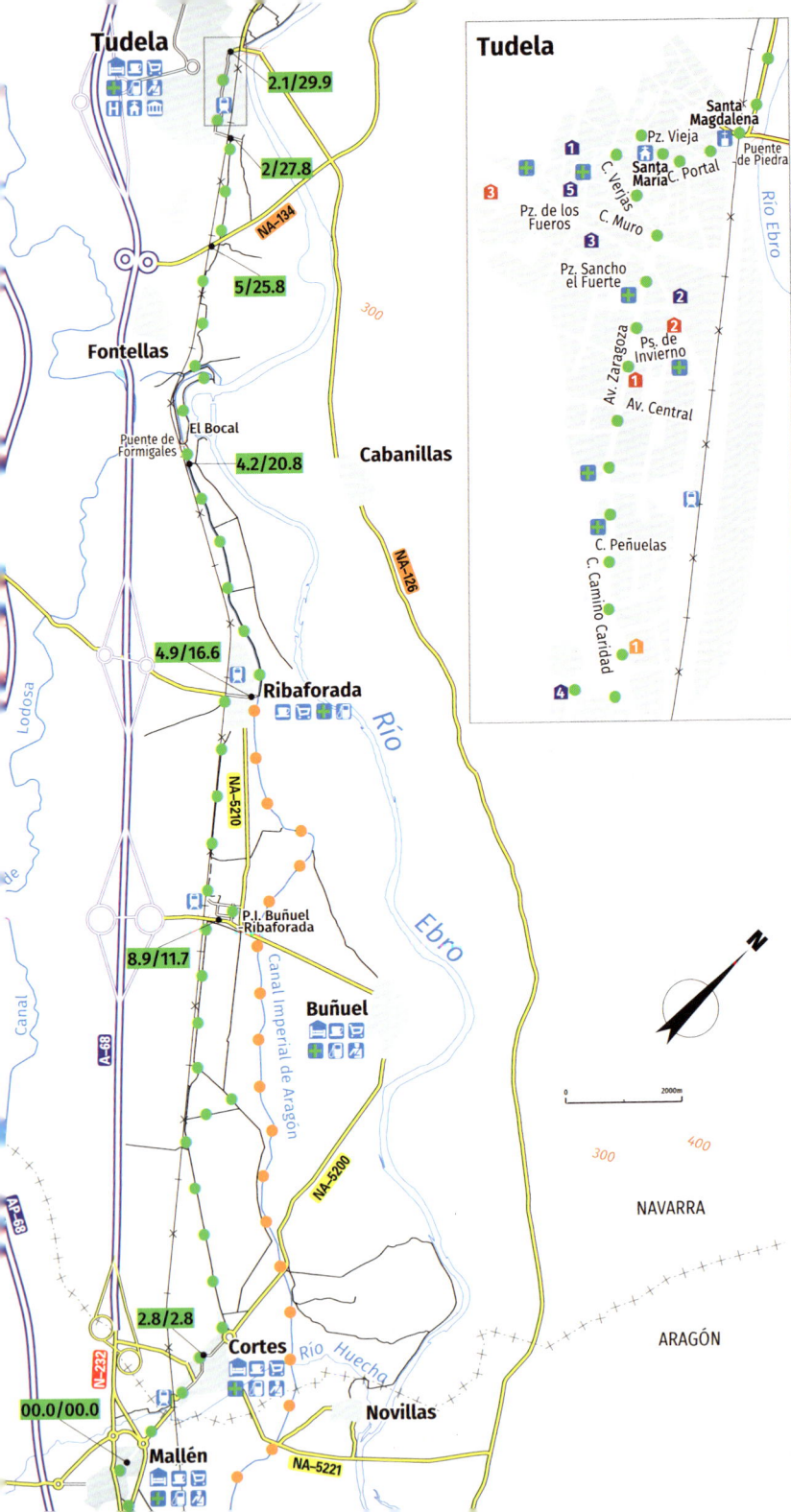

2km/27.8km Tudela. At the first street, turn left to cross over the railway. At the first roundabout turn right along C. Sancho Abarca. At its end, by the Plaza de Toros bullring, turn right and then left onto C. Camino Caritat and continue straight onto the city centre on Av. Zaragoza. At its end by a roundabout cross straight over and veer left and down a ramp into the narrow C. Verjas. Continue along and at Pl. San Jaime, turn right into the dog leg C. Roso (passing the 'Judgement Door' of the cathedral) to reach the Pl. Vieja. **2.1km/29.9km Tudela Cathedral.**

Tudela - pop. 35.000. Capital city of the Merindad of Tudela and the Ribera area. The second largest city of the Community of Navarre.

Cortes de Navarra
- **El Talón del Reyno**
  Tel. 948 821 400

Buñuel
- **Hostal Villa de Buñuel**
  Tel. 948 833 024

Tudela
- **1 Albergue Municipal**
  Tel. 664 636 175
- **1 Pensión La Estrella**
  Tel. 948 821 518
- **2 Pensión La Posada de San Marcial**
  Tel. 638 762 782
- **3 Hostal Remigio**
  Tel. 948 820 850
- **4 Hostal La Parrilla**
  Tel. 948 822 400
- **5 Hostal Pichorradicas**
  Tel. 948 821 021
- **1 Hotel Delta**
  Tel. 948 821 400
- **2 Hotel Santamaría**
  Tel. 948 821 200
- **3 Hotel Ciudad de Tudela**
  Tel. 948 402 440

Cortes de Navarra Castle. Well preserved C12th fortification that was once a residence of the Kings of Navarra.

Church of San Juan Bautista, Cortes de Navarra. Remodeled over the centuries. Nothing remains of the chapel where in 1333 Doña Juana, heir to the throne of Navarra, married Pedro IV 'The Ceremonious', heir to the kingdom of Aragón.

El Bocal, Fontellas. The hydraulic installations of the Imperial Aragón Canal and its attractive C18th workers' village, which also features the Carlos V Palace, a neoclassical church, a maze and a centenary oak!

Santa María Cathedral, Tudela. C12th - C13th late Cistercian Romanesque with many later additions. The Puerta del Juicio or Judgement Door is a unique work of western christian art due to the extensive treatment given to the scenes of Hell.

Santa Magdalena Church, Tudela. A Romanesque church of great beauty, built over a mozarab place of worship.

Puente de Piedra, Tudela. A magnificent medieval stone bridge with 17 arches of varying size.

12. Tudela - Alfaro: 24.3km

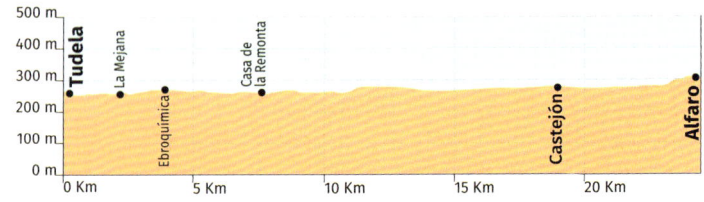

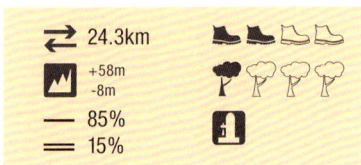

The Camino passes a multitude of market gardens watered by irrigation channels, before meeting the mighty Ebro once again. Flood plains produce a rich variety of flora and fauna, and the area provides rich pickings for the annual arrival of the White stork. From February they can be seen preparing their nests upon church towers and electric pylons.

0km Tudela. Follow C. Pontarrón along the rear side of the Cathedral and then turn left along C. Portal past the church of Santa Magdalena. Turn right and pass under the railway line. Turn immediately left, before the Puente de Piedra bridge and in a few metres, turn right to pass under the arch of Puerta Mejana. Turn left through a car park to join an earthen track. Now proceed parallel to a country lane, between an extensive area of market gardens and an irrigation channel. Continue straight on ignoring all turns.

2.2km/2.2km La Mejana. At the end of the track turn left to cross an irrigation channel and then turn right onto a country lane.

1.8km/4km Factory. Just after this small industrial area, turn right onto an earthen track. It soon veers to the left to cross part of a floodplain close to the river. At a junction of tracks, keep straight on past the ruins of a corral on a farm track. At a fork, take the less trodden track to the right, staying close to the river.

3.6km/7.6km Casa de la Remonta. Skirt around the right of these ruins then keep straight on. After 200m, fork to the right on the lesser of two farm tracks, between orchards and the riverside vegetation. Continue on, parallel to the Ebro

3.3km/10.9km Junction. Camino veers left to climb gently away from the river. It joins a country lane to cross a bridge over the nearby railway. Continue in a straight line for several kms on an earthen track alongside the rails ignoring all turnings. Continue under the bridge of the A-15 motorway. Eventually the track becomes asphalt and climbs a ramp to join a road. Turn left and enter the village taking the second street to the right, C. Navas de Tolosa.

8km/18.9km Castejón. At the end of this long street turn right and immediately left along C. Ruiz de Alda in a straight line towards the outskirts of the village.

0.8km/19.7km Double Roundabout. ATTENTION. Take the verge to the right following the Camino markings towards Alfaro by passing under the N-113 flyover. At the second roundabout join a cycle lane towards Alfaro that passes fields of orchards and vines. On the outskirts of Alfaro go straight ahead at a roundabout to enter the town in a straight line along C. Castejón and C. Araciel. At Pl. Chica take C. Argelillo to arrive at Pl. España.

4.6km/24.3km Alfaro. Collegiate Church of San Miguel Arcángel.

Alfaro - pop. 9500. Municipality of Rioja Baja, known for its Stork Festival.

Ciconia ciconia

Castejón
- Hostal Europa 🪙🪙
Tel. 948 814 468

Alfaro
① Albergue Municipal de Peregrinos 🪙
Tel. 666 041 958

① **Hotel HM** 🪙🪙
Tel. 941 180 056
② **Hotel Palacios Rioja** 🪙🪙
Tel. 941 180 100

🏛 **Church of San Francisco Javier, Castejón.** Neo Medieval style with a C16th mannerist altarpiece.
Collegiate Church of San Miguel Arcángel, Alfaro. C16th-C17th. The largest church in La Rioja. The choir stalls are noteworthy as are the 50m high twin towers and their stairwells.

13. Alfaro - Calahorra: 24.7km

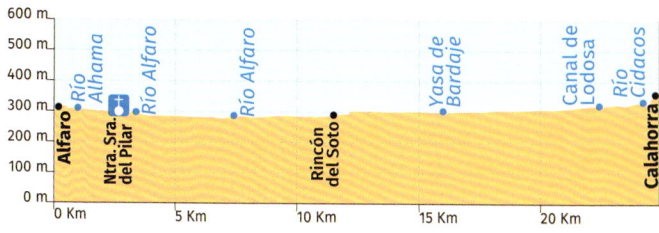

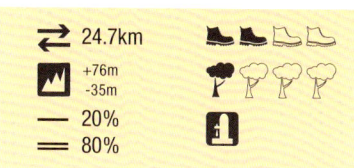

- 24.7km
- +76m / -35m
- 20%
- 80%

A flat stage dotted with marshes, market gardens, farms, irrigation channels and canals. On occasion, the bends of the river Ebro and its calm waters are glimpsed. Calahorra, another city with an important heritage awaits the traveller.

Observations: There is a much quieter and pleasanter route out of Alfaro (orange dots on map), for the first couple of kms to the Ermita del Pilar, that adds no extra distance and is described below. It avoids the signed route along very busy roads and roundabouts, often with no protected crossings (red dots on map).

0km Alfaro. With your back to the door of the collegiate church, turn right along C. Argelillo. In under 100m at Pl. Chica fork left along C. San Antón. At the end of the long straight street, continue a short distance to cross the rio Alhama. In 50m turn left onto a country lane.

0.6km/0.6km Camino Viejo del Pilar. Continue parallel to the river.

0.5km/1.1km Junction. The asphalt lane veers away from the river. Continue past fruit orchards and market gardens until you meet the LR-288 road. Turn right along the road verge (the Pilar chapel is on the opposite side) for 250m and then follow the adjacent lane still parallel to the road. After 400m, veer to the right.

2.1km/3.2km Lane. Cross the railway and then the narrow river Alfaro. After 100m, veer to the left still on the asphalt and at the next junction fork left. Follow the train tracks for a long stretch always along the country lane. After a small play park on the outskirts of the village take C. Cascajuelo to the right. Continue along C. Pozo to the church of San Miguel.

8.2km/11.4km Rincón de Soto. Turn left to cross the Pl. de la Iglesia and then turn right along C. Cascajuelo. Continue in a straight line past the town hall and the Pl. González Gallarza. Cross the Av. Príncipe Felipe to continue straight on along C. Ancha. Take the first turning to the left and then right onto the tree lined Av. de la Rioja to leave the village along an asphalt country road. Continue straight on at all junctions with an irrigation channel to your right. Cross a short bridge with railings over the Yasa de Bardaje stream.

4.6km/16km Junction. After 50m turn left on an asphalt country lane. The Camino crosses a plain of crops, vines and orchards always along the same lane.

6.4km/22.4km Lodosa Canal. Cross a bridge to follow the train line until you meet the LR-486 road. Turn left to continue under the railway. Follow the road past the Sanctuary of Carmen. At a crossroads turn right towards the city and cross the river Cidacos.

2.3km/24.7km Calahorra. Enter the city and follow the Camino waymarks to reach the Cathedral.

Calahorra - pop. 24.000. The second largest city of La Rioja Community, and the largest in the Ribera Baja area.

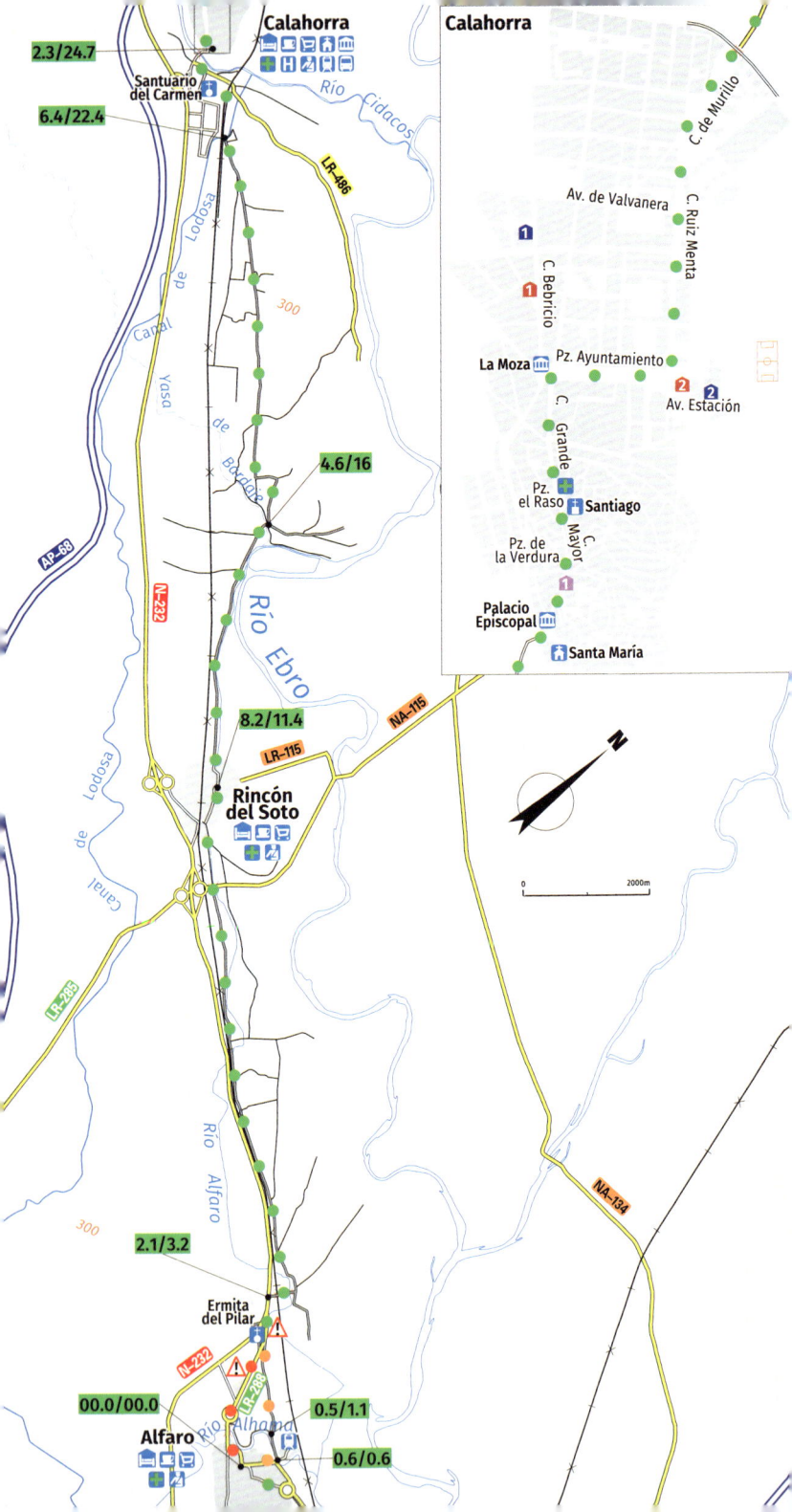

Santuario del Carmen (©Ayuntamiento de Calahorra)

Rincón de Soto
🏨 **Hotel Casa de mares y Sueños** ⚬⚬
Tel. 651 814 903

Calahorra
❶ **Albergue de Peregrinos San Francisco** ⚬
Tel. 941 590 511

❶ **Pensión Teresa** ⚬
Tel. 941 591 129
❷ **Hostal Gala** ⚬⚬⚬
Tel. 941 145 515
❶ **Hotel Ciudad de Calahorra** ⚬⚬⚬
Tel. 941 147 434

❷ **Parador Nacional Marco Fabio Quintiliano** ⚬⚬⚬
Tel. 941 130 358
🏨 **Hotel Zenit** ⚬⚬
Tel. 941 147 952

Church of San Miguel Arcángel, Rincón del Soto. C16th Baroque. Built in brick.
Calahorra Historic Centre. A Roman layout that retains remains of the circus, sewers, walls and gates.
Santuario del Carmen, Calahorra. C17th sanctuary with a large altarpiece. Currently inhabited by Carmelite fathers.
Cathedral of Santa María, Calahorra. C17th Baroque. Built on the site where the city's patrons, San Emeterio and San Celedonio were martyred.
Episcopal Palace, Calahorra. Former bishop's seat of the C16th.
La Moza, Calahorra. A column in the Plaza del Mercadal and symbol of a free city.
Church of Santiago, Calahorra. Built between 1626 and 1730. It has a cross shaped floor plan with a triple nave that combines baroque and neoclassical architecture.

14. CALAHORRA - ALCANADRE: 19.9KM

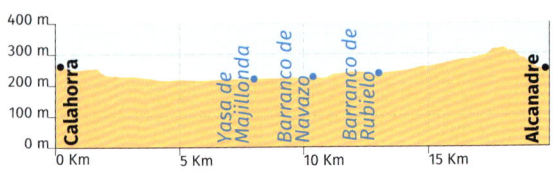

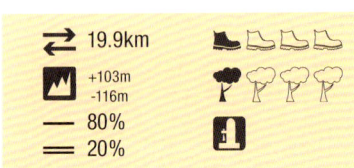

A flat agricultural landscape surrounded by bare outcrops characterize this stage. Olive groves, vineyards and plastic greenhouses are interspersed with a network of canals and irrigation channels that sustain a rich variety of crops.

0km Calahorra. From the Cathedral, follow Cuesta de la Catedral, then C. Mayor, to diagonally cross Pl. del Raso with its church of Santiago. Continue along C. Grande and C. Mártires until the roundabout Glorieta Quintiliano. Turn right along the Paseo del Mercadal to its end. Turn left along C. Ruiz y Menta. At an urban roundabout take the second exit to the left and keep straight on towards the outskirts.

2.3km/2.3km Roundabout to Murillo. ATTENTION. Care should be taken to navigate this junction, then keep straight on towards Murillo de Calahorra along the LR-482.

1.6km/3.9km Track to Left. 200m after crossing over the railway, take an earthen track to the left. Continue until a junction with an asphalt lane to Murillo. Cross straight over to follow the dirt track in a straight line. At a crossroads with a country lane, keep straight on along an earthen track and soon take a short detour to cross the Barranco del Navazo gulley where it passes through a large tube. Now follow a farm track to the left to continue between the railway and the Canal de Lodosa.

7.4km/11.3km Railway Bridge. Turn left to cross over the railway and immediately turn right to continue on, parallel to the A-68 motorway on an earthen track. Turn left to pass through a tunnel under the motorway and turn right to continue parallel to the A-68.

2.2km/13.5km LR-123 Junction. ATTENTION. Upon reaching this country road turn right. After 150m take an earthen track to the left, continuing parallel to the A-68 and ignoring all tracks to the left.

3.4km/16.9km A-68 Bridge. At a junction turn right to cross the motorway. After the bridge, keep straight on at all junctions until you enter the village of Alcanadre. Continue in a straight line along C. Pilares and then turn right to follow C. Dr Chavarría, past the town hall square.

3km/19.9km Alcanadre. You arrive at the Church of Santa María.

Alcanadre - pop. 700. A village of la Rioja.

 Alcanadre
1 Casa Azul de Ramón y Asu
Tel. 686 730 187
2 Apartamentos Fuente Vilda
Tel. 600 792 122

Church of Santa María, Alcanadre. C16th. Contains the Romanesque statue of a seated Virgin, taken from the chapel of Aradón.

15. ALCANADRE - LOGROÑO: 34.7KM

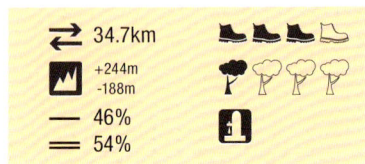

- ⇄ 34.7km
- +244m / -188m
- — 46%
- — 54%

The final stretch that accompanies the river Ebro traverses two different types of countryside: the vineyards and olive groves of the shallow valleys that run between low hills covered in scrub, and the riverside farm fields of asparagus and market gardens. The arrival into Logroño and joining the Camino Francés creates a dual impression in the mind of the pilgrim: on the one hand the sense of completion of the Camino del Ebro, whilst on the other feeling of starting out once again on the next stage of an unknown journey towards the final goal of Santiago de Compostela.

0km Alcanadre. From the church of Santa María, retrace your steps along the narrow C. Dr Chavarría and continue straight on along C. San Isidro to exit the village. Turn right onto the LR-260 road.

0.6km/0.6km Track to Right. After the bend in the road take the former Camino to Logroño, an earthen track to the right. Continue amongst vines and olive trees and after 500m fork to the left and continue straight on along the main track. Eventually, you pass near a farm building on the left of the track. After 700m the Camino encounters an area of multiple turnings.

5.7km/6.3km Junction to Aradón Chapel. Take the first turning to the right along a wide track, following a gulley that gradually becomes deeper.

1.9km/8.2km Aradón Chapel. The chapel is situated in a pretty spot, hidden away between a bluff and the river Ebro. The Camino turns to the left, parallel to the railway line. Ignore a track over the railway.

2km/10.2km Railway Crossing. The route crosses the railway and turns immediately to the left, just a few metres away from the Ebro. At a ruined farm by the river, continue straight on, with the railway to the left. Upon meeting an asphalt track, veer left and after 200m turn right onto a gravel track, leaving the railway behind.

5.1km/15.3km Arrúbal. Enter the village and fork to the left along C. Calvario. Continue along C. de la Cuesta, and at its end descend a concrete ramp. Cross an irrigation channel by a small bridge and take the earthen track straight ahead. Continue in a straight line ignoring all turnings. Upon reaching Agoncillo village, turn right along Av. del Polideportivo. On reaching the church of Nuestra Señora la Blanca turn left to cross Pl. del Castillo square.

3.8km/19.1km Agoncillo. Turn the corner of the castle and follow C. de la Ermita. On the outskirts of the village pass by the roadside chapel of Los Dolores. Further on, cross under the railway and climb a ramp to reach the N-232 main road.

2.1km/21.2km N-232. ATTENTION. Great care should be taken when following the right hand verge. Turn right to cross the river Leza. In 600m ascend an exit slip road to the right.

0.8km/22km Airport Exit. ATTENTION. At a junction, continue ahead to descend a slip road to rejoin the N-232. Follow the right hand verge onto El Recajo. Continue through this village and climb an exit slip road signed 'base militar'. At a roundabout turn right to cross a bridge over the railway.

3.3km/25.3km Track to Left. 300m after the bridge take an earthen track to the left. Follow the main track and pass under

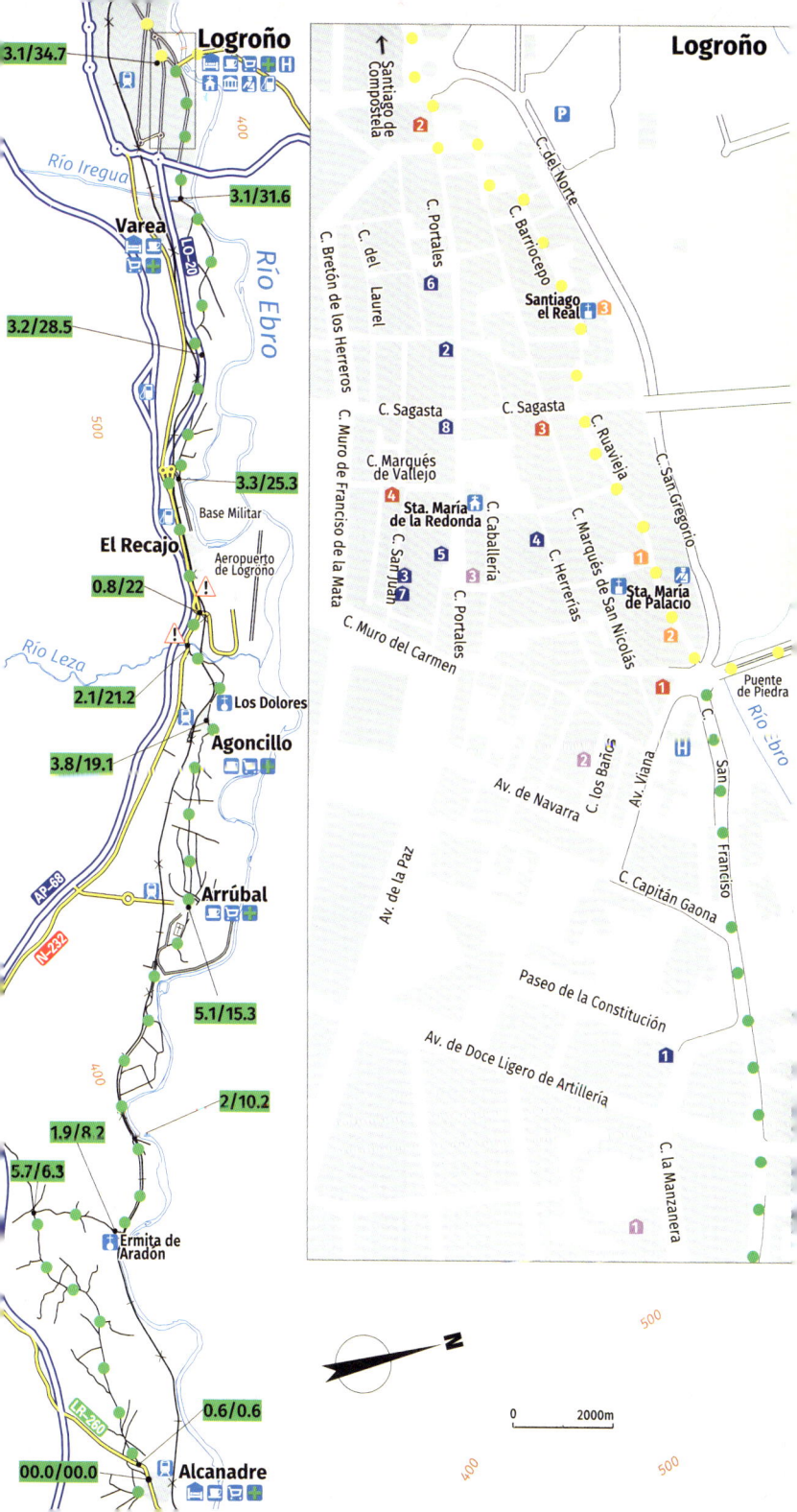

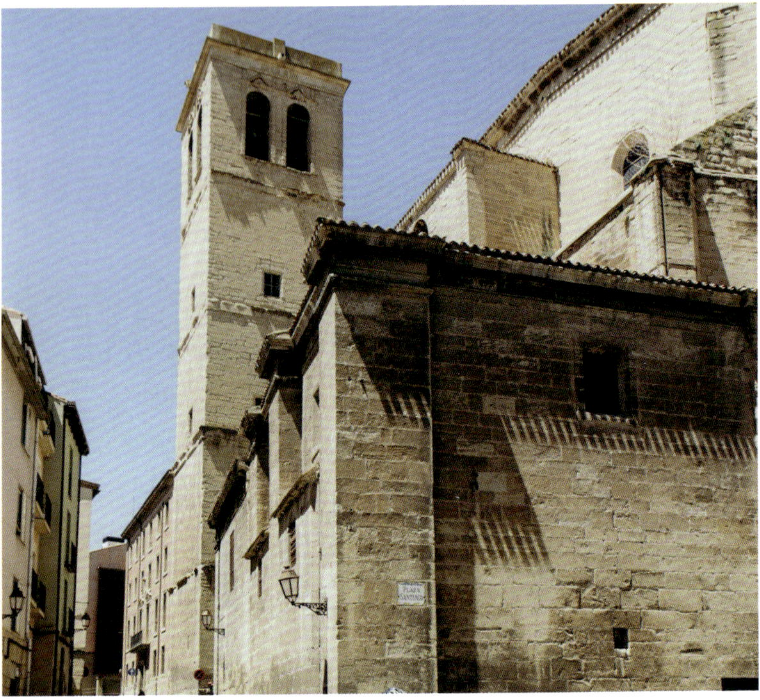

Santiago el Real, Logroño (©La Rioja Turismo)

Varea

Hostal Mesón Pepa
Tel. 941 234 011

Logroño

1 **Albergue Municipal de Peregrinos**
Tel. 941 248 686

2 **Albergue Santiago Apóstol**
Tel. 941 209 501

3 **Albergue Parroquial Santiago el Real**
Tel. 941 256 976

1 **Albergue Albas**
Tel. 941 700 832

2 **Albergue Check in Rioja**
Tel. 941 272 329

3 **Albergue y Hotel Entresueños**
Tel. 941 271 334

1 **Pensión Parque del Ebro**
Tel. 616 840 786

2 **Pensión La Bilbaína**
Tel. 608 234 723

3 **Pensiones Sebastián y San Juan**
Tel. 941 242 800

4 **Winederful**
Tel. 941 139 618

5 **Pensión La Redonda**
Tel. 941 272 409

6 **Pensión Entreviñas**
Tel. 607 414 747

7 **Pensión San Juan**
Tel. 665 974 651

8 **Hostal La Numantina**
Tel. 941 251 411

1 **Hotel FG Logroño**
Tel. 941 008 900

2 **Sercotel Portales**
Tel. 941 502 794

3 **Hotel Calle Mayor**
Tel. 941 008 900

4 **Hotel Marqués de Vallejo**
Tel. 941 248 333

the LO-20 motorway. The track becomes asphalted.
3.2km/28.5km LO-20 Tunnel. Turn right to pass under the LO-20 for the second time. Turn left along the asphalt track. The Way veers to the right to leave the motorway behind, then immediately forks to the left. The Camino crosses an area of small farms on the alluvial plains of the Ebro valley. A crossroads of lanes awaits at the entrance to the hamlet of Varea. Turn left for 20m and then right towards 'Centro Ciudad'. Continue straight on ignoring all turnings to follow the banks of the Ebro and to cross through an urban riverside park.
3.1km/31.6km River Iregua Footbridge. Turn right to cross the river and walk towards the embankment of the A-13 motorway. Turn left towards a crossroad. Turn right and pass under the A-13. Continue in a straight line along C. Madre de Dios and then C. San Francisco. At a roundabout by the Puente de Piedra bridge, go straight ahead along the narrow C. Ruavieja and continue in a straight line.
3.1km/34.7km Church of Santiago el Real.

Logroño - pop. 151.000. Capital of La Rioja Autonomous Community. An historic city and traditional crossing of Caminos to Santiago de Compostela.

El Ebro (@Darío Martínez Ibáñez)

Aradón Chapel. All that remains of the former abbey of Aradón and its medieval village.
Church of San Salvador, Arrúbal. C16th. Brick built with a narrow bell tower. The central nave has a barrel vaulted ceiling.
Aguas Mansas Castle, Agoncillo. C12th-15th with four towers, an impressive central courtyard and part of its moat.
Church of Nuestra Señora la Blanca, Agoncillo. C18th with a magnificent bell tower.
Würth Museum of la Rioja, Agoncillo. An important collection of landscapes and sculptures housed in an avant-garde centre.
Chapel of Los Dolores, Agoncillo. Notable for its C18th altarpiece.

Cathedral of Santa María de la Redonda, Logroño. Diocese seat shared with the cathedrals of Calahorra and Santo Domingo de la Calzada. C16th-18th with three naves and two huge towers. Gold leafed brickwork, the main altarpiece and a painting of the Crucifixion by Michelangelo are worthy of note.
Church of Santiago el Real, Logroño. Despite the present church dating from the C16th, it is thought that the crypt was originally a cave church. It was established on the site used by Saint James to spread the gospel. A Romanesque church of the C9th was completely destroyed by fire.
Imperial Church of Santa María, Logroño. C12th-15th. Notable for its C13th Gothic pyramidal tower.

LES - BERBEGAL

In the heart of the mountains, the secluded and beautiful Val d'Aran lies north of the Pyrenean watershed. Here, the ancient *Camin Reiau* (Royal Route) track has crossed the strategic Port de Vielha pass since Roman times. The gentle climb along the wooded river valley from the French border contrasts with the sudden ascent to the challenging mountain pass traditionally used by drovers and pilgrims alike. Heading south along the modern day border between the regions of Catalonia and Aragón, the steep sided valleys with their cascading waterfalls lead to upland meadows, slate topped villages and mixed woodland. Old drovers' routes cross Romanesque bridges and descend through the Pyrenean foothills following river valleys out onto the fertile plains.

Pilgrims travelled this rugged mountainous route during the accessible period from late Spring to autumn, when local mountain folk could provide them with a meal. During the long winter enemy incursions and longer journeys were impossible due to the harsh weather. The half hidden Monastery of Obarra and the hilltop Cathedral in the tiny village of Roda de Isábena were early bastions of Christianity whilst the nearby town of Graus and Barbastro remained under Moorish control.

Pardinella (©Juan Carlos Borrego Pérez)

La Noguera Ribagorçana (©Callum Christie)

The Vall de Boí provides a fascinating detour due to its natural beauty and unique towered churches built by stonemasons from Lombardy. Local lords grew rich on the spoils of war as they helped to push the Moors out of the valleys of the Ebro basin. This area seems to have been forgotten in time and its church architecture was rediscovered in the early C20th by scholars from Barcelona.

Pyrenees - With some 200 peaks of over 3,000m this formidable geographical border between Spain and France stretches 491km from the Atlantic to the Mediterranean. 120kms at its widest point the Pyrenees range has very few accessible passes and most are only found at high altitudes.
Historically the kingdoms of Navarra and Aragón extended on both sides of the mountains. Today, various different peoples inhabit the Pyrenees and a vibrant mix of folklore exists throughout. The Val d'Aran has its own dialect of Occitan known as Aranese, and a form of Catalan is spoken throughout much of this trans Pyrenean area even in the Aragonese villages. The traditional practice of annual transhumance along drovers' trails is slowly disappearing whilst the mountains are becoming a well known haven for climbers, skiers and walkers alike.
Bordering the Val d'Aran, the Parque Nacional de Aigüestortes i Estany de Sant Maurici and the Posets-Maladeta pristine nature reserves contain an amazing number of endemic species. They form a high altitude ecosystem, including the highest peak in the Pyrenees (Aneto 3,404m), glaciers and hundreds of blue water mountain lakes. Golden eagles and Lammergeiers soar above impressive waterfalls and precipitous cliffs.

1. LES - VIELHA: 20KM

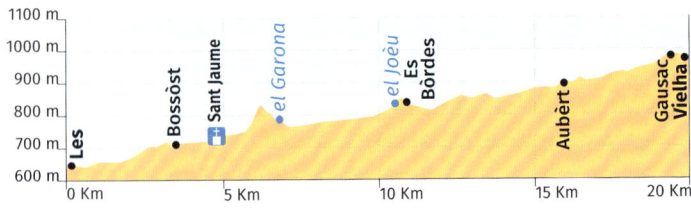

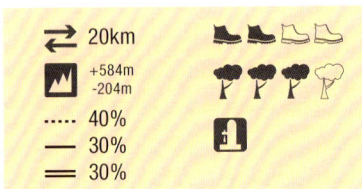

The river Garona is the only Catalan river that runs towards the Atlantic. It is a typical fast flowing mountain river, whose banks are dotted with picturesque Pyrenean villages with their slate-roofed dwellings. The pilgrim follows an ancient trail under a canopy of native riverside woodlands.

Observations: The Camino coincides with the red and white markings of the GR211 up to Era Bordeta, and then the GR211.1 to Vielha.

0km Les. Commence from the Pont de la Garona footbridge in the centre of the village. On the right bank, continue upstream along Carrer des Bahns and after 100m fork right to the outskirts of the village, keeping parallel to the river. Continue straight on to pass a campsite and a fish farm that produces caviar. Soon, pass an electric substation and after a few metres, take a path to the left.

2.2km/2.2km Pònt de Cledes. Join a track and turn left without crossing the nearby bridge.

1.3km/3.5km Bossòst. Enter along C. d'An- glades and leave the village along C. Sant Jaime without crossing the river. The street turns into a track that crosses an irrigation canal and several meadows. The Way passes a shrine to St. James, in a recess of a dry stone wall. Leave the metal Pònt de Hèr bridge to the right and continue straight on up a steep path before descending a pronounced slope through woodland.

3.4km/6.9km Pònt deth Saut deth Lop. Join a section of old road and turn right to cross the bridge over the Garona up to the main road. ATTENTION. Turn left and cross the road with care. After 100m ascend a lane to the right to enter the woods and cross the meadows of Era Bordeta. At a junction by a modern bridge, continue straight on through oak woods, always with the Garona river on your left. Pass by the bridge at Pont d'Arró and keep straight on through woodlands and fields on an earthen track. Cross the Pònt deth Joèu bridge over a tributary of the Garona.

3.9km/10.8km Es Bòrdes. Cross through this picturesque village along C. Major and then C. Real. Continue along tracks and paths under the leafy canopy between the steep mountainside and riverside pastures. At El Pont d'Arròs continue straight on along the wooded path until meeting a track that leads to Pònt d'Aubert.

©Callum Christie

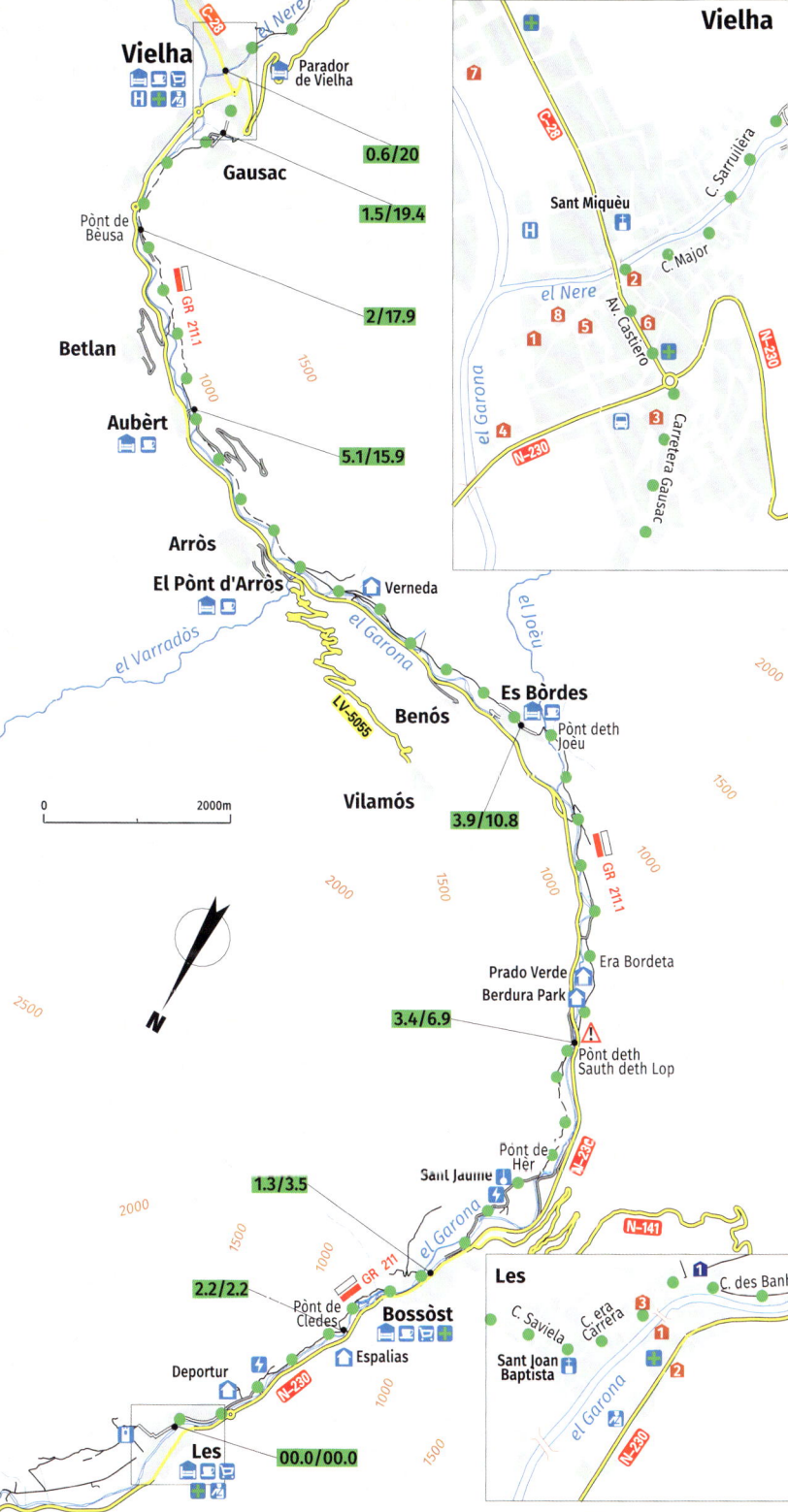

Vielha (©FTVA-KREAR)

5.1km/15.9km Pònt d'Aubert. Continue without crossing the bridge and after leaving the houses behind climb along a woodland path parallel to the river.
2km/17.9km Pònt de Beusa. Without crossing the bridge follow a path to the right that becomes an earthen track that leads up towards the village of Gausac.
1.5km/19.4km Gausac Crossroads. At the outskirts of the village turn to the left and follow the road to Vielha.

0.6km/20km Vielha. Continue along C. Carretera de Gausac and at a large roundabout continue straight on towards Baquèira until you reach a river bridge near the town hall.
Les - pop. 950. A village of the Val d'Aran. Located near the French border, renowned for its thermal springs since Roman times. The festival of the Haro on the night of San Juan includes the burning of a fir tree trunk in the village square.

Vielha - pop.5500. Capital of the Val d'Aran. Lying at the confluence of the rivers Nere and Garona, Vielha's old centre is an attractive example of traditional pyrenean architecture. The economic mainstay of traditional farming and livestock care has been practised since medieval times. These are gradually being replaced by involvement in year-round outdoor pursuits. This fast growing sector of the tourism industry has in turn driven modern urban expansion.

Les
- **Pension Es Neres** ⊖⊖
  Tel. 973 648 389
- **Hotel Europa** ⊖⊖
  Tel. 973 648 016
- **Hotel Juan Canejan** ⊖⊖
  Tel. 973 648 031
- **Hotel Talabart** ⊖⊖
  Tel. 973 648 011
- **Camping Deportur - Cauarca** ⊖
  Tel. 973 647 044

Bossòst
- **Hotel Garona** ⊖⊖
  Tel. 973 648 246
- **Hotel Batalla** ⊖⊖
  Tel. 973 648 199
- **Hostal Tina** ⊖⊖⊖
  Tel. 973 647 431
- **Hotel Shadow** ⊖⊖⊖
  Tel. 973 647458

- **Camping Espalias** ⊖⊖
  Tel. 973 648 310

Era Bordeta
- **Camping Bedura Park** ⊖⊖
  Tel. 973 648 293
- **Camping Prado Verde** ⊖⊖⊖
  Tel. 973 647 172

Es Bòrdes
- **Pico Russell** ⊖⊖
  Tel. 662 594 444

Pont d'Arròs
- **Hotel Penha** ⊖⊖⊖
  Tel. 973 640 886
- **Hotel Barradós** ⊖⊖
  973 640 309
- **Camping Verneda** ⊖⊖
  Tel. 973 641 024

Aubèrt
- **Osteria Roc 'n' Cris** ⊖
  Tel. 973 641 723

- **Hostal Era Nheuada** ⊖⊖
  Tel. 973 640 369

Vielha
- **Hotel Turrull** ⊖⊖
  Tel. 973 640 058
- **Hotel Riu Nere** ⊖⊖
  Tel. 973 640 150
- **Hotel Eth Pomèr** ⊖⊖
  Tel. 973 642 888
- **Hotel Eth Solan** ⊖⊖
  Tel. 973 640 204
- **Hotel Albares** ⊖⊖
  Tel. 973 640 081
- **Hotel Aran la Abuela** ⊖⊖
  Tel. 973 640 050
- **Hotel Tryp** ⊖⊖⊖
  Tel. 973 638 000
- **Hotel Fonfreda** ⊖⊖⊖
  Tel. 973 640 486
- **Parador de Vielha** ⊖⊖⊖
  Tel. 973 640 100

Parish Church of Sant Joan Baptista, Les. C17th Baroque style. Built on a Romanesque temple of which only the bell tower remains.
Parish Church of la Asunción de María, Bossòst. Built between C11th-C12th. One of the most important and best preserved churches of the Aranese Romanesque style.
El Pont d'Arròs. Medieval bridge of the Camin Reiau a 'Royal Road'.
Church of Mair de Diu deth Roser, Aubèrt. C12th Romanesque with a C16th bell tower.

Parish Church of Sant Martin, Aubèrt. C13th Romanesque. Once the chapel of the now disappeared monastery of Sant Agustí.
Tor deth Generau Martihnon, Vielha. C17th stately home that houses el Museo Etnográfico, the Aran Valley Museum. It has an octagonal tower with a pointed slate roof.
Church of Sant Miquèu, Vielha. Built in the transition style of Romanesque to Gothic. Its bell tower was formerly one of the towers of a medieval castle.

2. VIELHA - CONANGLES: 15.5KM

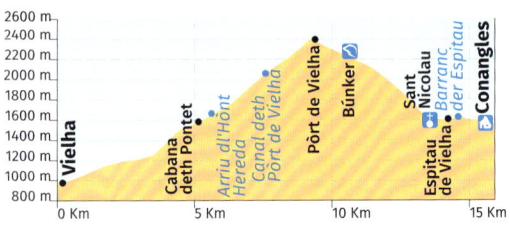

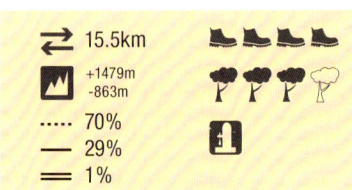

- 15.5km
- +1479m / -863m
- ····· 70%
- — 29%
- = 1%

This Pyrenean stage is not only the highest but also the toughest of this whole guidebook. The mountainous ascent to the pass of Port de Vielha is also one of the most stunning landscapes in this book. Snowy peaks, glacially formed lakes, forests of firs and alpine-like meadows create a highly attractive landscape that can be enjoyed if the weather is favourable.

Observations: During the winter season (November - June), the Port de Vielha pass is an impracticable and hazardous option. The red and white GR markings at the higher altitudes are mostly painted on rock faces and can be almost invisible to follow in heavy rain, mist or light snow. There is a daily bus service from Vielha and a bus stop at the southern end (Boca Sud) of the tunnel. You are advised to let the driver know where you wish to descend. There is also a bus stop at the northern end of the tunnel. This can be reached along a forest track off the stage route at km 4.1. *Bus timetables available at www.alsa.es.*

0km Vielha. From the Pl. Sant Antoni, opposite the rear of the town hall, follow the river Nere upstream along C. Major. Cross the river at the next bridge and turn right passing the modest chapel to Nuestra Señora de Lurdes. At the end of the village continue straight on, uphill along a cement track. Continue between woods and fields, always accompanied by the river Nere to the right.

3km/3km Eth Pontauet. A few metres before a bridge over the river, fork left uphill on the signed GR211.5. Continue along a farm track lined with hazel trees and bordered by grazed fields. The Way narrows to a path, climbing steeper ground as it enters a forest of firs.

1.1km/4.1km Sarraèra Forest Track. (Note: Turn right here to descend to the bus stop at the north end 'Boca Nord' of the tunnel). Cross the track and follow a path steeply uphill. The Camino soon joins a wider track and continues uphill.

1km/5.1km Cabana deth Pontet. The forest gives way to alpine meadows with a shepherds' cabin nearby. Now follow a path that continues up the mountain side parallel to a stream.

0.3km/5.4km Footbridge. Cross the Hònt Hereda stream by a wooden bridge and continue to climb a ridge following the GR waymarkings towards the cliffs at the head of the valley.

1.6km/7km Era Creueta. Reach this small flat area perched on the mountainside with views over the lake of Estanh de Hònt Hereda. With the cliffs to the right, turn their corner to enter the narrow mouth of a hidden valley. The path follows the floor of the valley, gently climbing whilst surrounded by the towering steep sided peaks of Tuc de Montanèro and Tuc deth Pòrt de Vielha on either side.

1.1km/8.1km Scree Slope. At the far end of the valley, the path meets a rocky scree slope and starts the short but steep climb towards the pass, at times in a zig zag fashion. Special care needs to be taken to pick out the GR markings on the rocks.

0.7km/8.8km Port de Vielha. Upon reaching the pass, slow down! The descent on this historic path, at times cobbled, is quite steep and worn. It has some loose stones, and is

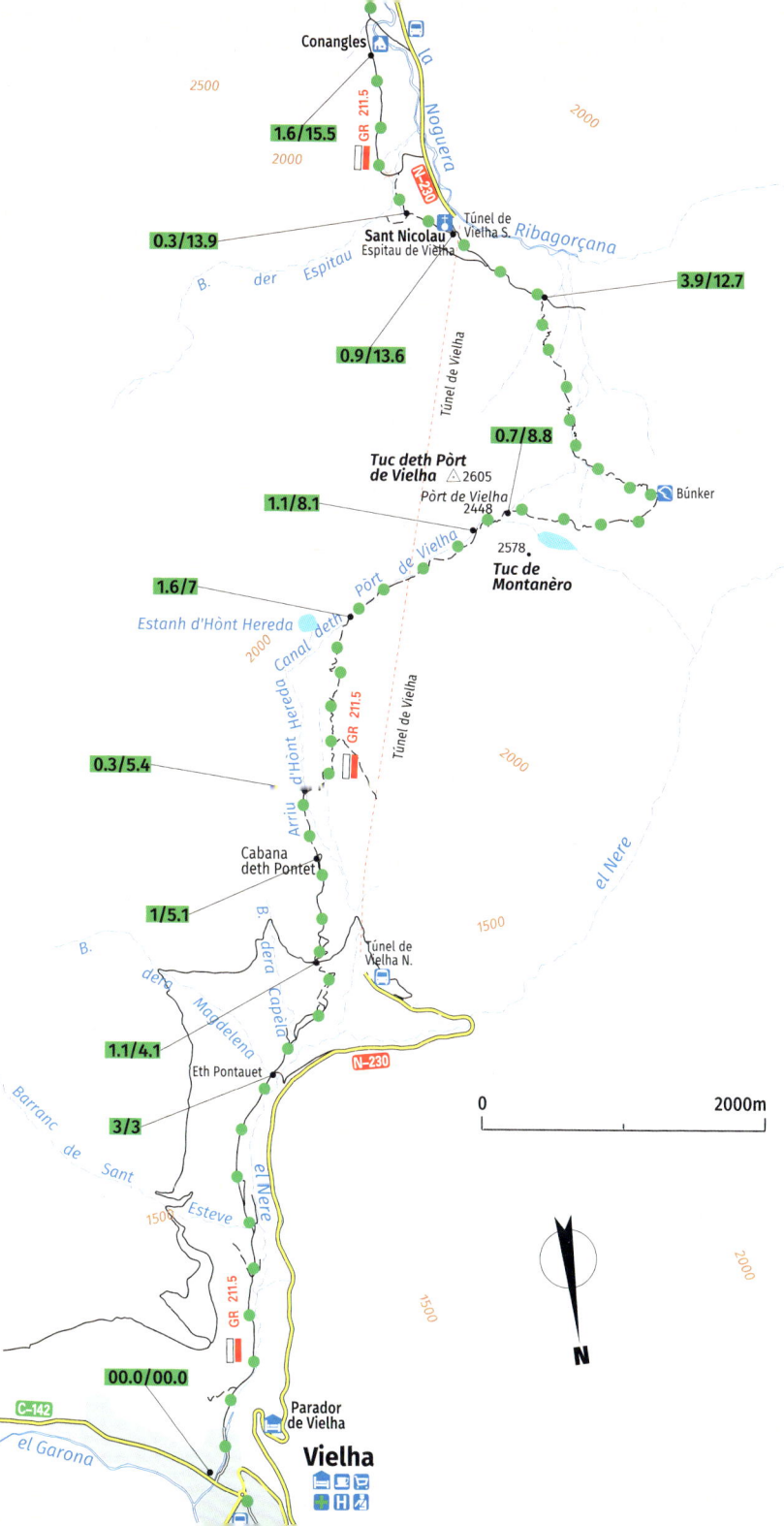

Fernando i José Antonio Subirà Gràcia (©Callum Christie)

slippery in places. Take care to follow the GR markings, which at times are few and far between. The path passes an old Civil War bunker and crosses grassy slopes before crossing a mountain stream and entering a young forest of pines. The path becomes heavily eroded and some areas are very uneven due to storm damage. The Way exits the trees and follows a boulder strewn gulley straight downhill with few waymarkings.

3.9km/12.7km Track. Upon reaching a wide track turn left.

0.9km/13.6km l'Espitau. A small hamlet by the southern end 'Boca Sud' of the Vielha tunnel. Turn left between the buildings and soon continue on a dirt track that at times narrows to a path.

0.3km/13.9km GR 11 Junction. Veer to the right to cross the Barranc de Espitau stream. On reaching a track, turn left following the GR 11 markings through Beech woods.

1.6km/15.5km Conangles Mountain Refuge. A mountain hut located in a beautiful wooded setting on an important GR crossroads. A much used stopover by walkers of the GR 11 trans-pyrenean route.

⌂ Refugi de Conangles 🛏
Tel. 696 649 871

Bus
www.alsa.es

🏛 **Espitau de Sant Nicolau dels Pontells, Boca Sud of the Vielha Tunnel.**
A hamlet of medieval origins that once offered shelter to travellers and pilgrims on their way to and from the Val d'Aran over the Port de Vielha pass.

3. CONANGLES - BONANSA: 31.9KM

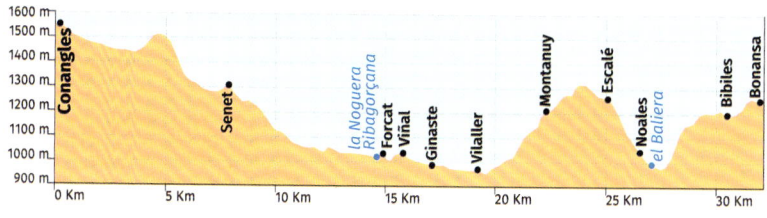

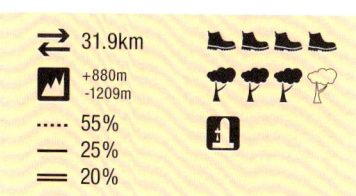

- 31.9km
- +880m / -1209m
- ····· 55%
- — 25%
- = 20%

A beautiful but long stage that follows the valley of the Noguera Ribagorçana river downstream to Vilaller. From there the route cuts across a range of foothills cloaked in oak woodland and small worked fields, passing through many small traditional Pyrenean villages along the Way.

Observations: The newly created GR 17 accompanies the walker from Conangles to the end of the chapter on Val d'Aran. During times of heavy rain or snow melt, care should be taken when crossing the numerous mountain gullies that are encountered between Conangles and Vilaller. A walking stick will be useful. Travellers may wish to split the stage into two by halting at Vilaller. The map suggests an alternative waymarked route (though not as a Camino) to explore the Vall de Boí. In parts it is a challenging route that crosses the mountain pass of Port de Gelada and should not be attempted when there is snow at this altitude.

0km Conangles. Continue downstream with the river Noguera Ribagorçana always to the right. Skirt the Baserca reservoir on an earthen track.

7.7km/7.7km Senet. At the entrance to the village there is a Tourist Info Centre with information on the surrounding area and the Aigüestortes i Estany de Sant Maurici National Park. Cross through the village to the Pl. Major and turn right to leave along an attractive cobbled track. Arrive at a waterfall that has a viewpoint and soon after, cross a stream bed that can be deeper in times of rain or snowmelt. The route crosses an area close to the river that can sometimes flood.

6.8km/14.5km Bridge over the Río Noguera Ribagorçana. Turn right to cross the river and follow a path up to the N-230 road, turning to the left. ATTENTION. After 100m, cross the road and pass through the small village of Forcat before returning to the N-230. Turn right to follow it for a short distance to the entrance of an electricity substation. Take a right, following a track past the rear of this installation and then climb to meet the lane to Viñal. Cross this small village with its pretty church and leave by way of a farm track surrounded by pastures, which then becomes an asphalt track. Keep straight on and then traverse the hamlet of Ginaste before continuing along an earthen track.

Gypaetus barbatus

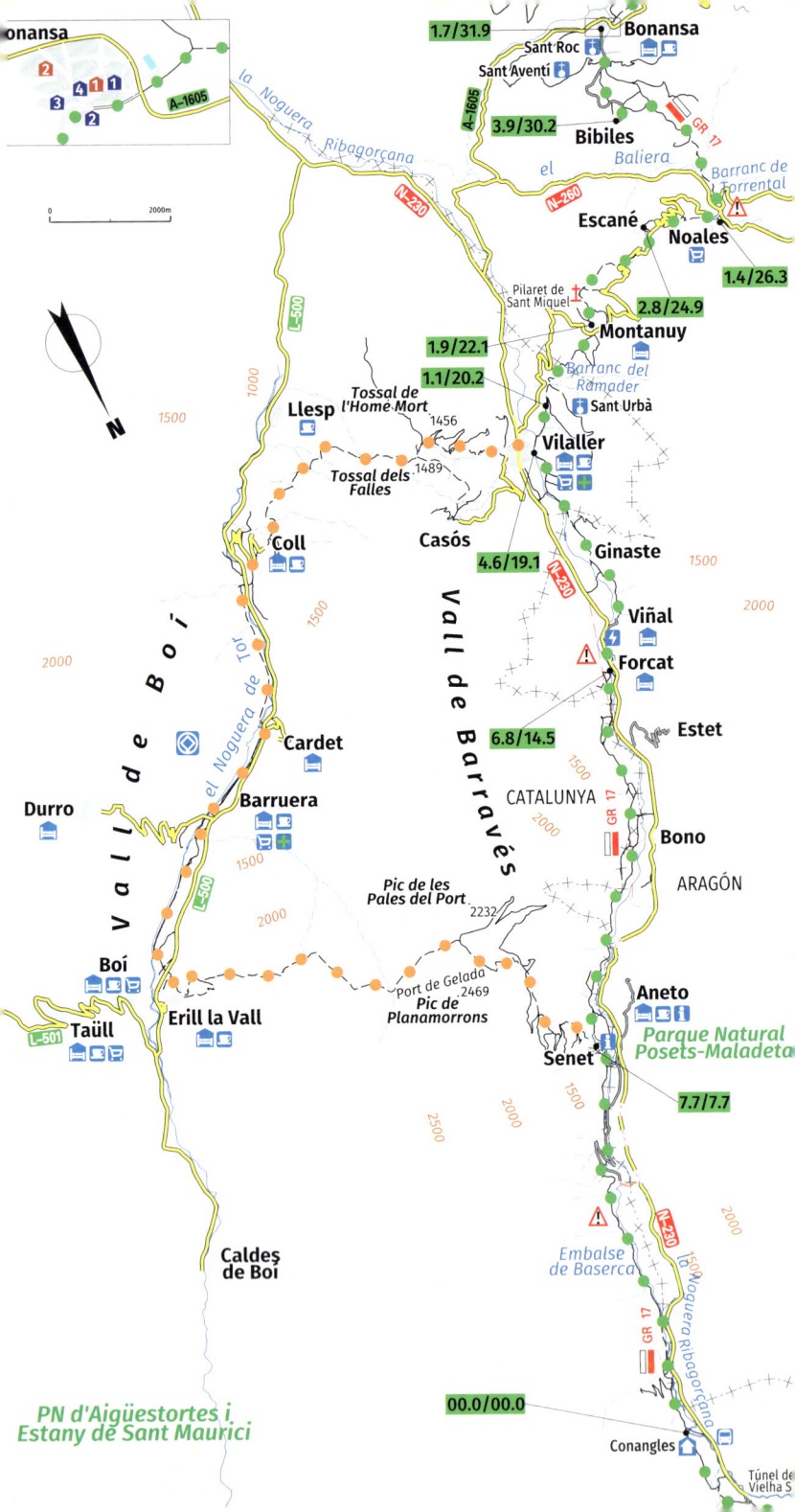

Les Falles (©Manuel Pueyo)

4.6km/19.1km Vilaller Bridge. Leaving the village of Vilaller on the opposite side of the river, the Camino climbs away from them both on a wide track past farmhouses and fields towards the Sant Urbá viewpoint.

1.1km/20.2km Path. After a bend in the track take a path to the left which begins with some steps. After 300m a detour to the right climbs to the viewpoint. The main path descends to the Ramader stream and then continues to climb through woodland and pastures.

1.9km/22.1km Montanuy. Leave the village on a track to climb past enclosed pastures onto a bare hillside. Cross a bridge over a water pipeline to arrive at the Pillar of Sant Miquel. The path broadens to become a farm track and continues straight on, soon crossing over a country lane. Descend to meet the lane again and turn right along the asphalt until a crossroads. Fork left towards Escané.

2.8km/24.9km Escané. Enter this small village and turn right along a dead end street that turns into a cobbled track. Proceed steeply downhill, crossing over the road to Noales and continue downwards on a path.

1.4km/26.3km Noales. Cross through the village to follow the lane downhill to the main N-260 road junction. ATTENTION. Cross the road and turn right towards Castejón de Sos and cross the river Baliera. After 150m take a track to the left that drops down to follow the river. Cross a couple of streams before starting a steep uphill section on a path that follows a firebreak in a zig zag fashion. Upon reaching flatter ground, veer left and follow a broader track all the way to the asphalt country lane. Turn left, then fork right at a junction on the outskirts of the village.

3.9km/30.2km Bibiles. Leave the village on a path that crosses meadows and then climbs gently over an exposed slope dotted with thickets of box, before it ends at the Sant Roc hermitage. Join the country lane and turn left to reach Bonansa.

1.7km/31.9km Bonansa.

Bonansa - pop. 88. Village of Ribagorza area. Situated on the watershed of the river Noguera Ribagorçana at 1256m above sea level.

Forcat
- **Casa Sastre**
Tel. 974 344 260

Vinyals
- **Casa Toni**
Tel. 653 471 357

Aneto
- **Casa Moliné**
Tel. 659 901 870

Vilaller
- **La Pomera**
Tel. 629 786 649
- **Casa Magí**
Tel. 973 698 119
- **Casa Pepedarro**
Tel. 689 507 927

- **Casa Txep**
Tel. 973 697 033
- **Casa Antonia**
Tel. 608 263 965
- **El Trinquet**
Tel. 689 50 79 27
- Hostal Maurín
Tel. 973 698 156
- **Fonda Muntanya**
Tel. 629 034 959
- **Fonda Mas**
Tel. 973 698 009
- **Hotel Montsant**
Tel. 973 698 025

Montanuy
- **Casa Ansos**
Tel. 677 645 002

Bonansa
- **1 Casa Farrás**
Tel. 649 58 66 27
- **2 Casa Maneló**
- **3 Casa Lluís**
Tel. 690 22 03 64
- **4 Era de Navarri**
Tel. 649 015 908
- **1 Bonansa Country Hotel**
Tel. 696 583 906
- **2 Hotel Terra**
Tel. 669 793 949

Vall de Boí
http://www.turismealtaribagorca.cat

La Serradora, Senet. A former sawmill converted into an Info centre for the Aigüestortes National Park (973 698 232).

Church of Santa Eulàlia, Forcat. C18th with a single nave.

Church of Sant Martí, Viñal. A small Romanesque church.

Pont Vell, Vilaller. A few metres downstream from the modern metal bridge lie the remains of the C17th bridge over the river Noguera Ribagorçana, that was destroyed in the floods of 1963.

Church of Sant Climent, Vilaller. C18th. Built with three naves and an octagonal bell tower. It replaced a Romanesque temple, traces of which can be observed in the interior.

Church of San Lupo, Escané. C12th Romanesque temple.

Chapel of Sant Roc, Bonansa. C12th-C13th Romanesque with lateral chapels and a semicircular apse.

Chapel of Sant Aventí, Bonansa. The horseshoe shaped apse indicates that this small C11th chapel is one of the oldest in Aragón. It stands on a hilltop overlooking the village on the spot where a fortress once stood.

Vall de Boí. This Pyrenean valley is listed as a UNESCO World Heritage site with a unique collection of nine Romanesque churches.

Las Fallas Festival. In many of the Pyrenean villages through which the Camino passes, the Fallas (Falles in catalan) summer solstice festival is celebrated. On the eve of St. John's Day (23rd June) residents gather outside their village and light their torches 'falles' before descending to the village square to light a bonfire and purify the streets with their flaming torches. The festival is listed as part of UNESCO Intangible Cultural Heritage.

4. Bonansa - La Puebla de Roda: 35.1km

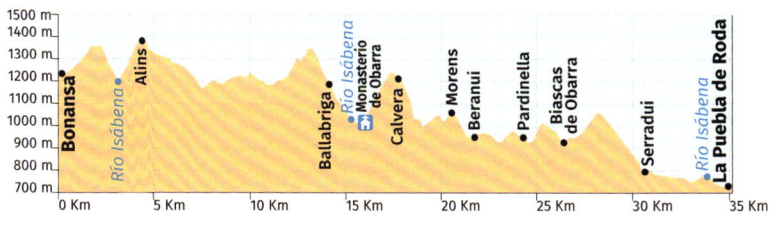

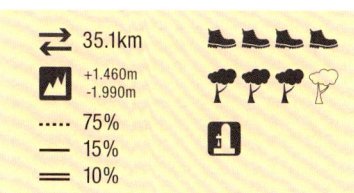

- 35.1km
- +1.460m / -1.990m
- 75% ·····
- 15% —
- 10% =

This long and arduous stage passes through many tiny and attractive villages, often following ancient drovers' routes. After the first 6km the main point of reference is the river Isábena. It cuts its way through the Pyrenean foothills forming a narrow gorge, the 'Congosto de Obarra', above the village of Ballabriga, before emerging into wider valleys that are flanked by wooded mountainsides, small worked fields and grazed pastures.

Observations: The length of this stage and the mountainous terrain it passes through, along with some overgrown paths, may well make it impossible to complete in a day. An alternative is to split the stage into two and arrange for a taxi pick up. An ideal site would be the car park at the Monastery of Obarra next to the A-1605 road. The majority of the villages en route are either without services or located at a distance from the main road. The red and white blazes of the GR 17 are the visual guide to the Camino and coincide at first with the GR 15 and later with the GR 18.1.

0km Bonansa. The way continues downhill through the centre of the village on C. del Medio to the main road. Turn right and then take the next lane left down past the municipal swimming pool. After 50m take an ancient drover's track to the right, advancing uphill between dry stone walls.

Upon reaching the A-1605 at Port de Bonansa, veer left without crossing the road, to join an all-abilities track through a pine forest. At a junction by a sign to refugio Pegà, turn left on a path through deciduous woods until you reach the A-1605 again. Turn left to follow the road over a nearby bridge.

3km/3km Bridge. ATTENTION. After the first bend, take a path to the right that starts to climb steeply before passing through a gap in the cliff to arrive at Alins. Pass by the church tower and in 50m turn right onto an old drover's track, downhill between dry stone walls.

3.5km/6.5km Junction of GR's. Turn left, (ignoring the GR 15 to Espés) then continue downhill on a path to cross a gulley and onto a wider track to meet the country lane to Espés. Turn right and after 250m, at the next bend, take a path to the left.

At the Font de Fusters path junction, keep straight on. The Camino climbs to a scenic pass above the Congosto de Obarra before beginning a descent to Ballabriga. Traverse this small village down to the church, and opposite its main door take a path downhill. Join the country lane that gives access to the village, continuing downhill to the A-1605 main road. ATTENTION. Turn right for a short distance before crossing over to turn left along a track down towards the Obarra Monastery. Cross the river Isábena by an impressive old bridge.

9.2km/15.7km Obarra Monastery. Continue on between the monastery and the chapel of San Pablo to join a path that starts at the rear of the chapel, climbing steeply. It ends on a farm track close to an isolated walled cemetery. Turn left downhill to a country lane and turn right to skirt the village of Calvera. After ignoring the turn off to the church, descend some wooden steps on the right to fol-

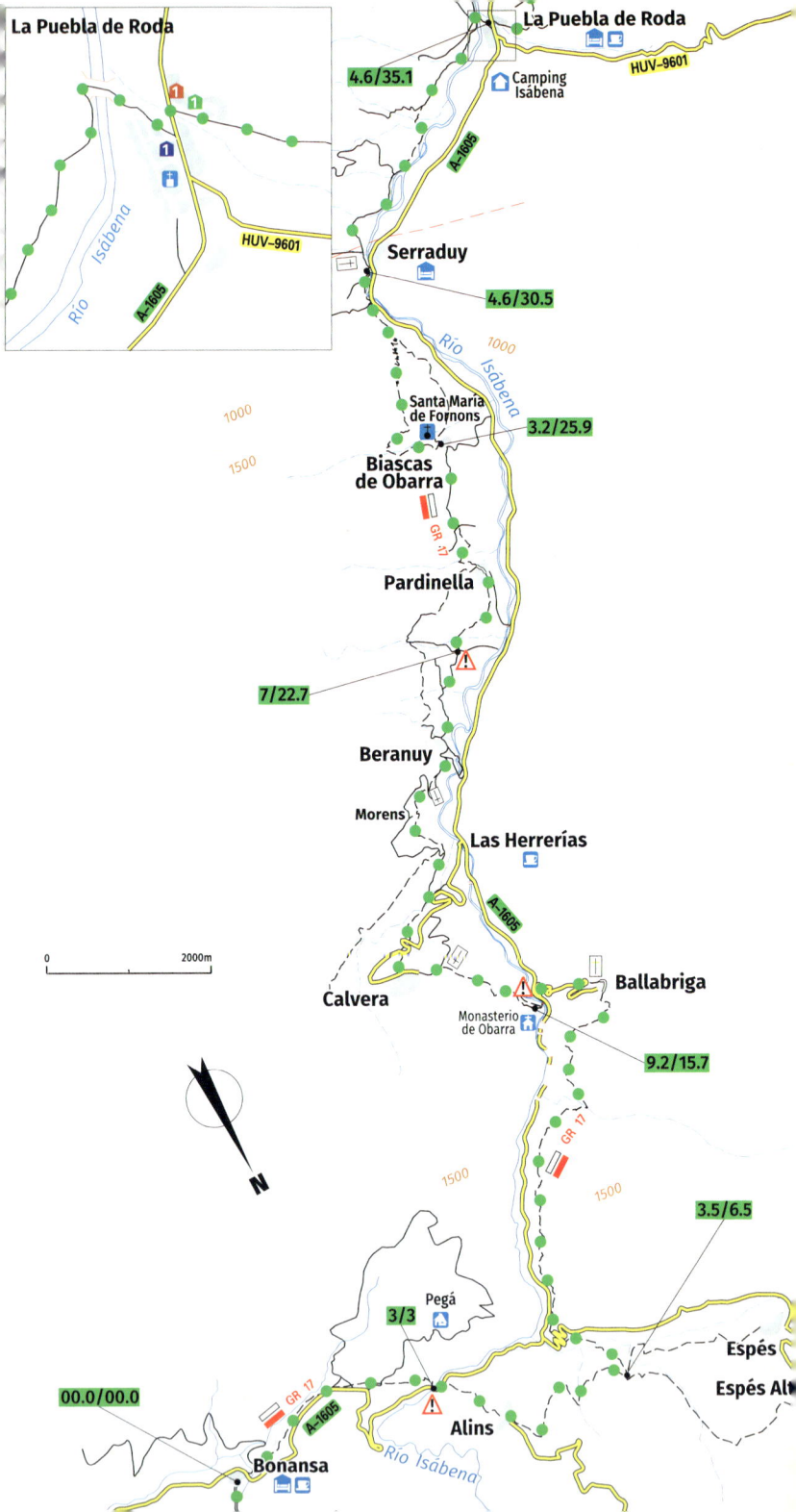

Santa Maria de Obarra (©Clara Borrego Muñoz)

low an old track between broken dry stone walls until you reach the same country lane again. Cross straight over to continue along a shaded walled track that soon narrows to a path before crossing a stream bed. The path climbs the opposite hillside and crosses a fire break and a line of electricity pylons to continue uphill to the tiny abandoned village of Morens.

Continue downhill, crossing a country lane with the cemetery of Morens close by. Upon meeting the lane again, follow it to the left, arriving at a junction where you turn left to reach Beranuy. Keep straight on, passing by the village and after the last house, fork right down a cement ramp. Follow this wide track that becomes a farm track. Continue straight on and at a fork, turn right downhill.

7km/22.7km Walled Track Turnoff. ATTENTION. At a bend in the farm track, look to the left to follow a narrow old way between dry stone walls. The way crosses a couple of small farmed fields and a gulley before starting to climb, on a path that contours the hill. Traverse the small village of Pardinella to pick up another historic path, soon crossing a gulley to climb steeply in a zig zag fashion. The path peters out and the way continues downhill on a farm track through oak woodland.

3.2km/25.9km Biascas de Obarra. Descend and veer left to cross through this modest village, passing the church and an open air washing place. Pick up a path that climbs towards the towering cliffs that enclose the valley. The way crosses a gulley and continues to climb steeply. It turns away from the surrounding precipices to reach a high point. Some 50m to the right, half hidden amongst the trees, are the ruins of the chapel of Santa Maria de Fornons. The path starts its descent along a series of tight zig

zags following the line of a ridge. At the foot of the hillside, cross straight over an asphalt track, following the path as it veers left to cross a wooden footbridge over a tributary stream.
4.6km/30.5km Serraduy. Proceed through the village past the church, reaching an elegant bridge. Without crossing the river, take the street to the left to leave the village. Immediately traverse a small stream and follow a track parallel to the river Isábena. At a left hand bend in the track, keep straight on along a fainter farm track which soon turns into a path alongside the river. Cross a tributary stream and veer left to climb a steep path before climbing a set of steps. Upon meeting a wider track, turn right downhill and soon follow the river downstream.
4.6km/35.1km La Puebla de Roda. Cross a bridge and take the first street right, uphill to the church of Santiago.
La Puebla de Roda - pop. 127. Capital of the Isábena municipality that also includes the village of Roda de Isábena, the hamlets of Merlí and Esdolomada and some ruined settlements.

Serraduy
🛏 **Casa Baltasar** 🪙🪙
Tel. 665 516 350
🏠 **Hotel Casa Peix** 🪙🪙
Tel. 974 544 430

La Puebla de Roda
🏠 **Camping Isábena** 🪙🪙
Tel. 974 544 530

🏠 **Casa Agustín** 🪙🪙🪙
Tel. 665 911 483
🏠 **El Prau de Vidal** 🪙🪙
Tel. 974 54 44 57
🏠 **Hotel Casa Custodio** 🪙
Tel. 974 544 414

TAXIS
Graus
Amable Guaño Rivera
Tel. 666 560 775
José Ramon Mascaray
Tel. 608 033 723
José Antonio Lacambra Enjuanes
Tel. 657 145 283
Taxis Graus
Tel. 630 684 279

Casa Castell Tower, Calvera. The only remaining feature of the local castle, now incorporated into a house.
Church of San Andrés, Calvera. This single nave church built with lateral chapels has an unusual octogonal tower that sits atop a square base and is topped with a charming spire.
Monastery of Santa María de Obarra, Calvera. A religious site since the C9th, of which, the basilica, the chapel of San Pablo, the abbot's palace and a mill remain. The Romanesque basilica of Santa María was built in the C11th by Lombard mastercraftsmen. It comprises three naves with the outstanding element being the exterior frieze that encircles the central apse.
Medieval Bridge, Serraduy. An unusual and ingenious design in stonemasonry spanning the Isábena with two unequal half point arches that balance on the rocky river bed.
Church of Santiago, La Puebla de Roda. A church of simple proportions. The open archway entrance topped by a belltower leads to a single nave with lateral chapels and a polygonal apse. The baptism font carries an inscription with the year 1598.

5. LA PUEBLA DE RODA - GRAUS: 33.1KM

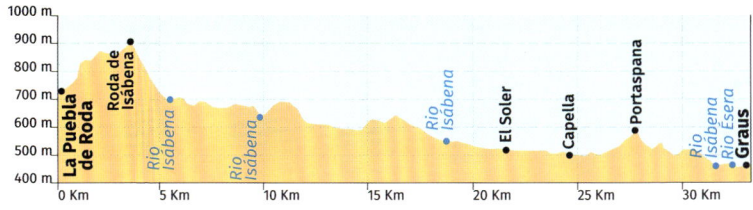

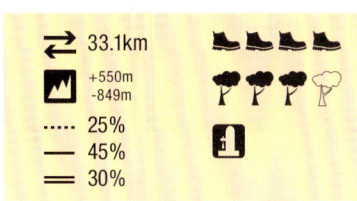

- ⇄ 33.1km
- +550m / -849m
- ····· 25%
- — 45%
- ═ 30%

The Camino follows the course of the river Isábena to its confluence with the river Ésera. Shaded paths and tracks traverse oak woods and pine forests interspersed with small cultivated fields. Roda de Isábena, a beautiful hilltop medieval village is complemented by the magnificent Romanesque bridges that span the river Isábena along the Way.

Observations: The length of this stage coupled with the undulating nature of paths, (sometimes overgrown after a wet Spring), could make it difficult to complete in one day. The walker may need to plan a pause at an intermediate point such as El Soler, with a taxi pick up.

0km La Puebla de Roda. On reaching the A-1605 main road, cross over and turn left. Take the first turn on the right to climb a cement track to a farm. A little later on the track forks left with a water deposit tank on your right. Continue along a steep path which soon broadens into an earthen track. Take a left turn after 1km to continue along the main track until you reach a country lane. Turn right, along the asphalt towards Roda de Isábena. Fork right uphill to the village reaching the foot of the medieval defensive walls. This historic village is the smallest in Spain with a cathedral and is well worth a visit before continuing along the Way.

3.1km/3.1km Roda de Isábena. Take a cobbled track to the right along the outside of the walls to skirt the village. Continue downhill along a farm track until reaching an old lane. Turn right, along the asphalt to meet the A-1605 road. Turn left and proceed along the protected verge for 150m.

ATTENTION. Cross the road to follow a track downhill to the river Isábena. Cross the C12th elegant single arched Romanesque bridge. On the far bank by a junction of GR paths, take the path ahead uphill. Cross a gulley and soon join a track. Turn right to follow the river along a combination of paths and earthen tracks.

6.4km/9.5km Colomina Bridge. Cross the river by this bridge.

ATTENTION. Cross the A-1605 and turn right for a few metres before turning left along a country lane towards Güel. Continue uphill passing the turn off to Mazana and keep straight on for another 300m.

2.3km/11.8km Track to Left. Turn left downhill on an earthen track. Descend on tracks and paths between small farmed fields. On reaching a small building, turn left onto a farm track down to the riverside. Turn right along tracks and paths to continue downstream. On entering a pine forest the dirt track turns uphill leaving the river behind. The Camino continues to climb by an intricate combination of paths that connect various stretches of tracks. After a couple of kms join an earthen track and turn downhill to the right. Another stretch of path and tracks continues through pine forests and farm fields until a small village is reached.

6.6km/18.4km El Soler. Follow the only street straight on and descend on a country lane. 100m before meeting the A-1065, turn left to cross the river Isábena by the older of two bridges.

ATTENTION. Cross the A-1065 main road and immediately take a dirt track to the right, parallel to the river. Cross a stream and in

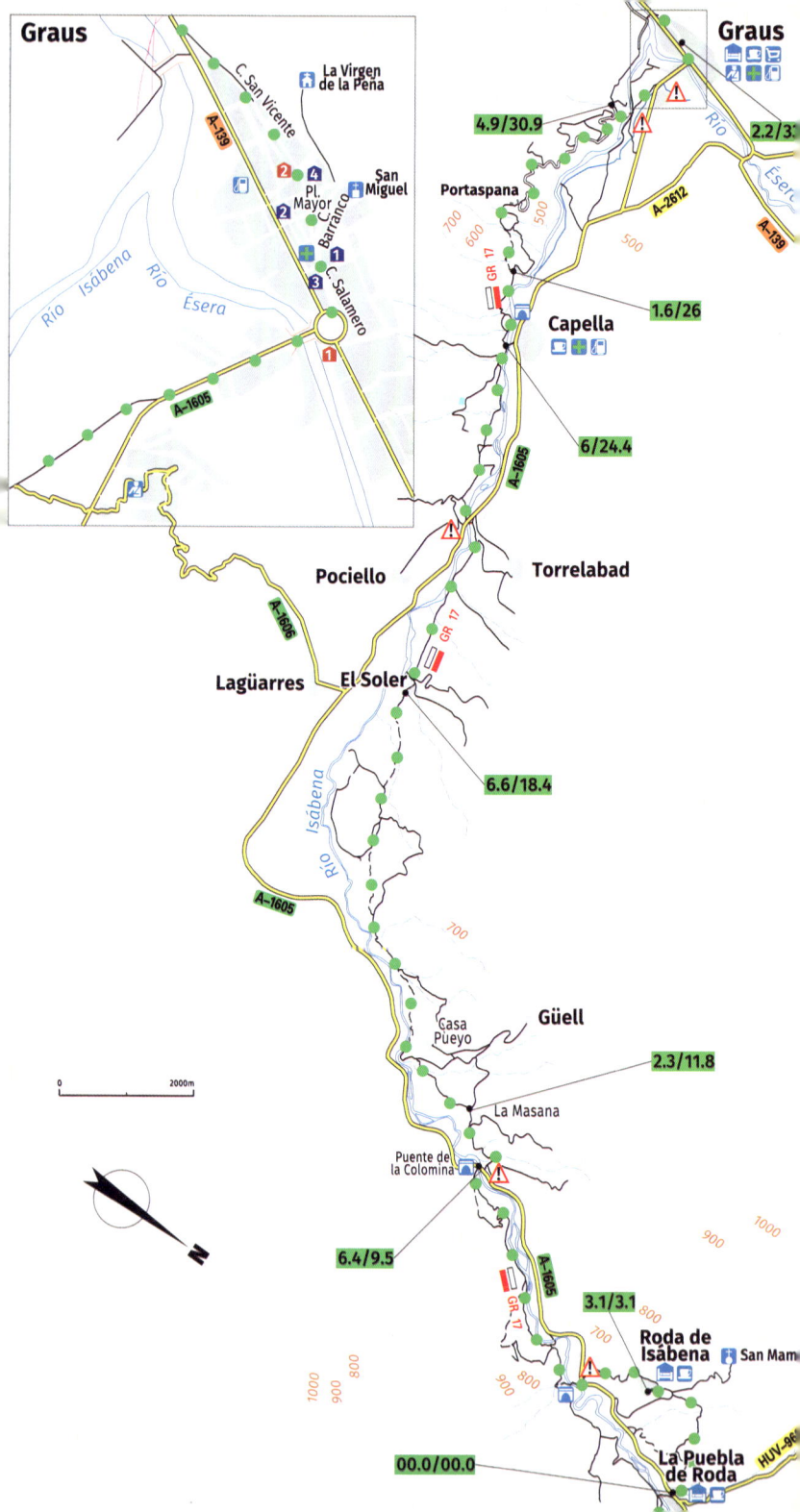

Capella (©Clara Borrego Muñoz)

50m at a junction, turn right. Follow the main track past farmed fields, staying close to the river

6km/24.4km Capella Bridge. Pass by this five arched bridge without crossing it. In 100m turn right to follow an earthen track. After a further 350m ignore another bridge over the river and continue along a farm track. Follow the main track up a short slope then after 500m of descent look for a path on the left.

1.6km/26km Path to Left. Take this path across open scrubland, climbing up a long slope towards a hill crowned by a forest of pines. Cross through the abandoned hilltop village of Portaspana with its roofless houses and a ruined church. Join a forest track and turn left to follow it for some 3kms, ignoring all minor turn offs.

4.9km/30.9km Junction. At a small building, leave the main track and turn right along a farm track downhill towards the river. ATTENTION. Cross a footbridge which can be subject to flooding (in which case return to km 30.9 and continue along the forest track to a bridge by the confluence of the rivers Ésera and Isábena). On the far river bank cross a track and follow a short path to pick up a dirt track. Turn left and soon meet the A-1065. ATTENTION. Cross the main road and turn left towards Graus. Cross the river Ésera to arrive at a roundabout. Take the third exit to the left along C. Salamero. Keep to the left and cross under the archway on C. Barranca to follow the narrow C. Mur until you emerge into the splendid Pl. Mayor.

2.2km/33.1km Plaza Mayor de Graus.
Graus - pop. 3400. A small town of the Ribagorza area. Located at a strategic crossroads between the Pyrenees and the plains of Huesca. The town's architectural heritage is linked to its heyday during medieval times

Roda de Isábena
- **Casa Simón** ⬤⬤
  Tel. 974 544 528
- **El Balcón de Roda** ⬤⬤
  Tel. 615 465 653
- **Hospedería de la Catedral** ⬤⬤⬤
  Tel. 974 544 554

Graus
- **Casa Serena** ⬤
  Tel. 974 541 035
- **Pensión Peperillo** ⬤
  Tel. 974 540 149
- **Hostal López** ⬤⬤
  Tel. 974 540 087
- **Casa Celia** ⬤⬤⬤
  Tel. 646 850 875
- **Hotel Lleida** ⬤⬤
  Tel. 974 540 925
- **Palacio del Obispo** ⬤⬤⬤
  Tel. 974 545 900

TAXIS
Amable Guaño Rivera
666 560 775
José Ramon Mascaray Graus
608 033 723
José Antonio Lacambra Enjuanes
657 145 283
Taxis Graus
630 684 279

Cathedral of San Vicente, Roda de Isábena. C10th Romanesque. It features a cloister, a tower, three crypts, a hospice, and an arched entrance. There is also the nearby fortified Prior's palace. The village was once the religious centre of the area.

Romanesque Bridge, Capella. Probably of C13th origins. It is a fine example of the 'donkey back' design. It has an impressive medieval span of 100m long with a central 10m high arch.

Plaza Mayor, Graus. A colourfully decorated square from the C16th with a continuous colonnade comprising a variety of styles featuring arches and pillars. It forms the heart of the town and includes the Town Hall, as well as many noblemen's houses; Casa Heredia, Casa Bardaxí, Casa Capucho, Casa Barón and Casa Loscertales. The outdoor market is held each Monday.

Basilica of the Virgen de la Peña, Graus. Built on a ledge in a cliff face. The existing collection of buildings date from the C16th. They comprise a church, a cloister and a hospice.

Church of San Miguel, Graus. A parish church of Romanesque origin that was much remodelled in the C16th - C18th. The main entrance and the ceiling of the single nave are all that remain of the original Romanesque design.

6. GRAUS - BARBASTRO: 38.1KM

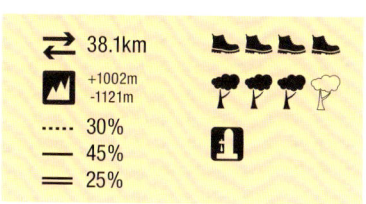

- 38.1km
- +1002m / -1121m
- 30% ....
- 45% —
- 25% =

A tough stage that traverses the Pyrenean foothills. Travelling between the Ribagorza and Somontano regions it skirts the extensive El Grado reservoir. Dry scrub clad hillsides are dotted with copses of holm oaks and small forests of pine. The valleys tend to be filled by fields of cereal crops.

Observations: This terrain is deceptively tough to cross, with frequent climbs and steep slopes. The length of this stage means most walkers may divide it into two parts. A good halfway point would be the Barrio Bajo de Cinca near El Grado.

0km Graus. From the Pl. Mayor continue in a straight line along C. Mayor, then C. San Vicente to pass under the arched Portal de Chinchín. Descend to the main road and turn right to follow a cycle lane as far as the cemetery.

2km/2km Cemetery. Take a dirt track to the right and after 200m take a left fork. Continue uphill on the stony main track. On reaching the crest, the track descends to meet a country road.

2.4km/4.4km HU-V-6432 Road. Turn right to follow the road and after 600m, at a bend, take an earthen track to the left. Cross a stream and follow a farm track to a junction at a round wash house. Choose a farm track that goes straight on between worked fields to meet a country lane. Cross straight over to enter the village.

4km/8.4km La Puebla de Castro. At the entrance to the village turn right to skirt the historic centre. Some 30m before the church, turn right, downhill to leave the village along the Camino de la Fuente. At the foot of the hill, just before meeting the road, turn right along a path. Continue on between farmed fields bordered by dry stone walls, following a combination of paths and farm tracks. Cross straight over a wide track to follow an old walled droving track. At its end fork left to enter the village.

2.6km/11km Ubiergo. The Camino follows the main street and forks right, descending to leave the village. By the last houses, turn right along an old faint walled track, continuing downhill to meet a dirt track in 200m. Turn left and follow the track 500m downhill to cross a stream. Veer left to cross a worked field and begin climbing a scrub filled hillside on a farm track. A path continues uphill to meet a country lane. Turn right and in 200m leave the asphalt, turning left to descend to a clearing. Look for a path to the right that descends a flight of wooden steps. Continue downhill through a mixture of woodland and open hillside to a junction of paths. Turn right and enjoy excellent views over the El Grado reservoir.

4km/15km Torreciudad. The path ends at a car park. Turn left, following the asphalt and at a minor crossroads continue straight on towards Ainsa. After 50m descend a flight of steps to the right and take a path that follows the road. On rejoining the road, turn right to drop down to a junction by the dam wall. Continue a few metres and take a path to the right, just before a small electric installation. Descend steeply before the path turns right onto a dirt track. As you meet a road, turn right towards the river Cinca.

3.4km/18.4km Bridge. Cross the river and veer left along a path with a wooden handrail. The Camino continues past a sports complex to meet the main road. Turn left and just before a roundabout, take a short dirt

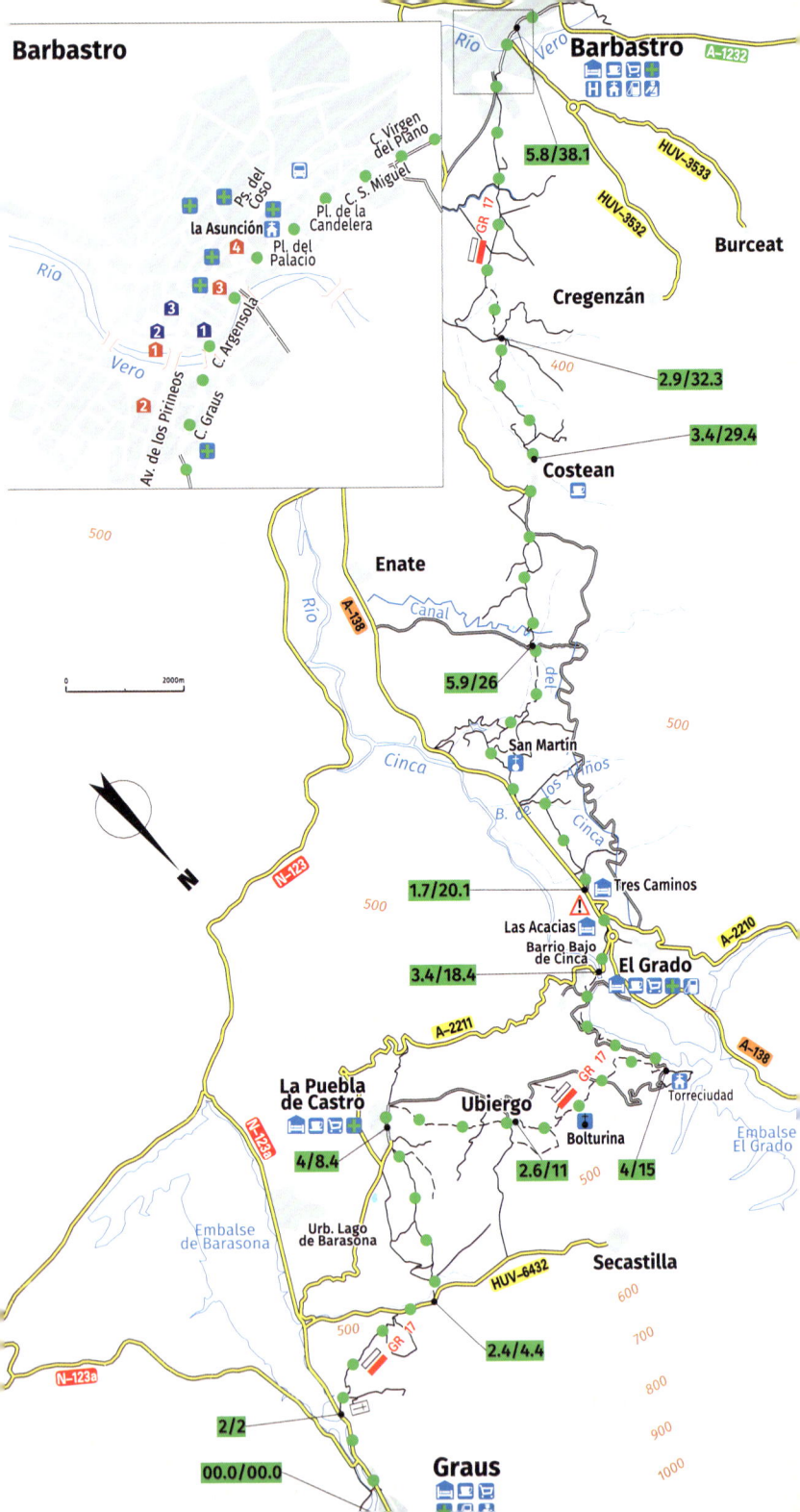

Barbastro (©Clara Borrego Muñoz)

track to the left that soon rejoins the road. ATTENTION. Cross the road and turn left, following a layby to its end. Recross the main road by a hotel and turn right. At the crossroads to the village of El Grado, keep straight on along the A-138 main road. ATTENTION. In 200m cross the main road to take the first asphalt track to the right.

1.7km/20.1km Asphalt Track. Ignore a street to the right and continue along the track. Just after a weighing platform you reach a junction of tracks. Turn left and immediately right along a farm track that crosses through an area of small worked fields. Eventually the track returns to the A-138 road.

Turn right, and a short distance ahead, cross a bridge over a stream. After a few metres turn right and immediately fork left along a farm track. The route passes closeby the modest chapel of San Martín, after which you turn right at the second fork and continue the steep climb on a dirt track. Ignoring two tracks to the left, keep climbing until just before a sharp bend (near a half hidden shed and corral), then take a path downhill to the left. Descend the scrub covered, thinly wooded hillside to meet a country lane. Turn left and continue 150m.

5.9km/26km Farm Junction. Leave the lane, turning right and proceed 100m along the edge of a farm field. Turn left around the rear of the farm buildings to join a dirt track uphill. After 200m, take a path to the right that passes under the Cinca Canal pipeline, before rejoining the dirt track uphill. Join a wider track and turn right. Ignore the minor tracks to both sides during the climb. On joining another track, take a path directly opposite that drops down, and in a short distance meets another wide earthen track. Follow it to the right and when it joins a road, turn right to enter Costean village. Continue along C. Mártires to the church.

3.4km/29.4km Costean Church. Leave the village downhill on a rough cement track. The track becomes a dirt one and crosses a gulley and continues uphill.

2.9km/32.3km Ford. Cross a ford and in 50m take a path to the left. Ignore a track to the right and continue straight on along the path until it ends at a dirt track. Turn right and climb along the main track ignoring several smaller track turnings on both sides. At a junction of tracks, cross an irrigation channel and fork right downhill. Follow this track to a small industrial estate and keep straight on to join Av. de los Pirineos. Turn right and

then follow a series of back streets before crossing the river Vero to reach the Pl. del Palacio.
5.8km/38.1km Barbastro Cathedral.
Barbastro - pop. 17.000. Capital of the Somontano region. A city nestling strategically between the Vero and Cinca rivers that has existed since Roman times and was conquered by the Moors in 717. It wasn't until 1101 that it was wrested from their control, after 40 years of sieges and several changes of hands between the kingdom of Aragón and the taifa of Zaragoza.

La Puebla de Castro
🏠 Casa de Castro ⚬⚬
Tel. 974 545 211
El Grado ⚬
🏠 Casa Flor
Tel. 667 969 677
🏠 Hotel Las Acacias ⚬⚬
Tel. 974 304 035
🏠 Aparthotel
Tres Caminos ⚬
Tel. 974 304 051

Barbastro
❶ Hostal Goya ⚬
Tel. 974 314 759
❷ Hostal Palafox ⚬⚬
Tel. 974 312 461
❸ Hostal Pirineos ⚬⚬⚬
Tel. 974 310 000
❶ Hotel Clemente ⚬⚬
Tel. 974 310 186
❷ Hotel Micasao ⚬⚬⚬
Tel. 974 308 884
❸ Gran Hotel Ciudad de Barbastro ⚬⚬⚬
Tel. 974 308 900
❹ Hotel San Ramón Somontano ⚬⚬⚬
Tel. 974 312 825
🏠 Hotel Sancho Ramírez ⚬⚬
Tel. 974 310 050

TAXIS
Alvarez Taxi (Barbastro)
Tel. 676 103 528

Lavadero de la Huerta, La Puebla de Castro. An elegant circular wash house whose pool also watered nearby vegetable gardens. The water comes from the nearby 'Corán' spring and supplies the local village.
Santa Barbara Church, La Puebla de Castro. A somewhat ungainly combination of architectural styles. The older nave is popular Gothic from the C15th, whilst the transept is C17th Renaissance.
Santa Ana Church, Ubiergo. A simple yet charming example of late Romanesque style.
Torreciudad. A modern centre of pilgrimage started by Opus Dei.
Cathedral of Santa María de la Asunción, Barbastro. Built atop a mosque, between 1571-1533. The exterior is Gothic in look but belies the Renaissance style of the interior. Of interest are the six narrow elegant columns ending in floral and decorated capitals that support the vault above three 15m high naves, forming arches and an intricate ribbed vaulted ceiling.
Episcopal Palace, Barbastro. C16th construction, extended a century later. The facade stands out with its three borders, an arched gallery and adjoining balconies.

7. BARBASTRO - BERBEGAL: 19.9km

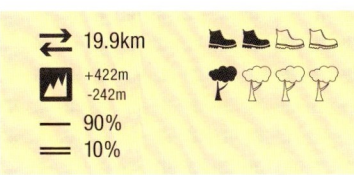

- ⇄ 19.9km
- +422m / -242m
- — 90%
- = 10%

Leaving the mountains behind, the Camino encounters the farmed plains that make up the heart of Huesca province. The hilltop Monastery of El Pueyo presides over the surrounding fields and the network of irrigation channels that distribute the waters of the Pyrenees. This stage joins the Camino to Puente la Reina just on the outskirts of Berbegal.

Observations: There are no villages or water fountains and very little shade on this route. Sufficient drinking water should be carried.

0km Barbastro Cathedral. From the main door turn left downhill to the Pl. de Aragón. Turn right onto Av. de Navarra and then climb the slope of C. Loreto and turn left onto C. Virgen del Plano to leave the city. By a stone cross, fork left along an asphalt track. After 100m, take a dirt track to the left. At a junction of tracks by another stone cross, take the right fork to climb an asphalt lane.

2.2km/2.2km Reservoir Junction. Continue straight on, crossing a bridge over an irrigation canal to follow an earthen track. Keep to the main track past all junctions. After almost reaching a road, the track starts to climb steeply. 400m after passing a farm with a small reservoir you reach a country lane.

3.2km/5.4km Road. Turn right towards El Pueyo Monastery, passing the chapel of San José. After 300m, turn right into a car park and at the far end take a dirt track downhill. After a few metres, fork right and continue until a junction of tracks, where you turn left.

1.5km/6.9km Asphalt Junction. Turn left downhill on a country lane to the N-240 main road. ATTENTION. Cross straight over to follow a dirt track and after 100m cross a bridge over the A-22 motorway.

1.1km/8km A-22 Bridge. 200m after the bridge, leave the main track and keep straight on along a farm track. After a further 400m, at a junction, turn right.

2km/10km T-Junction. At the end of a downhill slope, turn left onto a wide earthen track. Just before a reservoir, atop a rise, take a track to the right. Follow the main track between farmed fields and rocky outcrops.

3.3km/13.3km Crossroads. Turn right onto a dirt track and in 500m turn left along a farm track. Cross an irrigation channel and keep straight on uphill for 500m to a T junction. Turn right, then after 50m, turn left downhill along a farm track. At a junction by an irrigation channel, turn right and after 200m turn left to cross the channel. Start to climb gently towards the hilltop village of Berbegal.

2.5km/15.8km Road Crossing. Cross the asphalt to continue straight ahead along a farm track and cross a narrow irrigation channel by a bridge. After 250m cross another channel and veer right along a farm track. Keep straight on until you reach an asphalt track by the Canal de Terreu. Turn right and continue along the asphalt for 100m.

2.7km/18.5km Canal Bridge. Turn left to cross the canal and keep straight on along a dirt track to meet the A-1216 country lane. Cross straight over and in 50m turn right, soon joining the Camino to Huesca. However, to enter the village, take a path to the left, climbing to a road. Cross straight over

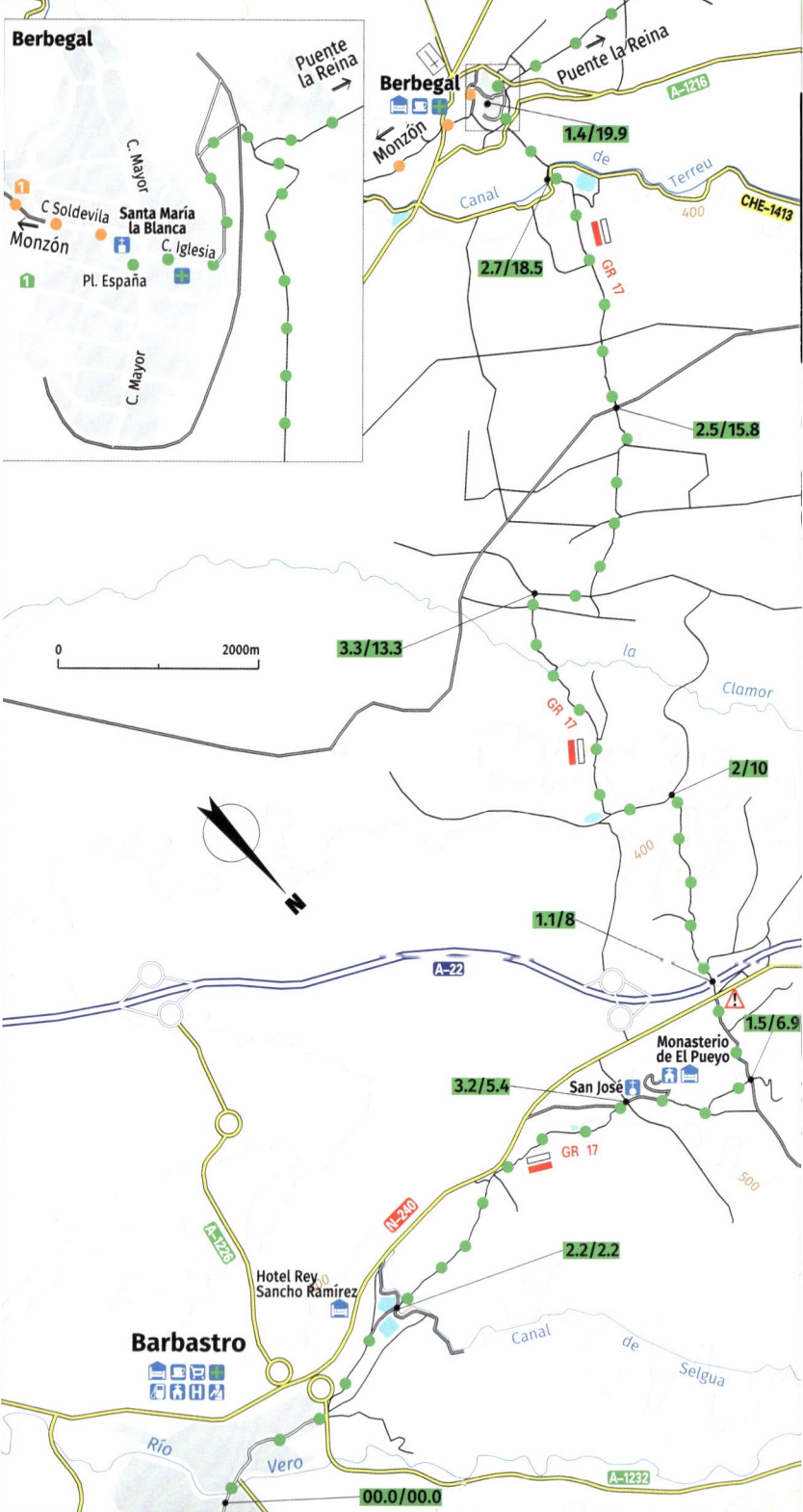

Tetrax tetrax

to climb a series of concrete ramps to the church square.
1.4km/19.9km Berbegal.
Berbegal - pop. 357.

Camino towards Puente la Reina - p. 100

Monasterio de Nuestra Senora del Pueyo
Tel. 974 31 09 34

Berbegal
Casa Rural Bergallo
Tel. 676 691 958

Albergue de Peregrinos
Tel. 974 301 001
  687 297 161

Nuestra Señora del Pueyo Monastery, Barbastro. The first chapel was built in the C12th on the spot where a shepherd had a vision of the Virgin Mary. The buildings were extended in the C14th and the present monastery was built in the C17th.

229

Key

The Way of St. James

- ● ● ● Main Camino
- ● ● ● Camino Francés
- ● ● ● Variants
- ● ● ● Hazardous stretch
- ▭ GR 6 Long distance trail
- 5.4/21.3 Km partial and total

Transport routes

- AP-2 Toll motorway
- A-12 Motorway
- N-II National road
- A-242 Regional 1 road
- C-153 Regional 2 road
- GI-601 Local road
- Asphalt lane
- Wide Track
- Earthen track
- Path
- Railway
- AVE High Speed Train

Accommodation

- Pilgrim hostel
- Private hostel
- Hostel, apartment
- Rural house
- Hotel
- Mountain refuge
- Camping, bungalow

Symbols

- Accommodation
- Bar, restaurant
- Supermarket
- Pharmacy
- Police
- Gas station
- Hospital
- Danger
- Museum, monument
- Cathedral, monastery
- Church
- Church (ruins)
- Hermitage
- Hermitage (ruins)
- Cemetery
- Castle
- Archaeological remains
- Dolmen
- Tourist info office
- Bus station
- Train station
- Greenway station
- Metro
- Bridge
- School
- Aerodrome
- Level crossing
- Ice well
- Picnic area
- Watchtower
- Bunker
- Electric sub station

- Distance
- Shade
- Difficulty
- Spring
- +611m / −462m Total metres ascent/descent
- % Road
- % Earthen track
- % Path